More Praise for *Preachers Dare*

"Preachers, I dare you to read this book. There should be a warning on the cover: 'Reading this book may cause you to burn all of your sermons and start your preaching ministry over again.' If you want to be admired as a great preacher, don't bother with it. If you want to turn your listeners' worlds upside down with the gospel, read on. But do it at your own risk."

—Charley Reeb, senior pastor, Johns Creek UMC; editor, *The Abingdon Preaching Annual 2022*

D0921653

WILL WILLIMON

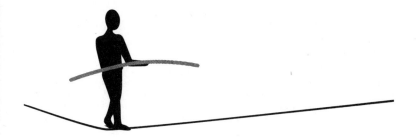

PREACHERS DARE

Speaking for God

Abingdon Press
Nashville

PREACHERS DARE:
SPEAKING FOR GOD

Copyright © 2020 by William H. Willimon

Library of Congress Control Number: 2020942266
ISBN: 978-1-7910-0805-5 .

20 21 22 23 24 25 26 27 28 29—10 9 8 7 6 5 4 3 2 1
MANUFACTURED IN THE UNITED STATES OF AMERICA

*For Fleming Rutledge, preacher,
and her minions, preachers Jason Micheli, Teer Hardy,
and Taylor Mertins*

Whoever listens to you listens to me.
Whoever rejects you rejects me.
Whoever rejects me rejects the one who sent me.

Luke 10:16

CONTENTS

INTRODUCTION

Christian preachers dare to talk about God. Even on the presupposition of the mediation of revelation by holy Scripture this venture would always be impossible without the . . . presupposition that God acknowledges it and will . . . speak as we speak, just as [God] spoke to the prophets and apostles and still speaks through them.

—Karl Barth, *Göttingen Dogmatics*[1]

After moving from his forlorn parish in Switzerland to the rarefied world of the University of Göttingen in 1921, Karl Barth began lectures on Reformed theology, opening with a thunderous "*Preachers dare.*"

Barth told his students that theology keeps preaching as risky as Jesus means it to be, testing preaching to ensure that preaching hasn't lost its nerve, daring preachers to get out of the way so God can use our sermons to speak.[2] God gives preachers guts. It's not a sermon until God shows up.[3]

"The ship is leaking even though the best preachers might be at the pumps. There is no lack of good preachers . . ."

What's lacking?

"Sermons that are meant to be God's Word and are received as such."[4]

Preachers dare to talk about God who, in Jesus Christ, by the power of the Holy Spirit, risks talk with us, making our sermons God's.[5]

Preachers dare. . . . They dare as though the history of philosophy had ended with the most satisfying . . . definite result—they dare to take the whole world, nature which is so incommensurable, . . . the sphinx of past history and the mystery of future history, the riddle of the individual, . . . destiny, guilt, and death—they dare to bracket all these things and deal with them from outside by tossing out

> such words as eternity, assurance, victory, forgiveness, righteous-
> ness, Lord, and life. . . . No homiletical . . . stupidity, ineptitude, or
> perversion can alter the fact. . . . [They] simply repeat what they
> have heard and learned from others, they do so boldly. . . . They dare
> to speak about God.[6]

This book is a dissent against homiletics as an exclusively human endeavor—rhetoric—or homiletics as a taxonomy of effective sermon forms
and styles—poetics. The only good reason to bother people with a sermon,
the sole rationale for investing a life in this vocation is theological.[7]

The dilemma of preaching is portrayed by a homiletic professor's
criticism:

> Today we see far more self-disclosure in preaching. Previously, ministers
> thought they should never talk about themselves in the pulpit because that
> would only get in the way of God speaking. Today's approach is much more
> incarnational: God speaks to us through our experience. The top-down
> mode has yielded to a more dialogical approach, an invitation to the con-
> gregation to explore the sermon's themes together. Authority is based on the
> authenticity and vulnerability of the speaker. Instead of announcing, "This
> is the Word of the Lord!", the preacher is willing to say, "This is how I see
> it—how do you see it?"[8]

If preaching is what everybody already talks about—our vaunted
subjectivity, our screwed-up democracy, our insatiable idolization of ourselves—who needs courage? "We don't preach about ourselves" (2 Cor 4:5),
and it takes courage not to cower at Jesus's brash, "Whoever listens to you,
listens to me" (Luke 10:16).

Barth can help contemporary pastors rediscover preaching as an es-
sentially theological endeavor: God speaking. When preaching degenerates
into moralistic advice, principles for better living, political commentary
of the right or left, helpful (but trifling) hints for humanity, Barth recalls
preachers to witness to the very voice of God.[9]

Every week the church, in wildly diverse settings and means, listens
to an ancient book and responds, "The Word of the Lord." This wonder
followed by another when God's people say, "Thanks be to God." As if this
were not enough, somebody like me stands up and presumes to speak for
God, thereby prepping the congregation to go back into the world as God's
designated speakers. That's the odd, miraculous chain of events I celebrate
in this book.

I left Yale Divinity School wondering how someone as flawed as I could preach from a disordered and poorly edited Bible. That's when I met Barth through the *Göttingen Dogmatics*, lectures that Barth said were born out of "the concrete situation of preachers mounting the pulpit steps."[10] I have experienced this vocation, not as trudging up pulpit steps but rather getting stuffed in the muzzle of a cannon by the biblical canon and God lighting the fuse, hurling me toward God's people. God only knows where I'll land next Sunday.

A gracious invitation by Dean Greg Sterling to give the 2021 Beecher Lectures at Yale prompted this book as preparation for the lectures to be given on the fiftieth anniversary of my graduation from the school where my enthusiasm for preaching was ignited.

Barth gave me the pluck to spend a lifetime attempting to talk to the God who has so recklessly, vividly spoken to us in Jesus Christ and then commanded cowards like us to speak of Jesus to the world. In this homiletical provocation, I double-dog-dare my fellow preachers again joyfully to risk the death-defying high-wire act of speaking for the God who has risked speech with us.

Preachers dare.

Will Willimon
2020

Chapter 1

CHRIST: *DEUS DIXIT*

Though we don't know all we would like to know of God, this we know: the God of Israel and the church is a big talker. Relentlessly, resourcefully revealing, refusing heavenly obscurity, not content to rule without telling us all about it.

That's why Barth begins his *Church Dogmatics* with the longest exposition of the Trinity in five centuries. Before we speak of God, God must speak. Good news: The Trinity reveals God to be lovingly loquacious.[1] The one God is triune—Father, Son, and Holy Spirit—which not only names the complexity and unity of the One in whom we live and move and have our being (Acts 17) but also points to God's life as self-communicative. Jesus the Son in constant communication with the Father, the Father in eternal interaction and revelation with the Son, and the Holy Spirit incessantly empowering, moving amongst Father and Son, as One. Barth says an arcane, esoteric, silent God "would not be God at all,"[2] at least not the God who greets us as Christ.

Preaching, as oral communication, is the uniquely suitable mode of discourse for so exceptionally dynamic and extroverted a God. And distinctively difficult.

The modern misunderstanding, Barth believed, was to suppose that a personal encounter with God was somehow given in the structure of human nature. The preacher need only uncover a connection within the listener's self and build a bridge to that innate point of contact.[3]

Gods to be had by human yearning are idols. Barth says this not because of his pessimism about human nature but rather because of his great optimism about the self-revelatory capacity of the Trinity. Finding a point of contact between God and humanity is God's problem, not ours. The Word "completes its work in the world in spite of the world."[4]

A trinitarian God who speaks, who shows up, who intervenes, was too much God for the modern world's illusions of human control. So beginning in the eighteenth century, God was made mute and divine revelation problematic. We're at last free to run the world as we please, with God safely tucked into the confines of human interiority. When this happened, Barth argued, two things occurred: First, Jesus Christ ceased to be understood unequivocally as the Lord; and second, we usurped the center that rightfully belongs to him. (I am virtually paraphrasing the first thesis of Barth's 1934 Barmen Declaration.[5]) Rather than understanding ourselves from God, we concoct God from ourselves. Christ—God's unique, binding revelation—is refashioned as a postulate of our experience—"as an ideal case or an idea of our possibility and our reality."[6] Any God who can be accessed solely through human consciousness can never be the Lord.[7]

With our natural laws, predictable processes, explicable humanity, and demystified cosmos in service to our Promethean aspirations, we neither expect nor want trinitarian address outside our subjectivity.[8] God deactivated, rendered interior and intuitive, silenced, is no God at all.[9]

Immanuel Kant's once courageous *sapere aude*,[10] dare to think for yourself, to demand evidence, to think rationally—that is, autonomously, godlessly—eventually became a means of merging into the herd. The modern state found that we are more easily managed if we think that we are sovereign individuals answerable only to ourselves. By naming forms of past servitude with relish, we're loathe to admit our own bondage. The murders of George Floyd and Armaud Abery are not aberration; they are apocalyptic revelation of who we are as a people. Two million Americans are incarcerated, millions more opting for slow suicide by opioids, a nation in thrall to a virus; we strut about, bragging of our freedom and liberation, even as we are tightly tethered to the market state, the great supermarket of desire, the USA Inc. Capitalism promises unrestrained freedom to choose what our lives mean—except the freedom to choose not to be servants of the market.

"I'm not listening to anybody standing up in a pulpit and telling me how I ought to live my life," explained a Duke student as his rationale for refusing to listen to my sermons. While free to resist my preaching, he was not free to make less than 1400 on the SAT, spend four of the best years of his life and thousands of dollars at Duke, marry someone of his race and economic level, or assume a half-million-dollar mortgage in Scarsdale where he could spend the rest of his days worrying about the wrong sort moving into the neighborhood.

Our most enduring American cliché is Ben Franklin's myth of shrewd self-invention. America is where you get to make up yourself, then keep remaking to give yourself the illusion that you are in control of your life.[11] As Stanley Hauerwas says, modernity tells us that we can choose whatever story we want (liberals call it "freedom")—except to choose a story other than the story that tells you that you must choose your story.[12] Our listeners think they are sitting through a sermon because they want to. Fancying themselves as controlling communication, they think that they can filter, unplug, and hit delete anytime they like. If you can decide who will be your Savior, that savior can't save you.

One of the characters in Marilynne Robinson's *Lila* says, "If there is no Lord, then things are just as they look to us."[13] It takes daring to address people who don't want an exterior word that changes what we see. Truth must be democratically available to all regardless of the nature of the knower. "Why?" or "Wherefore?" are answered through the exercise of our marvelously omnipotent, critical, innate rationality. What lies in front of us—in plain sight if we concoct the appropriate methodology to uncover it—is all we need to make sense of ourselves and the world. What you see is what you've got. This is it. Listen for no other. "God says . . ." is shushed by "In my experience . . ."

Our contemporary context makes outrageous the Barthian assertion upon which faithful preaching is based: *Deus dixit*. God has spoken (Scripture), God will have the last word (the eschaton), and—surprise—God speaks *hic et nunc*, here and now. *Deus dixit*. How? Primarily through preachers.

Impossible Possibility

Barbara Brown Taylor began a Lenten sermon in Duke Chapel by asking, "Has anyone dared to tell you truth, truth so painful, truth so true, that you wanted to kill them? Well, that's why Christ was crucified."

Preachers dare to speak with the truth-telling Christ. Artful rhetorical devices, grabbing our hearers' attention, propagating practical help for daily living, and comforting our cares is effective public speaking, not preaching. Preaching has a more unsafe mission: *talk about, with, and for God.*

Carnal, finite human limitations make human speech about God Almighty suspect. Is my talk of God just inflated verbiage about myself? Then there's the problem of my self-deceit. Can one deceitful as I—serving a congregation who, in the name of "love," encourages my self-duplicity and rewards me for preaching that falsifies—tell the truth about God?

Ludwig Feuerbach charged that "God is the mirror of man"; all theology is anthropology.[14] Much of what passes for theology these days confirms

Feuerbach's charge when discourse about "God" is "humanity" puffed up, sentimentalized, exaggerated in a resonant, beguiling voice.

Young Barth emerged self-confidently from seminary into his first parish. All might have gone well had he not been forced to preach. "I started to find it increasingly difficult to use what I had picked up at university when I stood in front of people in the pulpit, preaching to them." Barth's received theology "started to appear a bit thin to me: the talk about self-consciousness and the 'experience of Jesus's and whatever . . . I faithfully repeated what I had learned. [But] then it slowly started to get stuck in my throat, so that I could not say these things seriously any longer."[15]

Then came the war and the day Barth opened the paper and read the names of his favorite professors, all stepping patriotically in line behind German mobilization. If his honored teachers couldn't tell the difference between German *Kultur* and the kingdom of God, what possibility was there for a young preacher to align his words with God's revelation? Barth said, we can't preach.[16]

The impossibility of our speaking accurately or truthfully about God is not only in ourselves but more so in our subject matter, God. Most Americans say they believe in "God." It is easy enough to show that the "God" they believe in isn't the God who meets us in Jesus Christ. Lacking theological capacity, we have no epistemology and can cultivate no set of practices whereby we gain access to the Trinity. We may have inchoate hankerings toward the transcendent, but we must not make much of them; there's no way they'll get us to God as a Jew who lived briefly, died violently, rose unexpectedly, and returned to us, whether we wanted him or not.

Every attempt to heft ourselves up to God—inflating some alleged human virtue or extolling some incipient inclination, working to right some human wrong or striving toward some noble ideal—inevitably dead-ends in the concocted God-substitute of the moment. Empty-handed we ask, *Who are you Lord? What are you up to? How does it stand between us?* God speaks: *Jesus Christ.*[17]

Life had taken a twist since I knew her as a Duke undergraduate:

> I defied my parents, just like I told you I would, and went into high school teaching. I figured that was the end of my rebellion. God had other plans.
>
> A friend talked me into teaching a class at the Central Correctional Institution. Life-changing. So, one thing led to another and, long story short, I've quit my job with the school system, downsized to a studio apartment, sold most of what I had, and now I'm teaching four classes a week at the prison. Loving every minute.
>
> How did I end up here? I wouldn't have known this is what God wanted

out of me if it had not been for that sermon you preached in Duke Chapel about eight years ago, the one about the rich man and Jesus. You said that when Jesus told him to go, sell all he had and follow him, the man just walked away. Then you asked, "Got the guts to follow Jesus?"

That's when it clicked. I wouldn't have known a crazy God's crazy plans for me if it hadn't been for your crazy sermon.

Gratefully,

Jane

Sorry, psychology, sociology, gender studies, and economics: you lack the means to explain this woman's testimonial. Jane's story is vindicated only by the high-wire act we preachers venture on a weekly basis: *Deus dixit.*

Once God promised "I'll take you as my people, and I'll be your God. You will know that I am the LORD your God" (Exod 6:7), faithful preaching became the impossible possibility.

Christ, the Preacher

While bumming around Europe during my sophomore year, one night in Amsterdam a guy from Ohio grinningly asked, "Hey man, want to see God?"

He opened his fist and held before me a small white pill. I didn't take up his offer; I was nineteen and had not yet caught the spirit of adventure later instilled in me by being summoned to preach Christ.

"Please show me your glorious presence," begged Moses (Exod 33:18); a glimpse of God's backside was all he got (Exod 33:23). "Tear open the heavens and come down!" pled Isaiah (Isa 64:1). That anguished prayer for divine unveiling is rarely answered in the way we want; God's revelation is often ambiguous, not self-evident. Isaiah doesn't ask for more of God's words—Isaiah's eloquent oracles prove that Isaiah received a deluge of divine discourse. The prophet pleads for divine presence. One must have a body to be present to another. Yet bodies alone are not yet fully present; there must be self-revelation before the other can be said to be truly "present."

Cleophus LaRue says that African American congregations have little interest in hearing *about* God; they want to hear *from* God.[18] Speaking presence is the *modus operandi* of the God rendered in Scripture and whom we meet in Christ. *Deus dixit.*

Although *finitum non capax infiniti* (the finite is incapable of the infinite), thank God, *Deus capax humanitatis* (God is capable of assuming human nature). Determined to be our God, God relentlessly reveals, generously offers three forms of revelation whereby the Word of God comes to us:[19]

> The Word of God is first an address in which God and God alone is speaker [Christ, the *Logos ensarkos*], in a second address in the Word of a specific group of people (the prophets and apostles) [Scripture], and in a third address of a limited number of its human agents of proclamation [preachers].[20]

The first form of God's address: The Word has become a Jew who speaks. We asked for the truth about God. God addressed us, saying, "Jesus Christ":[21]

> The Word became flesh and made his home among us.
>> We have seen his glory, glory like that of a father's only son,
>> full of grace and truth.
>
> John testified about him, crying out, "This is the one of whom I said, 'He who comes after me is greater than me because he existed before me.'"
>
> From his fullness we have all received grace upon grace;
>> as the Law was given through Moses,
>> so grace and truth came into being through Jesus Christ.
> No one has ever seen God.
> God the only Son,
>> who is at the Father's side,
>> has made God known. (John 1:14-18)[22]

John says, "No one has ever seen God" (John 1:18), a statement that held true until we saw Jesus preach in Nazareth (Luke 4:16-30). Jesus reads from the Isaiah scroll. Things went well until he preached. His sermon transformed an otherwise sweet congregation into would-be murderers. It's not only a picture of our reaction to the truth about God; it's a vignette of Barth's three modes of divine unveiling: (1) Christ speaking; (2) Scripture speaking through reading and hearing; and, most surprising and daunting of all, (3) a preacher speaking and hearers responding.[23]

Trinitarian faith says that the one who preached at Nazareth is none other than the whole truth about God, repetition of God the Father and God the Holy Spirit as God the preaching Son.[24] "When [Jesus] came, he announced the good news of peace to you who were far away from God and to those who were near [echoing Isa 57:19]. We both have access to the Father through Christ by the one Spirit" (Eph 2:17-18). Jesus, as much of

God as we hope to see. No mere prophet talking about God or messenger from God, he is a brown-skinned Jew on whose body "the fullness of God was pleased to live, . . . and he reconciled all things to himself through him—whether things on earth or in the heavens. He brought peace through the blood of his cross" (Col 1:19-20).

The Father is Revealer, the Son the Revelation, the Spirit the Revealedness (revelation received); the one God is triune revealing agent, revealed content, and effect of revelation. Barth even says that we can substitute for the three forms of revelation—Christ, Scripture, and proclamation—the names of the divine persons, Father, Son, and Holy spirit "and *vice versa.*"[25] Revelation—God face-to-face with us.[26]

> Look! God's dwelling is here with humankind. He will dwell with them, and they will be his peoples. God himself will be with them as their God. (Rev 21:3)

We ask God to show up; God does so as the Incarnate Word, God with a name, a face, God speaking.[27] As Paul says, we have been given "the light of the knowledge of God's glory in the face of Jesus Christ" (2 Cor 4:6). First John 1, echoing John 1, reverberating from Genesis 1, is declaration of the possibility and necessity of Christian preaching:

> We announce to you what existed from the beginning, what we have heard, what we have seen with our eyes, what we have seen and our hands handled, about the word of life. The life was revealed, and we have seen, and we testify and announce to you the eternal life that was with the Father and was revealed to us. What we have seen and heard, we also announce it to you so that you can have fellowship with us. Our fellowship is with the Father and with his Son, Jesus Christ. We are writing these things so that our joy can be complete. This is the message that we have heard from him and announce to you. (1 John 1:1-5)

"What we have heard," that which is revealed, compels preachers to "testify" that God is uniquely present in human space and time—Jesus, revealed, revealer, revelation.[28] Having been revealed to us, we now "announce to you what we have seen and handled." The goal of the declaration called preaching? "Fellowship," human camaraderie with "the Father and with his Son."

"I am the way, and the truth, and the life. No one comes to the Father except through me. If you have really known me, you will also know the Father. From now on you know him and have seen him" (John 14:6-7). Jesus hasn't come to tell us the truth or point us toward the truth: "*I* am the truth." Truth is not an idea; truth is personal, a crucified Jew from Nazareth who returned to resume the conversation. God doesn't wait for us to discover truth; God comes as the truth who speaks, who calls us to follow. Preaching is Jesus—Truth speaking for himself.

My own denomination is splitting apart in a debate between "traditionalists" (who claim to stand upon "biblical authority," asserting that Scripture gives fixed and final sanction to their views on marriage and sexual orientation) and "progressives" (who claim that their individual consciences trump Scripture and tradition). Jesus never said, "All authority in heaven and earth is given to the Bible," nor did he say, "Just follow your conscience." The conflicting parties approach Scripture (and Jesus, Lord of Scripture) with minds made up in advance, unwilling to hear a word that destabilizes their preconceived positions. Let's all beware.

"Lord, show us who you are, what you are up to." God said: *Jesus Christ.* If the Word has not become flesh and moved in with us, then we preachers have nothing to say that the world can't hear as well elsewhere. Jesus Christ is the only thing that preachers know that everyone else doesn't. The word that the church speaks in the face of the world's injustice, struggles, needs, fears, and church fights, the word that the world cannot say to itself? *Jesus.*

When prominent evangelicals like Albert Mohler, Eric Metaxas, or *First Things'* Rusty Reno attempt to defend Trumpism, equating Christianity with Republicans, never, ever do they refer to Jesus.[29]

Good call.

Spread the News

Barth contended that the only difference between Christian and non-Christian is "noetic," a matter of having been given knowledge of God. A Christian is no better morally or intellectually. A Christian's modest claim is to have received news of who God is and thereby now knows how it stands between us and God. Revelation, given to and received by empty-handed, undeserving recipients makes a Christian, Christian.

The gospel is neither *photismos* (enlightenment), *musterion* (mystery),[30] *gnosis* (knowledge), nor *nomos* (law). Gospel is *euangellion*—Good News.[31] The gospel is news that stays news, a happening that demands to be shared, information that is not self-generated but demands to be self-delivered.[32] Announcers of the news don't spend much effort worrying about how to spread the news; broadcasters urgently buttonhole the first person they meet. News begs delivery. The nature of the gospel as news explains why preaching is the primary activity of the church (that community convened by the news for the purpose of giving out the news), God's main means of getting out the word that God is not against us (Rom 8:31).

We don't know why God has given us this news, but we know wherefore, to give away what we have received. Thus missionary preacher Paul says that faith is not only hearing but also passing on news:

> All who call on the Lord's name will be saved. So how can they call on someone they don't have faith in? And how can they have faith in someone they haven't heard of? And how can they hear without a preacher?. . . So, faith comes from listening, but it's listening by means of Christ's message. (Rom 10:13-14, 17)

The substance of the good news? Paul repeats it as he heard it:

> Brothers and sisters, I want to call your attention to the good news that I preached to you, which you also received and in which you stand. You are being saved through it if you hold on to the message I preached to you, unless somehow you believed it for nothing. I passed on to you as most important what I also received: Christ died for our sins in line with the scriptures, he was buried, and he rose on the third day in line with the scriptures. He appeared to Cephas, then to the Twelve, and then he appeared to more than five hundred brothers and sisters at once—most of them are still alive to this day, though some have died. Then he appeared to James, then to all the apostles, and last of all he appeared to me, as if I were born at the wrong time. . . . So then, whether you heard the message from me or them, this is what we preach and this is what you have believed. (1 Cor 15:1-8, 11)

There you have it. The good news of a Jew named Jesus ("God saves") who "died for our sins in line with the Scriptures, . . . was buried, . . . was raised on the third day, . . . appeared to Cephas, then to the twelve, . . . to more than five hundred brothers and sisters, . . . then . . . to James, then to all the apostles. Last of all, . . . he appeared to me"; so I announced, so you believed.

Gospel is not a set of ideas, a precious something tucked into our hearts, a decision we made, much less a feeling we experienced, nor is gospel a procedure for getting right with God. Gospel is news of what God has done and (because of resurrection) is now doing. Gospel is not how we wind up at an optimum ultimate destination, nor is it an exhortation to industriously work justice to make the world more habitable for victims of our injustice. Gospel—who God is, what God is up to, and how we are part of it—is a sermon that Paul did not come up with on his own, an announcement "which you in turn received, in which also you stand, through which also you are being saved," this story "that I proclaimed to you." Christians—saved by a true story of how Christ enfolds us into God's story.[33]

Most preachers learn that vagueness, abstraction, and generalization are the death of interesting preaching. Barth says that evasion of the concrete, particular, God-with-a-body-speaking personification of God leads to atheism:[34]

> The question can't be: What is God? The question must be: *Who is God?* And the answer can't be the description of an It; but must be the characterization of a person. This is the first and definitive depiction of God's identity that arises out of the fact that God is knowable to us through God's Word. What Christian preaching calls God's revelation is God's speaking, lightning that rends the darkness (what a lame comparison!), an unnatural occurrence, the Logos, the free divine Spirit who makes God's true self known. . . . The miracle or paradox of revelation is that God personally speaks to us this Word and that we can hear this Word as an address, person to person. . . . God is a person, Christian revelation is trinitarian revelation. This decisively rules out any possibility of seeing God behind, above, or apart from God's personality. This is an axiom of Christian proclamation—God exists as a person, Father, Son, and Spirit from eternity to eternity. Once we abstract or conceptualize God as detached from the speaking person who addresses us, once we dissolve God into a general truth or idea that is no longer a person, we are no longer thinking about God.[35]

Paul's "Gospel of God" or "God's good news" (Rom 1:2-4 NRSV, CEB) tells us more about who Christ is than what he says or does. Paul describes Christ's post-Easter epiphanies as "appearances," not "Risen-Christ sightings." Christ's presence is gift, not our discovery, God coming to us rather than from inside us, speaking words we cannot say to ourselves.

A prominent preacher launched a series, Learn How to Recognize God's Voice. In the first sermon, he promised to take the mystery out of revelation with "seven ways to test in order to know with absolute certainty you are hearing the voice of God." "You can't have a relationship with God if you can't hear God, if God never speaks to you." Still, "How do you know if your thought about God came from God or the Devil or a bad burrito you ate last night?"[36] His first example of hearing direct, unmistakable revelation? "Render unto Caesar." "If you're thinking of not paying taxes, it's a refusal to listen to God," says the preacher, guffawing.

Announcement of a New World

Barth's theological revolution began in 1918 through a close, creative reading of Paul's Letter to the Romans—and after a frustrating decade of attempting to preach. That which Barth received from Romans, leading to his bombshell of a book, was, "We have found in the Bible a new world, God. God's sovereignty, God's glory, God's incomprehensible love. Not the history of [humanity], but the history of God!"[37]

In a sermon on 1 Kings 17, Fleming Rutledge asks, "Why are the mainline churches having so much trouble?" She answers that mainline preaching is

> Not about a God who judges and redeems, who causes great movements to come to pass, who puts down the mighty from their seats and exalts the humble and meek. Instead, the messages are about human activity. They are about human potential, human hopes, human wishes, human programs and agendas. . . . The living God of Elijah does not seem to be in view.[38]

Mainline, liberal preachers in my part of the world preach mostly from the Gospels, rather than the earlier letters of Paul. Is that because the Gospels, replete with Jesus's words and deeds, couching Christology within narrative, appear to encourage human agency? Christ, the great exemplar of goodness, hanging out with the good country folk of Galilee, giving them a gentle nudge to love their neighbor as themselves; Christ, the beloved teacher who told stories that brought out the best in us; Christ, of use in our projects of the moment.

Maybe Christ as exemplar of good behavior is a First World problem. Paul, at work in 1 Corinthians 15, is strikingly disinterested in details of Jesus's birth, life, and death, as if the sheer, luminous identity of Christ overshadows his deeds and words, as if in his resurrection, Christ—bodily presence of God's eternal benevolence—needs no bolstering.[39] God raised crucified *Jesus. God* raised crucified Jesus. God raised *crucified* Jesus. This, the sermon Paul was dying to preach, is news that propelled Paul all over Asia Minor, planting churches where nobody knew they needed a church. Is Paul's "Gospel of God" (Rom 1:2-4) too hot for accommodated, well-adjusted-to-decline-and-death, self-help, bourgeois, progressive Christianity to handle?[40]

Years ago, the errant Jesus Seminar caused a stir by attempting to isolate and identify the few "authentic" words of Jesus, only to be surprised that Christians don't worship the words of Jesus; we worship the Word. While it's fair for preaching sometimes to offer helpful hints for persons in pain, therapeutic advice for the wounded, a reason to get out of bed in the morning, a spiritual boost for the sad, or a call to arms for social activists, human helpfulness can never be preaching's main intent because such concerns are of little concern to Jesus.[41] Besides, why get up, get dressed, and come to church at an inconvenient hour of the week to hear what is otherwise readily available anywhere else. At least Rotary serves lunch.

Christ's identity makes preaching in his name dangerous in its consequences and cosmic in its intentions:

> You previously heard about this hope through the true message, the good news, which has come to you. . . . He rescued us from the control of darkness and transferred us into the kingdom of the Son he loves. He set us free through the Son and forgave our sins.
>
> The Son is the image of the invisible God, . . .
> Because all things were created by him:
> both in the heavens and on the earth,
> the things that are visible and the things that are invisible.
> Whether they are thrones or powers or rulers or authorities,
> all things were created through him and for him.
> He existed before all things, and all things are held together in him.
> He is the head of the body, the church, who is the beginning,
> the one who is firstborn from among the dead
> so that he might occupy the first place in everything.
> Because all the fullness of God was pleased to live in him,
> and he reconciled all things to himself through him—
> whether things on earth or in the heavens.
> He brought peace through the blood of his cross. (Col 1:5-6, 13-15, 16-20)

Paul's story of God coming alongside us in the history of Jesus Christ, God's Son, clashes with what we think about God. So the good news bears repeating. Preaching is difficult because of Christ, God unexpected, God daring to entrust "the message of reconciliation" to frail envoys (1 Cor 5:19).

It's fine for preachers to call out human sinfulness, screwed-upness, bias, and idolatrousness. I do so frequently, which helps me feel better about my own moral compromises. Yet we are not free to belabor human depravity without stressing that we are sinners to whom God in Christ has turned, "For us and for our salvation," as the Nicene Creed puts it. Moralistic, judgmental preaching "is often mistaken for prophetic preaching," says Richard Lischer, moral hectoring rather than proclamation.[42] The good news is not that we might make moral headway but rather that the God from whom we sinners turned away has come out to meet us.[43]

Woe to the preacher who cuts Paul's Christ Pantocrator down to our size. Years ago, faced with the challenge of preaching four baccalaureate services to diverse congregations (that is, congregations clueless about Christ), I took the easy way out and preached Jesus's parable of the prodigal son (Luke 15) as a story about what sometimes happens when graduates at last leave home. Jesus the helpful human relations expert. The congregations received my conventional wisdom with a collective yawn. If Paul's claims for Christ are true, there's no way Jesus would have told that parable for that purpose. Fretting over better family life, what to do after graduation—such small potatoes for One on his way to a new heaven and earth.

When some challenged Paul's preaching, Paul's defense was, "I want you to know that the gospel I preached isn't human in origin. I didn't receive it or learn it from a human. It came through a revelation from Jesus Christ" (Gal 1:11-12). Paul's apostolic defense applies to every preacher. Authorization rests not upon an orthodox, faithful reiteration of church tradition or ecclesiastical reinforcement, and certainly not upon the expertise of the preacher. Sanction is "through a revelation from Jesus Christ" or nothing.

I know. This bodacious claim of received revelation could lead the claimant to self-delusion in which we preach ourselves as exemplars rather than preach Christ crucified (2 Cor 4:5). I'll admit that there are pompous preachers, though the world is giving most preachers less to be pretentious about. Few preachers would declaim with Paul, "I no longer live, but Christ lives in me" (Gal 2:20). More typical is to mumble, "Ur, uh, this is just how I see it."

In daring to hand over what they receive (1 Cor 4:7), preachers are given an assignment, commissioned as missionaries. Luther tells his flock that when we "hear how Christ comes here or there, or how someone is brought to [Christ], you should therein perceive . . . he is coming to you, or you are brought to him. For the preaching of the gospel is nothing else than Christ coming to us, or we being brought to him. . . . Christ is yours, presented to you as a gift. . . . [Then, after having received Christ,] it is necessary that you turn this into an example and deal with your neighbor in the very same way, be given to him as a gift and an example."[44] Listening to a sermon risks Christ's coming "to you, or you . . . being brought to him," *and* being placed under compulsion to hand over Christ to the neighbor.[45]

Paul preaches to the Corinthians as an externally authorized spokesperson for Christ: "From Paul, called by God's will to be an apostle of Jesus Christ" (1 Cor 1:1). And though he begins with praise for "God's church that is in Corinth, . . . made holy," Paul brags that he wasn't sent by Christ "to baptize but to preach the good news . . . and not with clever words so that Christ's cross won't be emptied of its meaning" (v. 17). Then Paul waxes homiletical: "The message of the cross is foolishness to those who are being destroyed. But it is the power of God" (1 Cor 1:18). "In God's wisdom, he determined that the world wouldn't come to know him through its wisdom. Instead, God was pleased to save those who believe through the foolishness of preaching. Jews ask for signs, and Greeks look for wisdom, but we preach Christ crucified, which is a scandal to Jews and foolishness to Gentiles. But to those who are called—both Jews and Greeks—Christ is God's power and God's wisdom" (vv. 21-24).[46]

To bolster his argument for the wise foolishness of preaching, Paul appeals to the Corinthians' experience of vocation, "But God chose what the world considers foolish to shame the wise. God chose what the world considers weak to shame the strong. And God chose what the world considers low-class and low-life—what is considered to be nothing—to reduce what is considered to be something to nothing" (1 Cor 1:27-28).

Preachers work with no foundation for preaching, no authorization, no safety net beneath our high-wire act except *Deus dixit*.

On the Sunday after the 2016 presidential election debacle I preached in a United Methodist church in the suburbs of Washington, DC. The pastor expected to lose as many as thirty families—Obama political appointees sure to be purged. My text was the assigned epistle, Romans 5, "Christ died for the ungodly." I reminded the faithful that gracious Jesus died for sinners, only sinners, and that Jesus liked nothing better than to party with tax collectors and whores.

My sermon concluded with, "OK, good for us. We have elected a lying, adulterous, draft-evading, bankruptcy-declaring, misogynistic, racist riverboat gambler with tacky gold plumbing fixtures. He is a national disgrace *and* [pause for effect] *one whom Jesus Christ loves, saves, and for whom he gave his life*. [Leaning over the pulpit, looking into the whites of their eyes.] *Are you sure that you want to worship* that *Savior?*"

I preached not as I pleased that Sunday and let Paul do the talking.

There have been times—such as the moments before a funeral for a toddler in our congregation—when I sat in my study and groused to the Lord, "I'm not going out there and making some lame excuse for your behavior," only to have the Lord shove me on stage and insist that Paul feed me the lines. Though at that moment I wasn't convinced, it was encouraging to hear Paul say, "Nothing can separate us from God's love in Christ Jesus our Lord: not death or life, not angels or rulers, not present things or future things, not powers or height or depth, or any other thing that is created" (Rom 8:38-39).

Jesus, Free Agent of Preaching

Jesus's first sermon in Nazareth (Luke 4:16-30) is preceded by Jesus reading from the Isaiah scroll. The congregation marvels at his beautiful recitation. "Today this Scripture is fulfilled." An excited stir runs through the assembly. Who is more worthy of salvation and liberation than we? Then Jesus preaches. That's when the trouble starts, of course.

The preacher reminds the chosen that on previous occasions when God showed up during a famine, there were hungry women in Israel. God's prophet fed only a foreigner. And when Elisha healed a Syrian army officer, surely there were afflicted in Israel more worthy than an enemy soldier.

And the congregation's adulation turned to wrath. To be reminded that God's previous appearances had been beyond the bounds of Israel, to realize the implications of praying, "Listen! Our God is the Lord! Only the Lord!" (Deut 6:4), to hear that God is not our patron—well, it was more than we good synagogue-going folk could take. To cluster around *our* God, only to have the preacher use our Scripture against us—well, we rose up as a body to silence the preacher.

"Never seen this congregation more united," they said as they dragged the preacher out.

The congregation failed. Jesus "passed through the crowd and went on his way" (Luke 4:30). Luke doesn't say that Jesus quieted them or miraculously vanquished them. Jesus came to his own, but his messianic intentions were beyond even the self-consciously elect. He appears to us, but he will not be captured by us. He talked directly from our Scriptures but preached them as the God we didn't expect. So we put him in a box, sealed the lid, posted a squad of soldiers to guard the tomb . . . only to have him go his own way.

What way? Toward a woman, Mary Magdalene, showing the news that needed to be told, making her the first preacher (John 20:1, 11-18). "Don't hold on to me," says the risen Christ (20:17), echoing Luke 4:30. Then the commission to preach: "Go to my brothers and sisters and tell them, 'I'm going up to my Father and your Father, to my God and your God.'" Mary Magdalene announces to the disciples, "'I've seen the Lord.' Then she told

15

them what he said to her" (20:18).[47] Mary sees, hears, and then obediently speaks: this, the dynamic at the heart of Christian preaching. With Mary we say, "I've seen the Lord," daring to tell the news that nobody expected.

Against attempts to make Jesus mean anything we want, the canon, Old Testament and New, stubbornly stands in wondrous irreducibility and noncompliance, keeping the triune God complicated and uncontainable, defying our idolatrous reductionism, breaking free of our smothering embrace so that he may go his own way. Who thinks about the Jesus Seminar anymore? I expect it will take Jesus less than a decade to trash this beloved book of mine.

He goes his own way, even when we are unable to walk his way. Though we try to silence, to contain, or to restrain him, here's the good news: he will go his own way with the whole world going after him (John 12:19).

Then our dilemma. Will we listen to him preach, even though his words were not those we wanted to hear? As he passes our way, dare we go with him?

He promised that when just two or three are gathered, he'll be there (Matt 18:20). But he does not promise to settle in, be constrained, or be controlled by us. *Gott nimmer ruhet,* said Barth, after the first Sabbath God never rests (Ps 121:4). Having been in the midst of us, Jesus also passes through the middle of us and goes his way.

I accompanied a group of church folks on a work team to clean up after Hurricane Katrina. For my sermon that Sunday I reached for an obvious text, Mark 6—Jesus coming to his disciples in the storm:

> We have just been through a terrible storm. Many of our churches and parsonages have been destroyed. Amid the devastation it's good to know that Jesus comes to his followers in the storm and speaks, reassuring them, offering peace. Sort of like what Jesus is doing for us today in this service. Right?
>
> Mark says, "Jesus made his disciples get into a boat . . . , while he dismissed the crowd.
>
> "After saying good-bye to them, Jesus went up onto a mountain to pray. Evening came and the boat was in the middle of the lake, but he was alone on the land. He saw his disciples struggling. . . . The wind was blowing against them. Very early in the morning, he came to them, walking on the lake. He intended to pass by them. When they saw him walking on the lake, they thought he was a ghost and they screamed, terrified by the sight. Just then he spoke to them, 'Be encouraged! It's me. Don't be afraid'" (Mark 6:45–50).
>
> Jesus "made his disciples get in the boat" (a midnight sail was his idea) while he went off to pray. Strange, considering the gathering tempest. But when Jesus "saw his disciples struggling" with the wind against them, "he

came to them." That's Jesus. In the storm, he comes to us. Many of you can testify that when the sky is dark, when the storms of life are raging, Jesus comes and stands by us.

But this time through this text I received a jolt, for the first time noticing a detail: "He intended to pass by them." *What?*

"Jesus, we're going down! Come save us!"

And Jesus, just out on the waves for a stroll, intending to go somewhere else important, interrupts his journey, stops, hears, and responds.

Intended to pass them by? What's that supposed to mean?

I couldn't shake the question "Can it be that Jesus has more important work than speaking to and rescuing his own followers?" Can Jesus's mission be greater and more expansive than our church in our time of need?[48]

Jesus, through Mark 6, pushed me into a sermon I didn't plan to preach and the congregation was unprepared to hear. I had meant conventional pastoral reassurance: Jesus comes to us in the storm. Smacking me with verse 48, Jesus spoiled my sermon and preached another.

Jesus comes to his people in the middle of our storms, yet his saving work is not limited to us. To be the church is to deal with our pain and tragedy but at the same time to be pushed to respond to someone else's hurt beyond the bounds of the church. Jesus calls us to venture forth with him into the storm, and then he entrusts to us a mission that doesn't end in the boat. The boat (*navis*, ancient symbol for the church, insignia of Duke Divinity School) is not Jesus's sole concern.

Much of systematic theology is an attempt to systematically stabilize, to housebreak and bind this free and living God. We can't, because Christianity is a revealed religion. Dealings between us and God are up to God. If you have a taste for adventure, are willing to be out of control of the communication, it's a great way to make a living, watching Jesus elude the church's smothering clutch and go his own way.

When we preach Christ, we refute Feuerbach's charge that when Christians say "God," we are projecting our pietistic feelings about God, naming our dreams and feelings "God." Really, Feuerbach, if we were merely casting our desires out into the cosmos and calling the echo "God," would we have come up with *Jesus* as Son of God?[49] Would we have devised poor old dilapidated church as Christ's presence in the world? We are capable of projecting gods easier to get along with than the Trinity, I assure you.

Revelation is an event whereby God lifts the veil and enables us to discern and then to speak about God.[50]

> Thought and speech about God must be ventured. But the final outcome must be left to God's own Word. We cannot repeat God's revelation or take [God's] Word on our lips. We can only bear witness to [God], and then God can speak . . . through our witness. . . . We must bear witness to God's Word with our human words so that God . . . may speak.[51]

Barth initiates talk about God by assuming God's determination to self-reveal, beginning not with nineteenth-century doubts but with wonder that we indeed know God here, now. We are not left to our own devices, forced to rummage in subjectivity, hoping to dig up some hint of transcendence. Rather, we relish the surprise that we really know God because in the Incarnation, God has lovingly objectified God's self.[52] The mercy of God is now knowable in the history of Jesus Christ, God entering history as a Jew from Nazareth who got down and dirty with us, God refusing to be suprahistorical.[53]

Dietrich Bonhoeffer says that the source of all preaching is the Word in the Flesh, Christ bodying forth among us:

> The proclaimed word has its origin in the incarnation of Jesus Christ. It neither originates from a truth once perceived nor from personal experience. It is not a reproduction of a specific set of feelings. Nor is the word of the sermon the outward form of the substance which lies behind it. The proclaimed word is the incarnate Christ himself . . . the thing itself. The preached Christ is both this Historical One and the Present One. . . . He is the access to the historical Jesus. Therefore the proclaimed word is not a medium of expression for something else, something which lies behind it, but rather it is Christ himself walking through his congregation as the word.[54]

When composing a sermon, I apply a theological test: *What is God doing in this biblical text, and what might God condescend to do in my sermon?* In every biblical text, even the most prosaic, God may take on our assorted idolatries. In the sorriest of sermons, Jesus may elect to show up and speak for himself.

At the Transfiguration (Mark 9:2-8), a couple of disciples are given a stunning vision along with a declaration from heaven. With Moses and Elijah standing by, the voice specifies Jesus. The baptismal voice heard by Jesus is now heard by Jesus's disciples. Earlier, the disciples were asked to "Follow me." In this transfiguring vision they are asked to do what the folk at Nazareth found difficult. Listen!

In Mark's account of Jesus's baptism, the descending Spirit calls Jesus "my Son, the Beloved" (Mark 1:9-11). At Mark's midpoint, in the Transfiguration, a heavenly voice designates Jesus as "God's Son." Only one human being calls Jesus God's Son in Mark. On the mount of Calvary, the voice is not from heaven but is that of a Roman Centurion, "This man is certainly God's Son" (Mark 15:39).

The *pneuma* leads to speaking, breathes upon Jesus in his baptism. Then, at the cross, when Jesus "breathed his last," after speaking a psalm from the cross, a Centurion exclaims, this was "God's Son." Surely Mark is making a connection between the breath from opened heaven, the Son of God's expiration from the cross, and the inspired exclamation from one of Caesar's finest. The Centurion says what Jesus's own disciples have been unable to confess. All the world has gone after him.

Barth said the best image of faithful preaching was Grünewald's "Crucifixion" from the Isenheim altar in Colmar, with John the Baptist's long index finger pointing away from himself, "impressively and realistically to what is indicated."[55] In Mark's Gospel, the one who speaks the truth about Jesus, pointing toward the crucified God, the one who gives testimony that Jesus's inner circle has yet to grasp, is a Centurion. The scandal of those whom God chooses to be preachers.

By the way, at Jesus's baptism the heavens were not "opened," as is the usual case with heavenly visions (Matt 3:16). Stephen's vision of Jesus at the right hand of God took place as heaven was opened (Acts 7:56); likewise, in the Revelation to John (Rev 19:11). But Mark 1:10 says the heavens were "torn apart," *skizomenos,* a Greek word used only eleven times in the New Testament. In Mark 15:38 "splitting open" is also used to describe the ripping of the temple curtain at Jesus's death.[56] Why "torn apart" (NRSV) rather than simply "opened"?

Isaiah begged God to "tear open" the heavens and come down (Isa 64:1). The veil that separates us from the Holy of Holies ("most holy place") is ripped in two. We are now unshielded from God's dangerous presence. The Heavens, the curtain separating us from God, the veil in the temple that disconnects God's earthly dwelling from the world, is now wide open. High priests, mediators who worked that exclusive sacred space in the most holy place, are no longer essential (see Heb 4:14-16). All that's lacking? Preachers.

Isaiah's prayer for God to rend the heavens and come down has received its answer. Jesus.

Chapter 2

SCRIPTURE: GOD'S ADDRESS

The theological rationale for Christian preaching, as well as its fiercest critic, is God speaking through a human being and a human book.

The Word that God spoke and that the prophets and apostles received, and we through them, wants to be spoken and received again. The problem of Christian preaching, . . . its only possible justification, is this: How can it be God's Word as a human word? . . . The point of the Bible is . . . *Deus dixit,* revelation. . . . The revealed Word becomes contemporaneous. . . . The record of this event becomes holy Scripture. . . . The same God will not keep silent today. [God's] Word is not buried in a book. The old witnesses speak in order that new witnesses may arise. We thus come up against living Christian preaching.[1]

Barth boldly based his Göttingen lectures upon a miraculous claim, *Deus dixit,* God has spoken, revealed through Scripture.[2]

Revelation is God's Word. . . . God's own speaking. . . . This is found in Scripture, this pregnant *Deus dixit,* God speaking personally as the subject, God as the author, God . . . speaking about [God's self]. This . . . makes Scripture the Word of God . . . the living hand which imperiously waves the rod, the canon [and the] . . . authority . . . in the relationship between the church and the Bible. . . . God is on the scene, speaking. . . . God as speaking subject, speaks through the medium of Scripture. This is how the permission and command to speak about God come into history . . . to which we ourselves belong.[3]

Two forms of revelation, Christ and Scripture, are the test for the third, which is preaching.

Christian preaching is measured, that is, critically purified, by the canon of Scripture and revelation.[4]

None of the three forms of revelation are revelation; together they "give witness" to God's revelation. Only God reveals God, "in statements, through the medium . . . of human speech."[5] Revelation can be received but never possessed; revelation is Jesus Christ, a free, living, speaking person, the action of God's revealing. Barth criticized Protestant scholasticism's "freezing of the relation between Scripture and revelation that equates the human words of Scripture as God's word."[6] By God's action, Scripture can become revelation but not independently revelation. After the Incarnation, nothing human is independent. Scripture becomes God's word when God takes up Scripture's human words and makes them God's word.[7] God's word is an event, not a given entity, an occasion to which we can only give witness.[8]

The prophets and apostles could no more talk about God than we can. Their witness, then, is: *Deus dixit*, God has spoken. Scripture is the basis of preaching, but it, too, [is only a] . . . witness to revelation. . . . The definition of Scripture as God's Word, or of God as its author, is a strictly paradoxical one. . . . Revelation gives rise to Scripture and itself speaks in it. This is what makes Scripture God's Word without ceasing to be historically no more than the words of the prophets and apostles, sharing the relativity, the ambiguity, and the distance that are proper to everything historical: the letters and words are flesh.

In revelation God unveils through human words, though even in unveiling, God is veiled:

Revelation means disclosure, *apokalypsis*, . . . revelation only in action, in the event of address, revelation is not a direct openness on God's part but a becoming open. God tears away the veil. . . . Later Protestant orthodoxy did incalculable damage [in not accepting] . . . the paradox that in Scripture God's Word is given to us in the concealment of . . . human words. . . . To deny the hiddenness of revelation even in Scripture is to deny revelation itself. . . .

The revelation that God enables through Scripture is not fixed and stable, so biblical exegesis is not a technique for grasping God's word; exegesis is empty-handed expectancy of fresh revelation.

God's Word is no longer God's Word when the truth that is new every morning is made into a sacred reality. . . .[9]

"Deus dixit means here and now" that occurred "then and there, for . . . there is no avoiding the offensive 'there in Palestine' and 'then in the years A.D. 1–30.'"[10] God, once active at a particular time and place, reiterated in our time and place. That's why we speak of a "passage" of Scripture, because in God's hands a text can be a path from one place to another.

Preaching is the reproduction, the spontaneous adoption of the biblical witness to revelation. Christian preachers are second-rank witnesses. They are neither prophets nor apostles but witnesses. As witness, preaching relates directly not only to Scripture but also to revelation. As Scripture is the Word of God in time and history, and as such the presupposition of the church and its preaching, revelation is the eternal Word of God. Both together are the basis of Christian preaching.[11]

And God Said

While it's true that before Christ, God had not been seen (John 1:18), from the first, we heard. Though averse to visual images, Yahweh loves conversation.[12] If the Trinity had been content to be self-contained—God alone, free of conversation partners external to the Trinity—for us there would be neither there nor here, only vacuous silence.[13]

Luther thought frivolous his student's question, "What was God doing before Creation?" I know the answer: Before God spoke the cosmos, God enjoyed constant colloquy—the Father engaging the Son, the Divine Logos (John 1 doesn't call Christ "the Word" for nothing) in conversation with the Father, all in the communicative power of the Spirit.[14]

Then, with linguistic fecundity overflowing, God began a conversation called Creation by saying, "Light," and it was so.

Reputed gods make matter by having sex with other gods, or through a grand, cosmic war between the forces of light and darkness. God creates by sovereignly saying a word, preaching to the "formless void," addressing, commanding, thereby making something out of the *tohu wabohu,* cosmos without shape or form. Dumb, mum darkness, audience for God's first sermon, "Light!"

> In the beginning was the Word
>> and the Word was with God
>> and the Word was God.
> The Word was with God in the beginning.
> Everything came into being through the Word,
>> and without the Word nothing came into being. (John 1:1)

"God said" occurs ten times in the first account of Creation; five times "God called," God calling, creating newness, something to say (and the means to say it) in a sermon on Sunday, the genesis of all: *Deus dixit.*

Word precedes world. Reality is linguistically constructed. Words do not arise from things; things are evoked by the Word. God said, "Light." And there was.[15]

Yahweh graciously relinquishes a monopoly on speech and allows the earthling, Adam, to enjoy a bit of divine creativity by christening "all the livestock, all the birds in the sky, and all the wild animals" (2:20). My candidate for the meaning of "Let us make humanity in our image" (Gen 1:26) is human speaking, even with its limitations, which is divinely permitted and authorized, imitating a defining characteristic of our Creator. "Image of God"—God's vocation of speech.[16]

God engages the earthlings in tête-à-tête, the remedy for human loneliness (Gen 2:18). In overflowing fecundity God says: "I've enjoyed being fruitful and multiplying; now you try it!" (1:28, paraphrased).

Paul brashly connected God's light-show, the first sermon, with his own preaching:

> We don't preach about ourselves. Instead, we preach about Jesus Christ as Lord, and we describe ourselves as your slaves for Jesus's sake. God said that light should shine out of the darkness. He is the same one who shone in our hearts to give us the light of the knowledge of God's glory in the face of Jesus Christ. (2 Cor 4:5-6)

In Paul's proclamation, God made something out of nothing all over Asia Minor and launched an ultimately victorious, nonviolent invasion of the Empire. When I preach Paul's letters, God condescends co-creation with me, invading North Carolina. Every time a preacher speaks, silence is broken, and someone emerges, mumbling, "I heard something today," it's Genesis 1 all over again.

God doesn't simply expound, declare, pronounce; God begins a colloquy. The Bible, God's relentless determination to be in conversation with God's people, in God's world, for God's purposes.[17]

The earthlings are not humanity's sole conversation partners. A smooth-talking, reptilian Questioner contests God's speech: "Did God say . . . ?" (Gen 3:1). (Theologians, with us from the first.) We immediately allow God's speech to be trumped by a snake, unable to distinguish the voice of God from that of Satan.

God had enjoyed easy conversation while walking in the garden with the woman and man, "during the day's cool evening breeze" (3:8). Now God interrogates: "Where are you?" "Who told you that you were naked?" "Did you eat from the tree, which I commanded you not to eat?" Then, "What have you done?" (3:9-11).

Pitiful blaming begins, "The woman you gave me. . . . The snake tricked me." It's all God's fault. Words once used for afternoon banter with God in the garden are now used to excuse and evade.

"Because you did this . . ." (3:14) "I will put contempt between you . . . ," "I will make your pregnancy very painful" (3:15-17). God is passionately invested in the earthlings, so God's discourse quickly becomes overheated. Soliloquy is more civil.

Fascinated by the Garden's forbidden tree, I preached in Duke Chapel from Genesis 3:

> It's a once upon a time sort of story. Once, we had it all—with no business more pressing than "to be fruitful and multiply." We were like children, naked but unashamed, . . . a two-year-old after her bath, romping gleefully through the living room, undiapered and unashamed, unselfconscious, once upon a time.
>
> But because it's a Bible story, it's a true story about *limits*. Enjoy the garden—only stay off that tree over there. Why that tree? We're only told it's the "tree of the knowledge of good and evil." Your student ears perk up because that's why you are here at Duke. You pay absurdly high tuition; we hand over knowledge.
>
> But because it's a true story, it's also a story of limits. We are different from God; we don't always know what is good, whereas God does. . . . Life, as good as it often is, has limits. (A) We don't know everything. (B) We shall die. . . .
>
> We wanted to be smart as God, so we disobeyed, ate from the tree of knowledge. Our innocent eyes were opened and we saw . . . our genitals. Congratulations on becoming an adult. Now, cast from the

good garden, innocence lost, we know only one thing for sure; we are naked and therefore afraid.

All culture, science, art, industry, philosophy arises as response to our nakedness. That is, we are (despite our marvelous brains) fragile, exposed, vulnerable, mortal. . . .

So, lacking immortality, security, meaning beyond ourselves, we write books, do research, endow chairs at universities, have children, make war, paint pictures—all as elaborate defense against the primordial awareness that we are naked and therefore afraid.

It's a story about the journey between your freshman and senior year. You have lost enough of your innocence to know that there's a world of things you don't know (midterms are only a week away), that relations between men and women are terribly conflicted. ("Nobody dates at Duke.")

You assume that your sense of vulnerability is temporary, that someday you'll know enough, be adult enough, to have overcome adolescent anxieties. By graduation, if all goes well, we will have succeeded in deceiving some of you into thinking that Duke has done this for you. Diploma in hand, you'll say, "I'm all grown up and can at last take hold of my life and stand on my own two feet because I got an A in organic chemistry." (The closest one can come, by senior year, to being as wise as gods.)

And yet someday, you may come to see that this was a great deceit; that, in truth, you are not self-sufficient but really quite small, finite— namely, *naked and afraid*. You will be sitting in your den, a martini in hand, but you will be naked. Once you needed a drink to party; now you need booze to forget. Your heart will skip a beat, you get a whiff of mortality. Then you will see yourself located, not in some gated Eden called "Westmont Estates" but in a weedy desert. And if asked "why?" you may blame your parents or an inadequate exercise program, . . . or you may say, if you muster as much honesty as Grandfather Adam, "I was naked. . . . I was afraid."

Which brings us to the end. . . . The story concludes, not with this curse of pain and enmity of thorns and dusty death but with the Lord God, Creator, Gardener, Accuser, becoming a *Tailor*. God made, for the two creatures, clothes.

Naked creatures need protective covering as they go out into a now difficult and bewildering world. They're not on their own. God gives what they need.

God will not abandon them to their destructive delusions of self-sufficiency. God refuses to give up on these two naked, frail earthlings. God gives them clothes and thus promises to continue to care for them, even in their silly presumption, even in their knowing too much for their own good.

Finite, frail, naked we are—yes, says the story. But also *loved,* clothed, fed, protected, in order to know not just the facts of life—death, good, and evil—but also trust in a God who makes us what we cannot make of ourselves.

From another tree, not in a Garden of Eden but overlooking a garbage dump called Calvary, God says: *My creatures, know this; I'll not let you go.*[18]

Adam and Eve's disobedience followed by God's tailoring were not the end of the story. Sorry to say, things turn from bad to worse, creation out of kilter. The woman's triumphant, "I have given life to a man with the Lord's help" (4:1) is followed by sibling violence. The first human progeny is the first fratricide (4:1-16). God's well-tuned ears hear Abel's blood preach from the offended earth (4:11). Though this could not have been the story God meant, it's the story God got once we learned to talk on our own. Iron and bronze are invented for tools (4:22)—and weapons. Music (4:21) was good for making love and for marching into battle. Human creativity is morally ambiguous.

Shortly thereafter, "people began to invoke the name of the Lord" (4:26). Amid our killing, avenging (4:24), and grief, did we humans sense that we badly needed someone to talk to other than ourselves? More likely, our calling upon God was responsive; even amid our head-bashing, God kept calling upon us.[19]

The gracious "have dominion" led to earth's despoilation. A garden, given to inepts and ingrates, becomes a desert. Seeing "that humanity had become thoroughly evil on the earth and that every idea their minds thought up was always completely evil" (6:5), launches the Lord into grief-stricken lament, "I will wipe off of the land the human race that I've created" (6:7).

Good news: God's soliloquys are short-lived. "God said to Noah . . ." (6:13). Noah is given detailed instructions on how to build and stock the salvific ark. God's justifiable regret at humanity's displacement of divine intentions, followed by remorseful silence, then God's redemptive resumption of the conversation shall be repeated time and again in God's conversation with God's troublesome creatures. Thank God.

An Anecdotal History of *Deus Dixit*: The Old Testament[20]

On a cloudless night God—self-identifying as "God Almighty"— summons a ninety-year-old nomad, Abram, and promises to make "a great nation" from him and his aged, childless wife Sarai (Gen 17). The world considered the couple "barren"; God promised descendants as numerous as stars (17:16). Though Abraham and Sarah mockingly laughed,

Isaac is conceived and born. With nothing to reassure them other than the promissory *Deus dixit,* the old folks venture forth, mocking laughter turned to joy.

I've got a bang-up sermon, preached numerous times at various venues, linking Sarah's laughter with Matthew 5:4: "Happy are people who grieve, because they will be made glad," tying in their geriatric, topsy-turvy redemption with Christ's work on the cross. But I won't bother you with it. For now, it's enough to note that God didn't wait until the advent of Christ to make redemptive announcements.

All is not divine decree; God calls for conversation. At first God secretly considers destroying wicked Sodom, then, remembering dialogue partner Abraham, God asks, "Will I keep from Abraham what I am about to do?" (Gen 18:17). Abraham dares to bargain and cajole. Fifty? Twenty? How do you like those numbers? God relents. If a mere ten righteous are found in Sodom, God will spare the city (18:16-32). "When he finished speaking with Abraham, he left," though in what frame of mind, after being worn down by Abraham's haggling, we don't know. (Many of Moses's arguments with God will be attempts to talk God out of destroying all Israel; divine-human bargaining doesn't die with Abraham.)

Abraham isn't only the recipient of blessing; he is the carrier. As Barth frequently noted, every gift (*Gabe*) is also a task (*Aufgabe*). God's election is borne into the world by an exasperatingly dysfunctional family.

The Lord chooses to work in concert with losers like Israel and the church. Surely Paul was thinking of God's Abrahamic covenant when he preached to squabbling First Church Corinth:

> By ordinary human standards not many were wise, not many were powerful, not many were from the upper class. But God chose what the world considers foolish to shame the wise. God chose what the world considers weak to shame the strong. And God chose what the world considers low-class and low-life—what is considered to be nothing—to reduce what is considered to be something to nothing. (1 Cor 1:26-28)

Though blessed to be God's blessing, God's relationship to Abraham is not merely instrumental. Israel is constituted by God's unwarranted love (Hos 11:1), an audience for God's exuberant self-glorification: "Have you not heard? The Lord is the everlasting God, the creator of the heavens and the earth . . . [who] gives power to the faint and strengthens the powerless" (Isa 40:28-29).

Conversation Resumed

Abraham's progeny became numerous, enslaved by the empire, desperate for some counter word to Pharaoh's pronouncements. Murderer Moses, though having been raised in the Pharaoh's court, is on the lam in Midian, playing the shepherd (Exod 3). A bush bursts into flame but is unconsumed. The bush speaks! Moses notices.

(Unaccustomed to Yahweh's speech, were verbal pyrotechnics required to get Moses's attention?)

"I've clearly seen my people oppressed in Egypt. I've heard their cry of injustice because of their slave masters. I know about their pain. I've come down to rescue them from the Egyptians in order to take them out . . . I've seen just how much the Egyptians have oppressed them" (Exod 3:7-9). God heard the groaning of the enslaved and recalled the covenant with Abraham, Isaac, and Jacob (Exod 2:23-25), though it took Yahweh four hundred years to remember.

Then, as shall reoccur in God's story, there is vocation: "So get going. I'm sending you to Pharaoh" to say, "let my people go." Wonder of wonders, God enlists slow-of-speech Moses to speak.[21]

God frees the Hebrews through the speech of a none-too-talented, untrained, unwilling Moses? "Who am I to go to the Pharaoh" and say . . . ?

"I'll be with you."

Yet speaking up for God doesn't guarantee listener assent. Pharaoh reacts to Moses's pleas and threats with stubbornness (Exod 8:15, 32). Pharaoh has a stake in squelching uppity speech among the slaves.

Exodus claims more than people at the top have trouble hearing the petitions of those on the bottom. "The Lord made Pharaoh stubborn" (Exod 9:12; 10:20, 27). Why? No answer is given. Lord, not only of speaking but also of hearing, a God easily explained, wouldn't be the God of the Exodus.[22]

The way I read it, Moses becomes the first notable instance of God speaking through a person.

"I'm sending you to Pharaoh to bring my people, the Israelites, out of Egypt" (Exod 3:10). Having no interest in speaking directly to Pharaoh, God sends Moses. Preachers, note how quickly, how easily divine resolve devolves to human speaking, "I have seen . . . I have heard . . ." then, "So get going . . . and *say* to Pharaoh."

Once free of enslavement, Moses is given a tougher task even than speaking to Pharaoh—talking for God to God's people. After leaving the land of Egypt for the Sinai desert, words are put in Moses's mouth:

29

Moses went up to God. The Lord called to him from the mountain, "This is what you should say to Jacob's household and declare to the Israelites: You saw what I did to the Egyptians, and how I lifted you up on eagles' wings and brought you to me. So now, if you faithfully obey me and stay true to my covenant, you will be my most precious possession out of all the peoples, since the whole earth belongs to me. You will be a kingdom of priests for me and a holy nation. These are the words that you should say to the Israelites." (Exod 19:1, 3-6)

Moses's sermon begins in remembrance of an event ("You saw what I did"), then moves toward exhortation ("So now if you faithfully obey me . . ."), from recollection to performance, from memory of God's acts to present responsibility.[23] Israel never tired of recounting the Exodus as the basis for its life with God:

We have heard it, God, with our own ears;
our ancestors told us about it:
about the deeds you did in their days, in days long past.
You, by your own hand, removed all the nations,
but you planted our ancestors.
You crushed all the peoples,
but you set our ancestors free.
No, not by their own swords
did they take possession of the land—
their own arms didn't save them.
No, it was your strong hand, your arm,
and the light of your face
because you were pleased with them. (Ps 44:1-3)

Says Walter Brueggemann, "This peculiar community is not self-generated, but understands itself in terms of a special authorization in a script available for steady and regular, attentive reiteration," that is, through preaching.[24]

The promise came unconditionally, but once liberated, there are conditions: "So now, if you faithfully obey me and stay true to my covenant, you will be my most precious possession out of all the peoples" (Exod 19:5). The blessing of unsought, undeserved covenant has a bite. The many allusions to the flood in Exodus 32–34 remind Abraham's heirs not only of God's redemption but also of the divine temperament. Conversation with Yahweh is reciprocal, demanding; God's got a peculiar notion of "freedom."

Along the exodus way, Moses is a relentless petitioner, frequently reminding Yahweh of past promises, bargaining, angrily complaining, and daring to sweet-talk the same God who made Pharaoh pay a heavy price for talking back to God. Preacher Moses not only speaks for God to God's people but also speaks to God on behalf of God's people, sometimes speaking without decorum.

Like Matthew, I find gospel, good news, all over the Old Testament. A critic complained that for three Easters in a row I preached from Old Testament texts. I replied, "Sorry, the same God who brought Israel out of Egypt thinks nothing of a stunt like raising crucified Jesus."[25]

It's awfully hard to keep in conversation with Yahweh, no matter how good our intentions. The verbiage of other gods is alluring. So God called Moses up Sinai and gave Ten Words (just ten, when God could have demanded so many more), *Deus dixit* set in stone. Israel won't have to find its way on its own. Apodictic directives to protect God's chosen from adulterous conversation with false gods and their lies that we love.

By the time we get to Deuteronomy, Moses is quite a preacher, delivering three eloquent farewell sermons (Deut 1–4, 5–28, 29–30). Moses begs Israel to stay in love with the God who has loved them: "Israel, listen! . . . Love the Lord your God with all your heart, all your being, and all your strength" (6:4-5). Israel's tasks are twofold: to love and to listen.

Poetic, Prophetic Speech

God's speech chiseled in stone doesn't make fidelity easier. We are adept at fashioning conversation partners less demanding than Yahweh. So *Deus dixit* moves from imperatives of the Decalogue to the vocative prophetic call. God expands the company of preachers into a curious consortium called "prophets," God-obsessed evangelists, personally chosen by God, to give Israel the bad news of their coming exile, sustain them through the horrors of Babylonian captivity, announce that they were going home, then direct reconstitution as God's Torah-loving, covenant people—with nothing but words.

The prophets are among the most intriguing of Yahweh's speech performances. As poet-preachers, the prophets dared, even in their full, flawed humanity, to preach unabashedly, "Thus says the Lord," making it hard to tell if it's God talking or Isaiah. Barth marvels that prophets "begin their addresses with 'Thus says the Lord.'"[26] While we preachers cannot "speak subjectively like the prophets" in direct divine address, "our objective talk about God, though unavoidable, is subject to inevitable suspicion" that our descriptive, secondhand God talk is idolatrous, "putting something different and improper in the place of God," prattling on about the God we wish we had rather than the God who is.[27]

Most prophets, like Moses, must be coerced. A sense of being under divine compulsion, conviction of unworthiness for speechifying characterizes prophetic vocation. "A lion roars; who will not fear? The Lord God has spoken; who can but prophesy?" (Amos 3:8). Jeremiah, beaten up by the rigors of preaching, resolves not to speak again about God, but then there's a burning fire in his bones. "I'm drained trying to contain it; I'm unable to do it" (Jer 20:9).[28] "Human one, I've made you a lookout for the house of Israel. When you hear a word from me, deliver my warning" (Ezek 3:17). Thus, John Calvin said that the prophet is distinguished by unoriginality— the prophet never gets to speak on his or her own.[29]

Amos was told by court chaplain Amaziah, "Never again prophesy at Bethel, for it is the king's holy place and his royal house" (Amos 7:13). Royal clerical lackeys insist on monopolizing speech that's counter to the presumptions of the regime.

When challenged, Amos blamed his preaching upon the Lord:

> I am not a prophet, nor am I a prophet's son; but I am a shepherd, and a trimmer of sycamore trees. But the Lord took me from shepherding the flock, and the Lord said to me, "Go, prophesy to my people Israel." (Amos 7:14-15)

Courage comes to the preacher who is able to give Amos's retort, "My being a preacher was God's idea before it was mine. I preach what I've been told to preach."

Jeremiah's call is paradigmatic:

> The Lord's word came to me:
> "Before I created you in the womb I knew you;
> before you were born I set you apart;
> I made you a prophet to the nations."
> "Ah, Lord God," I said, "I don't know how to speak because I'm only a child."
> The Lord responded,
> "Don't say, 'I'm only a child.'
> Where I send you, you must go;
> what I tell you, you must say.
> Don't be afraid of them,

because I'm with you to rescue you,"
declares the Lord.
Then the Lord stretched out his hand,
touched my mouth, and said to me,
"I'm putting my words in your mouth.
This very day I appoint you over nations and empires,
to dig up and pull down,
to destroy and demolish,
to build and plant." (Jer 1:4-10)

Quite a preaching future for a fetus. Old worlds deconstructed, dismantled; new worlds formed, reformed, with some of the pushiest, poetic, richly metaphorical speech ever. Still, just words. Note God's strenuous oratorical agency, "I consecrated you; I appointed . . . you shall speak whatever I command. . . . I am with you. . . . I have put words in your mouth" (NRSV).

Luther quipped that the prophets "have a queer way of talking."[30] Prophets preach poetry, pushy plucking and planting, a valley of dead, dry bones (Ezek 37), smashing pots (Jer 18:1-11), locusts, fire, and a plumb line (Amos 7:1-9).[31] God is an enthusiastic metaphor-maker, reveling in figurative speech that makes the guardians of the status quo exclaim, "How dare you talk like that?" God's propensity for metaphor requires preachers to become, if not poets, at least lovers of language.

Preachers beware: Prophetic judgment begins with God's own house (1 Pet 4:17), focusing first upon those who are doing the talking. While I've been close with alcoholics in my congregations, I'm embarrassed that Scripture's most extended condemnation of drunkenness (Isa 28:1-22) is applied specifically to Israel's priests and prophets, calling them drunks (28:7-8) who "stagger," "confused by wine," and "stumble from beer." Their inebriated proclamation is boring, babbling baby talk, "tsav letsav, tsav lestav; qav leqav, qav leqav," which the NRSV tries to translate "precept upon precept, precept upon precept, line upon line, line upon line, here a little, there a little" (28:9-10). Blah, blah, blah.

After the jabbering, tanked-up preachers have had their say, Yahweh speaks (28:11). Marauding foreign powers shall lay waste the land (28:17-22). There's a high cost when the Chosen People put up with lying, cowardly, stoned preachers:

Therefore, hear the Lord's word,
you scoffers who rule this people in Jerusalem.
You said, "We've cut a deal with death;

with the underworld we made a pact.
When the overflowing flood passes through, it won't reach us;
for we have made lies our hiding place,
and in falsehood we take shelter."

The congregation shares responsibility. Yahweh tried to speak, "but they refused to listen" (28:12). Unfaithful preaching requires someone to speak falsely and somebody who laps up lies.

Still, Isaiah insists that God's remedy for this sad state of homiletics is more words. Isaiah 40–50 follows—a luminous, lyrical poem in which the disaster of exile is countered with sweeping promises of homecoming. Conversation between Yahweh and Israel cannot be ended unilaterally by Israel's stupidity. Yahweh keeps saying, "Listen and hear my voice" (Isa 28:23).

God manages God's heavy investment in Israel through prophets. Words wasted from the pulpit shall be liable to judgment. Practice temperance in the use of alcohol and the custody of language.

If congregations only knew how dependent prophetic preachers are on truth-loving hearers. One morning I opened a powder blue envelope addressed with a flowery hand that I knew belonged to one of our older women at Duke Chapel. Within the note was a newspaper clipping that reported American troops had buried alive a score of Iraqi soldiers in their trenches after a battle.

"By the time we got there, nothing but arms and hands sticking out of the sand," said one GI.

"Did you preach on this?" she asked in her note. "I don't get out much, but I listen to your sermons on television, and I don't recall that you mentioned this atrocity. Where is the moral voice of our clergy? We are frighteningly dependent upon our preachers."

With your help, Alice Philips, one day I might become North Carolina's Isaiah.[32]

However, the urge to be a "prophetic preacher" often brings out the worst in mainline preachers, political posturing and preening slightly to the left of the Democratic Party.[33] (One year we had a run of anti-Trump diatribes by guest preachers in Duke Chapel, presumptive prophets who condemned the rascal from the pulpit of a left-wing university chapel—causing not a stir.)[34]

"The Lord God gave me an educated tongue to know how to respond to the weary with a word that will awaken them in the morning. God awakens my ear in the morning to listen as educated people do" (Isa 50:4). A prophet speaks because a prophet has been spoken to.[35] The vocal range of prophets like Isaiah (Jesus's favorite) is testimonial to how the prophets have been addressed. At Sinai, thunder, lightning, thick cloud, trumpet blast, and earthquake preceded God's address (Exod 19:16-19), though the Lord's voice seemed to Elijah "Thin. Quiet" (1 Kgs 19:12). Even Creation "speaks" of God's glory in a noiseless but highly visible way (Ps 19:1-6).

Mohammed's range, from what I read, is less poetic and metaphorical than Amos's or Isaiah's. I've never heard the Buddha rage, shout, or mock.[36] Shiva dances but does not exhort. By comparison, the scope of Yahweh's discourse is remarkable.

Rather frequently among the prophets, God displays an emotion that is usually banished from church talk: anger. Sorry if your God must be an even-handed, civil, dispassionate bureaucrat: Israel's God is not indifferent to evil or impartial in dealings with rich and poor.[37]

"Your sermon came across as angry," said a respondent.

"Take it up with Jeremiah," said I. "Like every pastor, I'm conflict-averse. I would never pick a fight with you on my own."

Having been called (enlisted, forced) into this peculiar vocation— words stuffed in my mouth that are not my own, speaking, if not to nations and kings, at least to a few soft-hearted folk in my congregation—while not a replica or replacement of the prophets, I'm bold to claim distant kinship with prophetic antecedents: Moses, Jeremiah, Micah, and Jesus.[38]

> Every great epoch of church history is characterized by a fresh attentiveness to the initial historical sources, which compel and instigate talk about God, . . . that is, attentiveness to a biblical text. Thereby the church shows why it dares to speak about God even though this is an impossible undertaking. Speaking from a biblical text shows that here we are not talking about God on our own . . . knowledge, courage, or authority. . . . We have no independent knowledge to present. . . . [In preaching from a biblical text] we acknowledge that . . . the prophets and apostles once talked about God and . . . now we are compelled to do likewise. We thus dare what they dared. Or rather, we do not dare not to do so.[39]

Rabbi Heschel says that prophetic preaching ventures "a ceaseless shattering of indifference." One needs "a skull of stone to remain calloused to such blows."[40] I've ceaselessly attempted to smack congregational unconcern, only to find that their skulls are fairly well fortified against sermonic wallops. Though Jeremiah called God's word a "hammer" (Jer 23:29), the prophets' frequent complaint is that they talk but nobody listens. Yahweh warns Jeremiah, "When you tell them all this, they won't listen to you; when you call to them, they won't respond" (Jer 7:27). While "Hear the LORD's word" occurs thirty times in the Major Prophets, Jeremiah 25:4 complains that "the LORD has tirelessly sent you all his servants, the prophets, but you wouldn't listen or pay attention," and Jesus noted that prophets are disrespected even in their hometowns (Luke 4:24).

Amos hears God prophesy widespread hearing failure:

> The days are surely coming, says the Lord God,
> when I will send hunger and thirst on the land;
> neither hunger for bread, nor a thirst for water,
> but of hearing the Lord's words. (Amos 8:11)

Let's be honest about preaching failure. While some preaching flops because of the prophet's poor speaking or the hearers' stubbornness, other preaching fails due to the inexplicable work of a heart-hardening, neck-stiffening God (Jer 7:27; Isa 6:9-10). God speaks to those to whom God speaks. My go-to response when they plead incomprehension after a too subtle sermon? "Take it up with the Lord."

There's little indication that hearers, high or low, heeded the words of the prophets. Still, prophets keep talking, and Israel bravely recorded and cherished this long record of prophetic malfunction. God is undaunted by our collective failure to hear the word of God, thank God.

We dare to preach, not backed up by a surefire rhetorical formula but by a *Deus dixit* promise. Isaiah predicts that eventually "the deaf will hear the words of a scroll" (Isa 29:18). How could Isaiah be both honest and hopeful? "Look! I'm creating a new heaven and a new earth. . . . Before they call, I will answer; while they are still speaking, I will hear" (Isa 65:17, 25).

Having Our Say

Whereas the prophets are noted for upfront, direct speech from God, sometimes Yahweh speaks more covertly. In Esther's story, God holds back, allowing full room for human witness, particularly the witness of a woman in a world where women are often enjoined to silence. Old Mordecai asks Esther, "Who knows? Maybe it was for a moment like this that you came" to "speak up?" (Esth 4:14). Esther will leverage her privileged position in the palace to dare to speak the truth about wicked Haman. God's people are saved through a woman's words made God's. Who knew?

In the disturbing story of Tamar (2 Sam 13), God is silent while sinful men rape. It's fearful to consider the consequences of humanity left to its own devices without the chastening, intrusive, inconvenient, accusatory *Deus dixit*. We are made uncomfortable by texts of terror like the rape of Tamar that draw us into raw, unsafe conversation.[41] Even without God directly speaking, there is revelation as we are made to see the violence against women that God sees all the time, to hear what God hears in the victims' cry.

Israel's hymnbook, The Psalms, unlike the prophets, are human speech without explicit claim to be revelatory *Deus dixit*. Psalms invite people to sing, notice, lament, protest, complain, and rejoice. Some psalms give people in pain an opportunity to get outside of themselves, an invitation for pain to go public. Psalms tend to be repetitious, in much the same way that young lovers or people in pain repeat themselves.

Friendship with a God so perplexing and demanding is not for the faint of heart, say the psalms. A God who never provokes you into shaking your fist and crying out, "Why?" is not the God so intensely engaged by the psalmists. No wonder Jesus counseled us to go into our closet and shut the door when we need a one-on-one meeting with God (Matt 6:6).

The psalms delight that we are not self-produced (Ps 100:3), a most un-American thought you might overlook because it's in a song.

Some psalms demand a hearing from God, "Answer me when I call, O God of my right!" (Ps 4:1, 3). Others promise divine speaking and action at long last, "Then the Lord will speak to them in his wrath, and terrify them in his fury" (Ps 2:5). Occasionally, the voice of the psalmist is the voice of God lamenting lack of human hearing, "Listen, my people. . . . If only you would listen to me!" (Ps 81:8).

The sheer wonder of *Deus dixit* is Psalm 29's theme:

The Lord's voice is strong;
    the Lord's voice is majestic.
The Lord's voice breaks cedar trees—
    yes, the Lord shatters the cedars of Lebanon. . . .
The Lord's voice convulses the oaks, strips the forests bare,
    but in his temple everyone shouts, "Glory!" (Ps 29:4-5, 9)

Augustine preached vigorously through the psalms, saying that here "the church discovers its voice."[42] In his commentary on Psalm 30, Augustine says, "If the psalm prays, you pray, if the psalm laments, you lament, if the psalm rejoices, you rejoice, if the psalm expresses fear, you fear."

Dietrich Bonhoeffer's *Psalms: The Prayer Book of the Bible* calls the psalms a school for Christian prayer.[43] It is a "dangerous error" to think that "the heart prays by itself" because "Prayer does not mean simply [to] pour out one's heart. It means rather *to find a way to God*," which cannot be done alone.[44] In the psalms, God teaches us what to say to God, just as Jesus's disciples asked, "Lord, teach us to pray." The psalter is "totally absorbed in the prayer of Jesus," says Bonhoeffer.[45] Faithful Christian prayer does not come naturally: "The richness of the Word of God ought to determine our prayer, not poverty of our heart."[46] More than just spilling our guts, Christian prayer is determined by the chief partner in divine-human communication.

Even "Heaven is declaring God's glory; the sky is proclaiming his handiwork. One day gushes the news to the next" (Ps 19:1-2).

Awkward Conversation

Conversation between God and Israel can be uneasy. Ask Job. God accepts Satan's gambit (the Lord has time enough to banter with Satan?). God's hand is withdrawn from Job, leading to horrible calamities. Though Job cries out, God holds back for over thirty chapters, allowing the laboriously long speeches of Job's comforters. Each speaker responds to suffering Job with rational justifications; stiff upper lip, Job, this is the way the world works.

Job hears them out, then explodes, raging that God is an unreliable liar (9:20-22). Even in his accusations, Job yearns for conversation with God.[47] When God finally speaks, it's with swaggering braggadocio and bombast (Job 38–41). Enough of "words lacking knowledge" (38:2). Now God interrogates Job with a series of questions that reveal an infinite qualitative distinction between Job and God. Bragging about the creation of wild asses, crocodiles, and hippopotami (making no mention of humanity), God is most proud of those creatures who have no earthly use for humanity, but aren't they wonderful? Explain that, Job and friends.

Sorry, if you prefer your gods to speak with civility and decorum, Yahweh has bet the house on Job. Go ahead, all you would-be comforters, state your theodicies, offer words of consolation and explanation. Job, clinch your fist and demand, "Why?" The Lord shall have the last word, even if not the word you just had to hear.[48]

If Job will not praise Yahweh for crocodiles and hippos, even in the middle of his pain, then Yahweh will do the doxology. Yahweh's self-adulation is not dismissive but takes the conversation to a new level, and Job is made different by the dialogue.[49]

Preachers note: after the Lord speaks to Job, the Lord takes on presumed spokesperson, Eliphaz the Temanite:

> I'm angry at you and your two friends because you haven't spoken about me correctly as did my servant Job. So now, take seven bulls and seven rams, go to my servant Job, and prepare an entirely burned offering for yourselves. Job my servant will pray for you, and I will act favorably by not making fools of you because you didn't speak correctly, as did my servant Job. (Job 42:7-8)

Job impugned God's goodness and righteousness, not the friends. But the Lord's anger is kindled, not against Job who called God a liar but against God's presumed defenders who have "not spoke of me what is right." Only seven bulls and seven rams can set things right.

In a sermon on Job 42, Brent Strawn noted that the Hebrew rendered by the NRSV as "of me" in verses 7 and 8 could as well be translated as "to me," suggesting that Eliphaz has spoken *about* God (explanation and interpretation) when he should have been talking *to* God (prayer and supplication).[50] Maybe Yahweh prefers direct address ("Oh God, why?") to overhearing our discussions on theodicy ("Maybe your misfortune is best explained by . . . ").

Barth says that "If . . . it is the questioning Job who is in the right and not his friends . . . , this probably means that if there is any pointer to God or proof of God . . . , it will be found where we come up against the mystery of God."[51] Isaiah taunted hearers who "Listen intently, but don't understand; look carefully, but don't comprehend" (Isa 6:9). A frequent Barthian theme: the more distinctly God speaks to us, the greater our sense of distance between us and God, *Deus dixit*, but not on our demand, nor saying all we wish God would say. Neither does God keep silent in order to preserve our comfort.

Wisdom

Since my youth I've had an aversion to the Bible's wisdom literature—Proverbs, Ecclesiastes, a few of the psalms. Do this. Do that. Six principles for a long life. Three steps to success. Don't drink too much. Early to bed, early to rise. Don't be a fool. The Lord has set up an allegedly orderly universe with immutable moral laws that the wise uncover and to which they adhere. Then the Lord retired.

God makes a cameo appearance in Ecclesiastes or Proverbs. In general, the aspirations of wisdom speech are modestly nontheological: common sense, good advice, the pedantic pontificating that we old so often inflict upon the young. God steps back and lets the sages give the kids advice.

In Ecclesiastes, the pushy speech and daring imagination of the prophets becomes tired, grumpy, resigned. Daily work, pleasure, and money— "chasing after the wind." "There's no end to the excessive production of scrolls. Studying too much wearies the body" (Eccl 12:12), sighs this weary preacher.

Not much redemptive, salvific interest; who needs redemption if you are good at being chaste, obedient, and sober? What need have we of God when our sages are so successful at uncovering the twelve steps, six biblical principles, thought for the day, helpful hints for homemakers? Listen up, kid! Pay attention to your elders and intellectual betters.

Still, there is something to be said for Proverbs' advocacy for human responsibility. Our decisions are not trivial. God has set before us life or death (Deut 30:15). Everything matters. Proverbs' dozens of "Better than . . . " statements do not shrink from making value judgments: this way leads to life and wisdom, that way to foolishness and death. "It is the glory of God to hide something and the glory of kings to discover something" (Prov 25:2). No wonder the sages of wisdom literature get a hearing amid our regal confidence that the world can be explained without reference to the "supernatural." We don't need divine rescue; we need a purpose-driven life, deeper meaning, reason to get out of bed in the morning. Face facts. Adjust to the status quo. Don't waste time theologizing, the question is, Who am I and how can I manage the world to my advantage?

Much preaching today is in the wisdom mode; not a positive sign. Wisdom literature's genius is to present the world as an orderly, reliable cosmos. Wisdom's temptation is to reduce God's dealings with us to bourgeois respectability, maxims for the self-satisfied and the secure, the well-fixed and the smugly prosperous. At its best, wisdom embraces ordinary life. God doesn't talk much because God has set up an orderly, purposeful, predictable world. We can find our way without recourse to revelation or confessional speech. "Faith" is in our God-given ability to uncover the tidiness of reality and work it to our advantage. When you get your life in sync with the fundamental coherence of the cosmos, you will prosper. Want your life to count for something? Here's how I did it. Listen up, fools!

Alyce McKenzie surprised me by showing how Proverbs can be subversive, a "counter-view of life" that challenges "what passes for wisdom in a violent, individualistic, acquisitive culture."[52] Each fall Proverbs makes a brief appearance in the lectionary. In spite of my distaste for proverbial wisdom, I was weirdly unmethodist: I stuck with the NRSV text, Proverbs 22:1, "A good name is rather to be chosen than great riches."

"Nice thought. Except nobody matriculates at Duke for a good name. We go for the gold. Somebody get The Donald on the phone and ask, 'Hey, I'm a college student and wondering, what's the life worth living? I could try for a good name, or I could act like you. What do you advise?'" (Note: My sermon was preached back in Trump's adulterer/casino days, long before his Birther Movement. Not to brag, but I was the first to condemn the rascal from a pulpit—Duke Chapel, September 1993, prior to others piling on.)

"Put Proverbs 22:1 on a tee shirt. Wear it on campus. Let me know how you do in fraternity rush." And so on.

End of service, a young man emerged, thanking me for my "pastoral sermon." *Pastoral? I aimed for obnoxious.*

"Such a comfort. I'm calling my dad tonight to tell him that I'm not applying to law school. I'm going into elementary teaching, and if he doesn't like it he can go to hell."

Don't tell him where you were at 11:30 this morning![53]

God took a trivial, anthropological, hortatory text and made it theological. God used a cowardly, compromised, Southern-accented preacher to speak, so determined is Jesus to have his say.

Wisdom becomes more interesting when moving from sage advice to personification as Woman Wisdom. While she is elusive in Ecclesiastes (7:23-24), Proverbs incarnates wisdom as a woman calling out in the street (Prov 1:28), hawking her wares, God not awaiting our discovery of wisdom but raucously shouting at passersby in order to save us from our downward tumble into foolishness.

Sometimes the Old Testament is the word of God, but not a word that is best heard in the present moment. If you don't care for Ecclesiastes, wait until your sixty-fifth birthday; it will make more sense. If Jonah is a joke you don't get, when the Lord forces you to go somewhere you hate, Jonah will become the funniest thing you've ever heard, in a dark humor sort of way. I hope that you will never be in horrible pain and anguish, but if you are, Job awaits.

Once, after I had ripped into Trumpism, a listener asked, "But doesn't the Bible say that God sometimes uses even nonbelievers to do God's will?"

"Intriguing. Trump is the equivalent of Nebuchadnezzar? America has made some mistakes, but, geez, don't you think God's being a bit harsh? Still, you've got Scripture on your side." Anything in the canon, even the least apparently theological passages, can be an opportunity for *Deus dixit*.

If you're too young, too adventurous, too frightened, or too angry to tolerate the reasonable, measured cadences of Wisdom, be of good cheer. Before the Old Testament is done, there is a visionary outburst in places like Daniel and Ezekiel called "apocalyptic." Beasts and night visions, dry, dead bones taking on flesh, weird talk, even for Yahweh.

Apocalypticism arose as classical prophecy was on the wane. Apocalyptic visions speak of the future but also make a claim about the present. Don't be fooled by the seeming solidity of the present. God has more things up God's sleeve than you can imagine.

Divine discourse tends to be in the promissory mode; God's "I will act" being more plentiful than "I have acted." The Bible handed to me at my Confirmation listed a dozen pages of divine promises: Guilty? 2 Samuel 14:14; Psalm 130:3-4. Dejected? Psalms 119 and 116; Isaiah 65:25. Afraid? Psalm 4:8; Isaiah 35:4. Because divine/human conversation is constantly oriented toward the future, trust is required. It's a conversation that takes place on the way, moving from the present to the future, now but not yet, hoped for but not yet seen (Heb 11:1). Apocalyptic, exuberant crescendo of a promissory God.[54]

When somebody at First Church Corinth accused Paul of vacillation, he defended himself by characterizing his preaching as a first installment on the eschatological, old age ending–new age beginning promise of God's eternal Yes to us:

> But as God is faithful, our message to you isn't both yes and no. God's Son, Jesus Christ, is the one who was preached among you by us—through me, Silvanus, and Timothy—he wasn't yes and no. In him it is always yes. All of God's promises have their yes in him. That is why we say Amen through him to the glory of God. (2 Cor 1:18-20)

As Susan Bond has said, preaching apocalyptic literature requires a "homiletic of folly," which may be one reason liberal, mainline Christianity has always been embarrassed by the apocalyptic.[55] Dis-ease with apocalyptic, dismissal of this futuristic literature that leans into a new heaven and earth, is a sign of our ease in Zion (Amos 6:1): working the present age to our benefit, content with things as they are, hoping for progress rather than death of the old and birth of the new, keeping your dreams to yourself. Yet whenever people dare to think, "We are slaves, slaves in the land that you gave to our ancestors" (Neh 9:36), the soothing reassurances of mainline liberal preaching are inadequate. Nothing less than eerie visions of a new heaven and earth will do. The nightmarish visions of Daniel said little to me. Then came COVID-19, the body counts on each evening's news, impotent men raging in high places, and people cowering behind locked doors for fear. The penny dropped.

Apocalyptic literature is a fitting crescendo of the Old Testament. God's creativity doesn't end at Genesis 1; dismantling and disruption presage New Creation. God will get what God wants: bad news for those of us too tightly wedded to and profiting from the present, good news for those who need a different future in the worst way. Ezekiel's apocalyptic visions too rambunctious for you? Wait until you hear Jesus.

Hard of Hearing

An anecdotal survey of God's discourse in the Old Testament reveals God to be quite a talker, though God is burdened by lousy listeners. Typical is the time Jesus is speaking, and though some listeners hear a voice from heaven (John 12:28), others hear thunder, some the sound of an angel. God's voice can be the "song of thunderstorm" (Ps 29), where seven times God's voice is tempestuous. "Is there anyone who has heard the living God's voice speaking out of the very fire itself, like we have, and survived?" (Deut 5:26). "Once more I will shake not only the earth but heaven also" (Exod 19:18) connects Christ with earlier divine rumblings (Heb 12:26). The voice of God is judgment in Isaiah 30:31, similar in tone to John the Baptist's "voice in the wilderness" (Isa 40:3; Matt 3:3). Though Jesus says that the Scriptures (the Old Testament) "testify about me" (John 5:39), most of us are hard of hearing.

Get over your squeamishness about anthropomorphism. God's got eyes, lips, arms, and, above all, voice. Deuteronomy 4:12 says that the Lord spoke with fire. Onlookers "saw no form; there was only a voice." Yahweh is more person than idea. Hearing another's voice makes a bodily, personal connection. The lover in the Song of Songs yearns to hear the beloved's voice, so sweet in the hearing (2:14). Mary Magdalene thought she had met the gardener on Easter morning until the risen Christ addressed her (John 20:14-18). Upon returning to the disciples with the announcement, "I've seen the Lord" (v. 18), what she meant was, "Only when I heard him call my name did I know he was Jesus."

Scripture's voice is modulated. A raised, "loud voice" often precedes some prophetic pronouncement, as in Ezekiel 11:13 (and later in Matt 27:46, or when Lazarus is raised, John 11:1-10). A soft, quiet voice draws us nearer so that we might better hear what's being said. What the Holy Spirit whispers in our ear we are to shout from the housetops (Matt 10:27).

Biologist Richard Dawkins says God's Old Testament speech reveals God to be "The most unpleasant character in all fiction: jealous and proud of it; a petty, unjust, unforgiving control-freak; a vindictive, bloodthirsty ethnic cleanser; a misogynistic, homophobic, racist, infanticidal . . . capriciously malevolent bully."[56]

If I were to weigh in on Dawkins's evolutionary biology, my comments would be as valuable as his assessment of God's speech.[57] Any put-down of fundamentalist, narrow biblical literalists applies to Dawkins's flat, ham-fisted reading of the Old Testament.[58] For instance, Brent Strawn notes Dawkins's indignant complaint that Christians and Jews artfully present the Leviticus 19:18 love command as a universal, inclusive exhortation. But the "neighbor" we're to love is our fellow Hebrew, rendering Leviticus's injunction tribalistic and exclusive: go love another Jew.[59] Dawkins conveniently ignores that a few verses later—in the same chapter (Lev 19:34)—love of "neighbor" is applied even to the sojourner and immigrant.

Dawkins is unaware that within Scripture there are not only Godly assertions but also Godly counter-assertions, divine testimony and counter-testimony, critique and nuancing divine discourse within the discourse itself. Complexity and subtlety are not Dawkins's strong suit.

Strawn compares Dawkins with Marcion, who rejected the Old Testament because he found the language "too difficult, . . . too complex, too irregular," and opted for God talk that was "more reduced, compressed, and simple; something far more consistent, coherent, and logical."[60] That Dawkins's sensibilities are too delicate for untamed divine discourse reminds us of how much training it takes for Christians to listen to the Old Testament without resenting God for talking in ways that are not immediately accessible. Though the Oxford don can't hear God speak, many ordinary Christians do, listening to the Old Testament not because it's either interesting history or great literature but because (as Barth told his students) here "we can expect to hear the voice of God." So too in preachers' use of the Old Testament, everything depends upon "whether or not they expect God to speak to them here."[61]

I have steadfastly used the Common Lectionary as a source for preaching texts, though the lectionary is ungenerous with the Old Testament. Some of the most interesting things God says (that is, the most controversial) are omitted altogether. That's a pity. Preachers know that too-hot-to-handle texts provide some of our best preaching opportunities. Even a three-year cycle of Old Testament readings does injustice to the Old Testament—God has so much to say to Israel. In 3,000 sermons, I have been a Marcionite in Methodist clothing. I shall die before I wring a dozen sermons out of

44

Deuteronomy. Somebody else must mine Proverbs; too late I overcame my youthful aversion to proverbial wisdom. Though I'm finally at the age where Ecclesiastes makes sense, the curtain comes down on my preaching.

Habakkuk apocalyptically predicts that one day "the land will be full of the knowledge of the Lord's glory, just as water covers the sea" (Hab 2:14). Until then, preachers will never be unemployed.

That God talked so copiously to sinful Israel is our best hope. Preachers have so much to say because God does, *Deus dixit*.

The sheer cultural, linguistic, historical otherness of the Old Testament is the preacher's friend. Fleming Rutledge says, "Without total and continual immersion in 'the strange new world of the Bible,' the preacher will only be able to tell stories from his or her personal human perspective, . . . thereby failing to transmit the world-overturning, kosmos-re-creating nature of the Voice of God."[62]

The Old Testament will live again in the church, says Ellen Davis, when it is heard as an "urgent and speaking presence" that puts "pressure on our lives."[63] Only a few weeks after 9/11, Bishop Kenneth Carder was guest preacher in Duke Chapel. Like many other churches, we had experienced an attendance bump after 9/11. Widespread fear, grief, and pain make church look good.

Carder dutifully took the assigned First Lesson—Jeremiah 29:1, 4-7 (Jeremiah's word to the exiles in Babylon)—allowing the text to put the squeeze on us.[64] Carder opened "Finding Peace in Enemy Territory" by noting that in the weeks since the twin towers fell, Americans were feeling like exiles, pushed unwillingly into frightening territory. On a September morning, we were given kinship with these Jews from long ago. Our once-secure home felt like enemy terrain.

And yet, there is a major difference between us and those Jews—we lack a preacher like Jeremiah. When the Babylonians swooped down and laid waste to Jerusalem, metropolitan center of national pride and power, Jeremiah told the nation that the blame lay upon the devastated nation itself:

> The Lord of heavenly forces proclaims:
> Zion will be plowed down like a field,
> Jerusalem will become piles of rubble. (Jer 26:18)

"Can you imagine a preacher talking like that to suffering, hurting, bereft people?" Carder asked. Why is your city in ruins, the temple destroyed, and you are now homeless exiles? The Babylonians are instruments of my wrath. You were warned! You wouldn't listen to my pleadings. Now, in exile, you'll have time to ponder my commandments and return to who you were created to be.

Carder admitted, "Jeremiah's message sounds traitorous, then and now." Tag team tough sermon by Jeremiah and a United Methodist bishop.

Carder noted that the sermons given by Billy Graham and others at the big service at the National Cathedral contained no speech like Jeremiah's. Whereas Jeremiah cast the destruction of Jerusalem as a matter of God's judgment, we speak of ourselves as innocent victims of evil people.

"What sort of God would speak to suffering, hurting people as God spoke to Judah through Jeremiah?" Carder paused to allow the congregation to chew on that.

> What sort of people would have dared to be in conversation with a God who not only is merciful and loving but also truthful? In our pain we want consolation; in their pain God gave them accountability, a mission to undertake before the nations.
>
> Sometimes we come to church and meet the God we thought we needed. Sometimes, by God's grace, we meet more of a God than we knew we had. Are you willing to be in conversation with this much of a God?

Subsequent attendance at Duke Chapel took a dive after Carder's sermon as people resumed their search for preachers who don't talk like Jeremiah.

An Anecdotal History of *Deus Dixit* : The New Testament

From the Old Testament to the New, there is little alteration in the timbre of God's voice. The range, phrases, and patterns of God's speaking in the Gospels sound like God's speech to Israel through Micah or Joel. It's impossible to comprehend the language of and about Jesus without reference to the way God talked in Exodus or Ezekiel. Preachers like Paul quite easily addressed Jesus like Isaiah spoke to Yahweh. When Jesus spoke, it sounded to Paul like *Deus dixit*.

The angel Gabriel visits Mary. She sings a battle cry, first Christian sermon: The child in Mary's womb "will be great and he will be called the Son of the Most High. The Lord God will give him the throne of David his father. He will rule over Jacob's house forever, and there will be no end to his kingdom" (Luke 1:32-33). "He has shown strength . . . scattered those with arrogant thoughts . . . pulled the powerful down from their thrones and lifted up the lowly. He has filled the hungry, . . . and sent the rich away empty-handed. He has come to the aid of his servant Israel" (1:46-55).

Jerusha Neal shows Mary as bodily overshadowed to bring God with Us into the world, and then to publicly sing about it (Luke 1:46-55), prototype of all who have been overshadowed, put into labor by the vocation to preach.[65]

The Old Testament saves apocalyptic until the end. In the New Testament, from the get-go, it's all about a new heaven and new earth, world turned upside down, the rise and fall of many, and bad news for the rich.[66] Malachi foretold a great "day of the Lord" (Mal 4:1), urging people to forestall God's wrath by remembering the instruction from Moses and by preparing for the advent of Elijah. If Israel thought that "great and terrible day of the Lord" was imminent, they discovered once again that an eternal God doesn't keep our time.

Silence is broken at last not only by the song of Mary but also by the shouts of John the Baptist preaching in the wilderness, calling people to be washed in the Jordan.

The beginning of the good news of Jesus Christ, the Son of God, happened just as it is written in the prophecy of Isaiah,

> Look, I am sending my messenger before you.
> He will prepare your way;
> a voice shouting in the wilderness:
> "Prepare the way for the Lord,
> make his paths straight." (Mark 1:1-4)

Listen to John's sermons and you'll know why no pulpits were available. Though from a priestly family (Luke 1:5), John dresses like Elijah. But John's most prophetic attribute is not his dress; it's his (what else?) speech (Luke 16:16). A "voice" preparing the way (Mark 1:1-8), John calls out the agents of Empire (soldiers and tax-collectors—Luke 3:12-14), and even King Herod fails to escape John's jeremiads (Luke 3:19).

Like Malachi, John threatens a coming cataclysm that demands repentance. To those who took comfort in the old order, bragging of their lineage to Abraham and Sarah, John warns that God can call forth family out of the stones in the river if God must (Matt 3:9; Luke 3:8).

God had done it before. God's promise to Abraham formed a people out of nobodies. In John's preaching, the Jordan becomes the watery abyss of Creation, Genesis 1 once more. A new Exodus through the sea, creation, restoration, regathering through the words of a wild-eyed, camel-coated, fire-breathing, locust-eating preacher. Word makes world.[67]

We had asked, "Is God really with us or not?" (Exod 17:1-7). In response, God comes alongside as Word made flesh, preacher John as precursor to the definitive Preacher, John's cousin. Emmanuel's occupation? "Jesus came preaching" (Matt 4:17 NRSV). Luke says Jesus's first apocalyptic assault upon the world-as-it-is was from a synagogue pulpit, quoting his favorite prophet, "The Spirit of the Lord is upon me . . . to preach good news" (Luke 4:18).

Newness is wrought by resumption of the conversation between God and Israel.[68] Prophetic words from the past are echoed in Nazareth. "Today this Scripture is fulfilled just as you heard it" (Luke 4:21). *Deus dixit.*

The congregation marvels that Joe and Mary's boy reads Isaiah's poetic prophecy so well. But when the preacher does midrash, reminding them how God's prophets Elijah and Elisha gave healing and bread to those outside Israel, their initial adulation turns to rage.

"Now after John was arrested [preachers take note], Jesus came to Galilee, announcing God's good news, saying, 'Now is the time! Here comes God's kingdom! Change your hearts and lives, and trust this good news!'" (Mark 1:14-18). They

> went into Capernaum. Immediately on the Sabbath Jesus entered the synagogue and started teaching. The people were amazed by his teaching, for he was teaching them with authority, not like the legal experts. Suddenly, there in the synagogue, a person with an evil spirit screamed, "What have you to do with us, Jesus of Nazareth? Have you come to destroy us? I know who you are. You are the holy one from God."
> "Silence!" Jesus said. (Mark 1:21-25)

Sabbath centering and quiet ruined by Jesus. Demons move into action, the first to recognize his threat. Has Jesus come as destroyer? Jesus responds, "Shut up." Quite a sermon!

After the brouhaha at Capernaum, Jesus slips away for a rare moment of contemplative prayer (Mark 1:35). The disciples seek him, saying, "Everyone's looking for you" (eager for him to continue his healing, no doubt). Jesus answers, "Let's head in the other direction, to the nearby villages, so that I can preach there too. That's why I've come" (Mark 1:35-39).

Demon-provoked truth-telling more important than medical care? Though Jesus heals a man with skin disease (Mark 1:40-44) he sternly warns, "Don't say anything to anyone" (1:44), presumably to give time for Jesus to have his say. Jesus "went out and started talking freely and spreading the news." So many people came "from everywhere" to hear him that he "wasn't able to enter a town openly."

Jesus assaults the world, not in the manner of most liberators—with violent deeds—but with a barrage of words; parables that shock, amuse, tease, and disclose; sermons that end with a riot, as in Nazareth or with a mass feeding by the Sea of Galilee (Matt 15); blessings, curses, proverbs, and prophecies. He heralds a regime change. There's no evidence that Jesus sprang anyone out of jail; for him it was enough to preach, "Let 'em out!" (Luke 4:18). Some—not many wise and powerful, but enough to make bigwigs jittery—heard him gladly, hailed him as "King." To inaugurate his reign? He talked.

And he commissioned others to speak. Jesus, the Great Delegator, not content to preach solo, sends his disciples into the world to preach (Mark 16:15) the same sermon as his: "Here comes the kingdom of heaven!" (Matt 4:17; 10:7), urging his disciples to beg "the Lord of the harvest to send out laborers into his harvest," lamenting that "the harvest is bigger than you can imagine, but there are few workers" (Luke 10:2).[69]

> [The church consists of a] very specific hearing and making heard, the Word which it receives and passes on.[70]

Vocational Speech

Jesus's sending of preachers reminds us that God's speaking tends to be vocational. Paul claimed not only that Christ had appeared to him but also that God had commissioned, called, summoned, enlisted, and thereby defined him: "Paul, a slave of Christ Jesus, called to be an apostle and set apart for God's good news" (Rom 1:1).[71] Having received an address that is also a summons, Paul raced all over Asia Minor founding churches, broadcasting news that draws a crowd.

While it's fine to love reading Scripture (Ps 119:103), preachers take love up a notch and publicly proclaim Scripture. "The preacher reads the book, then speaks it. The text passes from heart and mind through the lips of the speaker and emerges into an assembly of people," said Richard Lischer in his Beecher Lectures.[72] "The word is near you" (Deut 30:14), asking more than the intellectual, "Do you agree?" but rather the vocational, "Will you join up and join in?"

The vocative intent of the Christ who speaks through Scripture challenges those who are deceived into thinking that we live free from constraint by any text other than the one we make up in our heads.

"Never again will any man tell me how to live my life!" she said in a church Bible study, adding, "*Unless* he is the Son of God."

Amen.

Though Scripture is the church's toughest critic, the church is the primary location for listening to Scripture, the source and purpose of Scripture. Ironically, this book saves us from thinking that this faith is about a book (fundamentalism) or from thinking that these ancient Jews have little to say to people so wonderfully progressed as we (progressivism). The Bible is interpreted best by "those who consider themselves active players in its drama," says Lischer.[73] Anything Christians lack in interpretive sophistication is compensated by their knowing that the toughest task is not interpretation but rather performance. It's good to read *Julius Caesar*, better to see a performance of *Julius Caesar*, best of all to win a bit part in *Julius Caesar*.

Preachers presume to give our people a more fulsome script than the one they think they are fated to live. Who better to do that than preachers, since most of us did not decide to be preachers? The life of every person who enters a pulpit has been imaginatively rewritten by God. Having had our lives commandeered by God, we preachers tell others that the life you are living is not meant to be your own.

Preachers perform the Word in our sermons so that the congregation might visibly perform the Word in the world.[74] Even after hammering one of his most troublesome congregations, Paul said, "You are the body of Christ" (1 Cor 12:27). An invisible church is as worthless as a silent church. The church, for better or worse, is how the risen Christ takes up room. We preach to the Body so that the church might be the visible Body of Christ in motion, Christ making his appeal through us (2 Cor 5:20).

Revelation is undemocratic. Though in Jesus Christ there's a surfeit of words and a plentitude of revelation, it's not given equally to all. Who knows why God self-revealed to Mother Teresa or to Ms. Jones who cleans toilets at City Hall and yet refuses to converse with Richard Dawkins? Why does God say something really interesting to the chair of my church board—whom I don't particularly like and who is a drag on my visionary leadership—but is miserly with me, even though I need a word in the worst kind of way for next Sunday's sermon? God's ways are too high for understanding (Ps 139:6).

When they haul you into court and, before judges, trouble not over what you are to say, Jesus told his disciples, "I'll give you the words" (Luke 12:11-12, paraphrased). The Preacher promises to enable preachers to fulfill our vocation by telling us what to preach. When Jesus's disciples asked, "Lord, teach us to pray," he did not urge them to cultivate a proper attitude; Jesus loved them enough to give them words. "When you pray, say it like this . . ." (Luke 11:1-13, paraphrased).

"I've had a hellish week," she said after service. "My son has started drinking again. The boss is in town, and I think he's got it in for me. So I came to church this morning seeking consolation and comfort."

"I hope my sermon was helpful," I said.

"Not particularly," she replied. "I came here looking for comfort only to receive an assignment!"

Parabolic Preaching

Somebody named Mark, sometime during the first century, somewhere in the Levant, invented a literary form as a means of recruitment. Biography (sort of), travel saga (of a kind), Mark's Gospel is a distinctively narrative way of presenting a unique Messiah. Something about Jesus just couldn't be conveyed without this rambling travelogue replete with excursions such as, "Jesus told this parable to certain people who had convinced themselves that they were righteous" (Luke 18:9). Jesus, teller of stories, becomes the master story that subsumes our stories.

The church is story-formed; we preachers enable listeners to renarrate their stories into Jesus's story. Maybe that's why Jesus's preaching is distinguished for his parables—pithy, deceptively simple stories drawn from everyday life that subvert everyday life.[75] If you must have your revelation theoretical or immediately practical, obvious, and straightforward, go worship Obviousness and Practicality rather than Jesus. On the other hand, if you delight in being teased, cajoled, surprised, jolted, there's nobody better than Jesus when he's on a roll with his stories.

"Tell us who God is," we asked. "You're not the God we craved or expected."[76]

And Jesus replied not with a three-point lecture or an enunciation of practical principles but with a story: "A farmer went out to scatter seed . . ." (Matt 13:1-16). A farmer goes forth to sow, carefully, meticulously preparing the ground, removing rocks and weeds, sowing one seed six inches from another . . .

No! This farmer just slings seed.

51

A dragnet full of sea creatures is hauled into the boat. Sort the catch, separating the good from the bad? No. The fisherman cares more for the size of the haul than the quality of the catch.

A field is planted. But when the seed germinates, weeds grow alongside the wheat.

"An enemy has done this!" cries the farmer. Enemy, my foot. You get an agricultural mess when your idea of sowing is to so carelessly sling seed.

Cull the wheat from the weeds? "No, good plants or bad, I just love to see things grow," says the casual farmer. We preachers love these parables as we throw out the dragnet every Sunday and put good seed at risk by sowing with abandon.

Which one of you, having lost a sheep will not abandon the ninety-nine (who lack the creativity to roam), leaving them to fend for themselves in the wilderness, and beat the bushes until you find the one lost? When found, which of you will not put that sheep on your shoulders like a child and say to your friends, "Come party with me; I found my sheep!"?

Your friends respond, "Congratulations. Most of your flock wandered while you saved one stupid sheep."

Which of you women, if you lose a quarter, will not rip up the carpet and strip the house of heavy appliances, and when you have found your lost coin, run into the street calling to your neighbors, "Good news! I found my quarter!"?

Which of you would not do that?

And which of you fathers having two sons, the younger leaves home, blows your hard-earned money on booze and bad women, then comes dragging back home in rags, will not throw the biggest bash this town has ever seen, saying to the prodigal, "Harold, you wanted a party? I'll show you a party." And shouting to the whole town, "My son's come back from the dead! Party time!"?

Which one of you parents would not do that?

And which of you, journeying down the Jericho Road, upon seeing a perfect stranger lying in the ditch half dead, bleeding, would not risk your life, put the injured man on the leather seats of your Jaguar, take him to the hospital, max out your credit cards in his recovery, and more?

None of us would behave so unseemly, recklessly, and extravagantly.

These are not stories about us. *They are stories about God.*

Mark and Matthew say that Jesus said nothing except in parables (Mark 4:34; Matt 13:34), which seems an exaggeration until we realize that Jesus *was* a parable: the storyteller become the story. Mohammed, from what I read, rarely told stories.

Why was a nice rabbi like Jesus crucified? After an especially creative rendition of Jesus's story of the Laborers in the Vineyard (Matt 20), when a sophomore complained, "These stories! That's an injustice, paying less those who worked more." I replied, "Just for your information, a few weeks after Jesus told that parable we got organized and tortured him to death in a vain attempt to stop the stories."

Listening to his stories helps explain why crucifixion is the world's verdict on the preaching of Jesus. An appropriate evaluative criteria is to ask, at the end of my sermons, "Why would anybody kill a preacher for this sermon?" Ouch.

In a story aimed at my income cohort, the rich man is prudent and carefully calculated (Luke 12:13-21). The speech of this secure, self-satisfied businessperson is mostly monologue, "'Soul,' I say, 'Soul,' take ease." Then the word of God intrudes, addressing him as "Fool!" Like most of us, he knew neither his foolishness nor his mortality until *Deus dixit*.

When John the Baptist (jailed because of his preaching against incestuous politicians; back in those days, preachers had guts) sent his disciples to ask Jesus, "Are you the one who is to come, or should we look for another?" Jesus responded by reference to what we can "hear and see": "Those who were blind are able to see. Those who were crippled are walking. People with skin diseases are cleansed. Those who were deaf now hear. Those who were dead are raised up. The poor have good news proclaimed to them" (Matt 11:3-5). Jesus is best recognized by his voice: "My sheep listen to my voice. I know them, and they follow me" (John 10:27; 10:3-5).

"Happy are those who don't stumble and fall because me" (Matt 11:6). Most were offended. I'm a bit ashamed that my homiletic retelling of Jesus's provocative stories has cost me little. Even in my most earnest attempts to cause trouble, I've never reached Jesus's level of contentiousness. Maybe my listeners are slow on the uptake.

As in his story of the sower and the seed, most of what Jesus preaches is wasted, falls upon barren ground, is consumed by birds, choked by weeds. Hearing, we don't hear, seeing, we don't see. The Sower is recklessly willing to imperil good seed in the confidence that though much is wasted on the likes of us, those few kernels that bear fruit make worthwhile the risks and losses of sowing.

When you listen to one of Jesus's stories and reply, "Sorry. I just don't get it," his typical response, "Try this: There was a woman who hid yeast in a huge lump of dough . . . Not helpful? Here's another: There was a father who had two sons . . ." Untroubled by our incomprehension, he keeps talking.

And the humor. What can you say about a God who, in response to our stuffed-shirt self-righteousness, told another joke about people who think they are righteous and look down on everybody else (Luke 19:9)? Or the way a damn Samaritan bested both clergy and pious laity on Jericho Road (Luke 10:25-37)? You can say God was in Christ, blissfully reconciling us laughable, silly, so silly sinners to God (2 Cor 5:19).

Jesus is astoundingly free of the compulsion to put his truth on the bottom shelf, to beat us over the head with obvious meaning. He never asks us to write it down. Rarely ties up his stories with a bow whereby you can say triumphantly, "I got it!" More typically, his parables led a few listeners to stagger away muttering, "It got me."

Jesus risks misunderstanding and rejection, as if getting the point—figuring him out, fully grasping his intent—is not the point. Many's the time I've retold one of Jesus's more outrageous parables (and there are many), and have been forced rhetorically to ask the congregation, "Are you sure you want to follow a Savior who tells stories like this to people like us?"

> God reveals . . . as the irremovable subject: I am who I am. The objective knowledge of God which comes through [God's] incarnation in faith and obedience, . . . which is effected by the Holy Spirit, is thus a knowledge of his mystery, . . . the incomprehensibility his incomprehensibility.[77]

Thank goodness Jesus asked us to follow rather than to comprehend him. In twenty years as preacher at Duke, when some student emerged from the chapel scratching his head, complaining, "I just didn't get the point," I've responded, "How high did you score on the SAT? . . . 1350? Well, that's just average here. I'll tell Jesus that his story shook the intellectual self-confidence of an oh-so-smart Duke sophomore. He'll be thrilled!"

Barth emphasizes that "mystery," "limit" is not due to modern skepticism but rather to God's christological knowability; Christ's concealment is in his revelation. God reigns from a cross so the one who reveals himself through his parables is also concealed.

> To deny the concealment in which God is knowable by us, the indirectness of the knowledge of God, is to deny revelation. [God] . . . cannot reveal . . . in any other way without ceasing to be God. The indirectness of our knowledge is the correlate of the concealment in which God gives himself to be known. . . . We should not violently try to grasp more than is proper for us. We will only finish up with less.[78]

His exasperated disciples complained, "Why speak in riddles?" (Matt 13:10, paraphrased). Jesus quoted Isaiah: people shut their eyes and close their ears; looking, they don't see; listening, they don't hear. Fortunately, Jesus liked nothing better than healing the blind or opening the ears of the deaf with, "God's realm is like . . ."

"I got nothing out of that sermon," laity complain. I remind them that Jesus ordered us to love our neighbors. Don't resent God for ministering to your neighbor in the pew, giving a word that was not, at least this Sunday, addressed to you. Jesus also commanded us to love our enemies, so as a forgiving preacher, I promise not to hold your incomprehension against you.

In Matthew, Jesus says that he tells parables so people can better understand the realm of God. Stories open eyes, unstop ears. In Mark 4:12, Jesus says the opposite: the purpose of parables is "so that they can look and see but have no insight, and they can hear but not understand. Otherwise, they might turn their lives around and be forgiven." My parables harden their hearts, strike them deaf and blind and rob them of their damnable certitude.

Don't ask Preacher Jesus not to be unruly. "Whoever comes to me and doesn't hate father and mother, spouse and children, and brothers and sisters—yes, even one's own life—cannot be my disciple" (Luke 14:26). Who dares talk that way about Mom and Dad?

Jesus's preaching helps explain why, in twenty years of sermons at Duke Chapel, a parent never phoned saying, "Help! My student is sexually promiscuous!" (though many are). Over the years I had at least two dozen anxious, often angry parental phone calls saying, "Help! I sent my child to Duke to be a success and she has become a religious fanatic!" (fanaticism defined: she dares to believe Jesus isn't dead).

In telling his truth parabolically, Jesus requires us to accept some of the responsibility for the meaning. Few can sit passively when Jesus aims a parable our way. Our interpretive devices go into action. We look for the star of the story, hoping the hero looks like us. We attempt a sorting of the good from the bad—notoriously difficult task when it comes to Jesus's stories. How often we, the unheroic, exclaim, "Hey, you're talking about me!"

I've been preaching nearly fifty years; Jesus still manages to shock, causing me to toss the two sermons I earlier preached on a story—my beloved previous interpretation trashed by Jesus. As Robert Jenson said, the difference between a dead god (idol) and the living God is that a dead God will never shock.

I've had the embarrassing experience of preaching at least five sermons on the Dishonest Steward (my label; Jesus is too sly to entitle his stories),

Luke 16:1-15, and have ended with confession, "I can read this in the original Greek, got at least twenty books on my shelf that purport to explain this parable, and God help me, I still am unsure why Jesus told it."

"That's irresponsible, telling us you don't know what this text really means," said a huffy businessman after service. "That's why you go to seminary, so you can set us straight." A guy who works for Goldman Sachs calling me irresponsible?

After battering them with a barrage of parables, Jesus asked, "Have you understood all these things?" (Matt 13:51).

His disciples respond gleefully, "Sure! We get it."

They lied.

Sometimes people attempt to (overly) simplify Jesus's message as, "Love God and your neighbor" (Mark 12:30-31). Then Jesus complexifies the question. Not "Who is my neighbor?" (Luke 10:29) but who is this God who is neighborly to me, in preaching by a Jew from Nazareth who lived briefly, died violently, and rose unexpectedly? This, the God we're to love with all our strength and might?

Still, a favorite designation for Jesus was "Rabbi," teacher. Jesus really wants to share the mysteries of the kingdom (Mark 4:11). Trouble is, the subject matter Jesus taught required a willingness to endure pedagogical failure. His language is no more obscure and difficult than it need be, considering Jesus's peculiar way, truth, and life.

> [There is] a knowability of God which can be calmly asserted over—against all historically or psychologically grounded skepticism because it is self-established.[79]

Refusing to waste time speculating on why many misunderstood his parabolic teaching (everybody knows that human stupidity is ubiquitous), Jesus congratulates his gaggle of followers, "Happy are your eyes because they see. Happy are your ears because they hear. I assure you that many prophets and righteous people wanted to see what you see and hear what you hear, but they didn't" (Matt 13:16-17). Though Jesus's talk can be hard to hear, Peter asked for all of us, "Lord, where would we go? You have the [sometimes incomprehensible, disturbing] words of eternal life" (John 6:68; cf. 3:15-16, 36; 4:14, 36).

We disciples may not be the brightest candles in the box, but at least we few know a true story when we hear one, entrusted with a divine mystery as yet unknown to nine out of ten Americans.

When questioned about his parabolizing, Jesus quoted Psalm 78:2, "I will open my mouth with a proverb. I'll declare riddles from days long gone." Refusing to allow us to relegate God to a transcendent blur, God in Christ lets us in on the public secret of who God is and what God is up to here, now, alluring us, turning narration into vocation: Now that I've let you in on who God is, don't you want to hitch onto God's vast retake of what belongs to God? Follow me! Go tell somebody!

Sent Out to Preach

Because God had spoken and, in speaking, transformed these nobodies, they responded by going forth into the world eager to talk to anybody about God's surprise. As Kavin Rowe describes their public speech, "no neighborhood was too lost for them to write them off; no Roman official was too powerful to reach; no poor drunkard was beyond help; no abandoned child should be left to fend for itself; no sick and helpless person should suffer and die alone."[80]

Revelation in Christ is a twofold miracle, a circle that begins in Christ's speaking and is complete only in our hearing.

> (a) God meets us and (b) we stand before God. . . . Concretely and objectively something . . . takes place in human space and time—the humanity of Jesus Christ which . . . , becomes luminous, it unveils even as it veils, it causes to shine, it bears witness, it imparts.[81]

Around academia, on rare moments when God creeps into conversation, someone is always standing by to respond, "God? Can't say much about God. God is large, distant, unknowable. It would be intellectually narrow and dishonest to claim knowledge of God."

We wish.

Barth said that preaching, talk about God, rests on the presupposition that God is knowable because God has turned to us.

> As preachers talk about God, they declare that they know God. . . . For theology the real problem . . . does not lie on the side of the human capacity for knowledge. . . . [The challenge is in] what God says. . . . The content of God's Word is God alone, wholly God. . . . God turns to us. . . . The possibility of Christian preaching is finally based [in this], . . . Christ reveals God to us.[82]

Though Barth doesn't make much of Jesus's parables, when Barth thinks about our reconciliation to God, Barth focuses not upon the cross and atonement but rather upon the prodigal son. Jesus is "the running out of the father to meet his son." Jesus is "hidden in the kiss which the father gives his son," Jesus, who dares to go out to the "far country" and then returns to the arms of the father. In this story, Barth says, we have an "illuminating parallel to the way trodden by Jesus Christ in the work of atonement, to His humiliation and exaltation," the "way back" to God where we are accepted in "full fellowship," "without hesitation or reservation."[83]

Sometimes Jesus paused, between preaching gigs, to restore sight to the blind or to shout at death and unbind a corpse (John 11:1-44), proclaiming with deeds rather than words. Coming upon a man who had been made mute by a demon, Jesus cured him. When accused of practicing magic, Jesus responded by characterizing his healing work politically, a power struggle with "Beelzebul, the ruler of the demons." A person now free to speak is a sure sign that "the kingdom of God has come to you." How? Jesus explains, "When a strong man, fully armed, guards his castle, his property is safe."

> When a strong man, fully armed, guards his own palace, his possessions are secure. But as soon as a stronger one attacks and overpowers him, the stronger one takes away the armor he had trusted and divides the stolen goods.
> "Whoever isn't with me is against me, and whoever doesn't gather with me, scatters." (Luke 11:14-23)

Any more questions?

In working these wonders Jesus enabled God's Kingdom to come, God's will to be done. The definitive miracle is Jesus, the living, revealing bodily presence of God's will "on earth as it's done in heaven" (Matt 6:10). His occasional exorcisms and healings are spontaneous, gratuitous out-breakings of the Kingdom he inaugurates, as if Jesus can't wait to get to cross and resurrection for his Kingdom to come.

Thus, Jesus's followers learned to pray, "Maranatha" (1 Cor 16:22), "Bring it on, Lord!"[84]

Jesus's preaching often attracted multitudes, at other times mockery and scorn, but it was effective enough to get him tried, tortured, and horribly, publicly, humiliatingly executed. Though his metaphors were sometimes obscure and his parables hard to follow, he spoke clearly enough for even the governmental and religious authorities to get his point. They crucified him to shut him up.

For three days the silence was deafening.

The accounts of what happened afterward on the third day, first of the week, are diverse and conflicting, as if the witnesses knew not how to bring to speech what they had seen and heard. Women (where were the men?) came to his tomb in the early morning darkness. There, they were met by a young man (Mark) or two men (Luke), presumably divine messengers. "Why do you look for the living among the dead?" the messengers impudently asked. "He isn't here, but has been raised" (Luke 24:5-6). "He is going ahead of you into Galilee" (Mark 16:7).

In Matthew's Gospel an angel says not, "He is risen! Now you will see your loved ones when you die." The angel's Easter announcement is vocational, homiletical, "Go, preach!"

The startled women race back to the male disciples and proclaim, "He is risen!" First witnesses to the resurrection, first evangelists to spread the good news, "He is loose! The story is not over; it is just beginning!" First preachers.

Why, on the first day after his resurrection, did Christ go to Galilee, an inauspicious location to launch revolution? Galilee is where his preaching began. Returning to the hinterland, Christ resumed preaching, now as unboundaried resurrection proclamation.

A couple of the disciples were walking that very afternoon from Jerusalem to a little village of Emmaus. A stranger appeared and walked with them. The stranger "opened the Scriptures" (Luke 24). They bid the stranger, "Stay with us; it's nearly evening." That evening, seated around the table, when the stranger took bread, broke it, and gave it, they saw. The stranger vanished. They raced back to Jerusalem, shouting, "The Lord really has risen!" John says that very evening the disciples where gathered "behind closed doors because they were afraid" (John 20), having witnessed what the powers-that-be did to Jesus. Alone, mourning dead Jesus and their betrayal, words failed.

The risen Christ stood among them, said, "Peace," offered his risen body as validation of his resurrection, breathed upon them (there's that holy breath from Genesis 1 again), giving them his Spirit, and commissioning them (best friends and most notable betrayers) to repeat his words. Then he vanished.

Why would the risen Christ appear first to these fearful ordinary men and women, his disciples, who had demonstrated their failure to follow? Why not appear to a powerful, influential, public figure like Pilate?

He came to the ones who had fled the conversation once the going got rough, those whom he had so patiently taught and yet who had so patently misunderstood. "As I was saying before I was so rudely interrupted," making them witnesses to the resurrection.

Shortly thereafter the authorities arrest Peter and John, "incensed that the apostles were teaching the people and announcing that the resurrection of the dead was happening because of Jesus" (Acts 4:2). Asked to explain the commotion, these first preachers replied, "Jesus Christ the Nazarene—whom you crucified but whom God raised from the dead" (4:10).

Hearing these "uneducated and inexperienced" preachers (4:13) the authorities respond as they had to Jesus. They ordered them to shut up. But Peter and John answered, "It's up to you to determine whether it's right before God to obey you rather than God. As for us, we can't stop speaking about what we have seen and heard" (4:19). Peter responds to the official order by praying for the Holy Spirit to give them the guts to speak "God's word with confidence" (4:31).[85] Just a few weeks before, Peter lacked the courage to admit he had even met Jesus (Matt 26:72).

The reason the powerful were troubled by Easter preaching? Here's the politically subversive reason:

> The community of believers was one in heart and mind. None of them would say, "This is mine!" about any of their possessions, but held everything in common. The apostles continued to bear powerful witness to the resurrection of the Lord Jesus. (4:32-34)

Don't tell me preaching can't be powerful.

And thus was the church born, and we were made witnesses of resurrection and preachers of good news. Jesus's preaching ministry is no longer geographically confined. Resurrection news explodes into Judea, Samaria, even to the ends of the earth (Acts 1:8). Israel was promised that the nations would eventually come to Zion to receive God's revelation (Micah 4:2; Zech 8:22; Isa 2:3; Jer 3:17). Jesus is God's Word no longer willing to wait for the nations to come to God, but God's speech surging into all the world in a great company of preachers (Ps 68:11).

Are we bold enough to state that the human possibility for knowledge of God can become a reality only by the path of Christian proclamation?[86]

Josephus explained that Jesus was just one more failed Messiah, gone the way of others who dared to mess with Rome, though Josephus is baffled that even into the Nineties of the first century the followers of Jesus are still around, proliferating, even. The explosion known as the "church" is testimony to the resurrection's facticity. One must say not only, "He is risen!" but in light of the phenomenon of ecclesia, one must add, "is risen and has resumed the conversation between us and God."

God is whoever raised crucified Jesus from the dead *and* sent out preachers to give the news.[87] Time and again in our history, when we have betrayed God's love with our infidelity, misunderstood, fled into the darkness, stopped up our ears, and hardened our hearts, God has returned to us and restarted the dialogue. Thus, Paul prayed that God might "open for us a door for the word" (Col 4:3), acknowledging that divine/human intercourse is at God's initiative. Easter all over again.

When I got pushback after my retelling of one of Jesus's parables, my only defense was, "The only good reason for my retelling that story, the only way it makes sense, is that the one who first told that story just happened to be the one God raised from the dead."

If God should stop talking, withdraw, even for a moment, into apophatic, contemplative, empty silence, the lights will go out and death will have the last word. Yet God's creative, life-giving, people-forming, intrusive Word keeps creating, being made flesh, pushing in, having its say. Preaching.

Luther admitted that 1 Peter 3:19-20, Christ's preaching to the souls in hell, is an "obscure passage." "I do not know for a certainty just what Peter means." Luther read this as a parable of Christ's preaching. So intent is Christ that the gospel be universally heard that he even descends to preach to those "that lie captive in the prison house of the devil."[88]

> We must not be ashamed of the gospel. No relativism, no skepticism, no personal timidity should prevent us from talking about God very naively, very definitively, and in the same matter-of-fact way as we talk about any other data. God is a datum in revelation by the Spirit. Happy are we, then, if we can speak about [God] with this certainty, *en pneumati*. And woe to us if we do not.[89]

Luke's last glimpse of Paul is as a jailhouse preacher, who "continued to preach God's kingdom and to teach about the Lord Jesus Christ" (Acts 28:31). Nothing shall hinder the expansion of the Word. Lest we preachers despair that our talk about Jesus is not half as interesting as Jesus is, Barth reassures us:

[People] with their various (but by nature unanimously hostile) attitudes towards the Word of God come and go. Their political and spiritual systems (all of which to some extent have an anti-Christian character) stand and fall. The Church itself (in which somewhere the crucifixion of Christ is always being repeated) is to-day faithful and to-morrow unfaithful, to-day strong and to-morrow weak. But although Scripture may be rejected by its enemies and disowned and betrayed by its friends, it does not cease . . . to present the message that God so loved the world that He gave his only-begotten Son. If its voice is drowned to-day, it becomes audible again to-morrow. If it is misunderstood and distorted here, it again bears witness to its true meaning there. If it seems to lose its position, hearers and form in this locality or period, it acquires them afresh elsewhere. The promise is true, and it is fulfilled in the existence of the biblical prophets and apostles in virtue of what is said to them and what they have to say. The maintaining of the Word of God against the attacks to which it is exposed cannot be our concern and therefore we do not need to worry about it. Watchmen are appointed and they wait in their office. The maintaining of the Word of God takes place as a self-affirmation which we can never do more than acknowledge to our own comfort and disquiet. We can be most seriously concerned about Christianity and Christians, about the future of the Church and theology, about the establishment in the world of the Christian outlook and Christian ethic. But there is nothing about whose solidity we need be less troubled than the testimonies of God in Holy Scripture. For a power which can annul these testimonies is quite unthinkable.[90]

The longest Gospel ends, "Jesus did many other things as well. If all of them were recorded, I imagine the world itself wouldn't have enough room for the scrolls that would be written" (John 21:24). With so lavishly revealing a God, there's always more to be said next Sunday.

The prophet hears a divine promise related to the divine word:

So is my word that comes from my mouth;
it does not return to me empty.
Instead, it does what I want,
and accomplishes what I intend. (Isa 55:11)

This, the basis for Christian preaching, this, the good news. *Deus dixit.*

The Lord's glory will appear,
and all humanity will see it together;
the Lord's mouth has commanded it. (Isa 40:5)

Speaking Scripture

The church assembles, Scripture is read, the lector says, "The word of God for the people of God," the people respond, "Thanks be to God," the preacher stands and dares to speak, venturing out on the tightrope between text and sermon. Hold on to your hats.

"To a large extent the pastor and boredom are synonymous," said Barth. "Against boredom the only defense is again being biblical. If a sermon is biblical, it will not be boring. Holy Scripture is in fact so interesting and has so much that is new and exciting to tell us that listeners cannot even think about dropping off to sleep."[91]

Palm/Passion Sunday, amidst the pandemic, the Episcopal Bishop of Washington took as her text the "Serenity Prayer," urging us to adopt a serene attitude amid the ravages of COVID-19. "To change what we can change and to accept what we can't change and the wisdom to know the difference." Good advice, eloquently delivered in just the right tone. Yet is it not striking that after reading the long narrative of Jesus's last week, trial, torture, and death, a preacher finds nothing of note in Scripture?[92]

As one of the three ways that the one Word of God is revealed, Scripture beats the boredom of self-induced serenity.

> [Christ] a first address in which God . . . and God alone is the speaker, [Scripture] in a second address in which it is the Word of a specific category of people (the prophets and apostles), and in a third address [Preaching] in which the number of its human agents or proclaimers is theoretically unlimited. . . . Three addresses of God in revelation, Scripture, and preaching, yet not three Words of God, three authorities, truths, or powers, but one.[93]

Principles for daily life, hints for happier homes, tips for trauma recovery, maxims for meaningful lives are rarely Scripture's interest and therefore of little concern to preachers.[94] As a rule of thumb, Scripture everywhere speaks about God; only secondarily or derivatively about us.[95]

Scripture presumes to be "the place where we can expect to hear the voice of God." Therefore, "The proper attitude of preachers does not depend on whether they hold onto a doctrine of inspiration but on whether or not they expect God to speak to them here."[96]

> Christian preachers dare to talk about God. [Because of the] . . . address of God in [God's] revelation, there is a contemporaneity

> between people of every age and revelation. The Word of God in this second form, as the communication of God in history, is Scripture . . . the witness of the prophets and apostles to Jesus Christ in which, and over against which, God the Holy Spirit bears witness.[97]

"I myself will be with you every day until the end of this present age" (Matt 28:20). "I won't leave you as orphans; I will come to you" (John 14:18). Not the product of fertile ancient imaginations, a projection of the highest and best aspirations of human spiritual striving, or some mythic figuration of the human psyche, Scripture is the self-attestation of God; sermon preparation is thus the practice of various forms of prayer.[98]

That's why whenever I'm engaged by a biblical text and say, "Now, I understand," Origen says it's a "visit from Jesus."[99] In preaching, our subjectivity is commandeered, our cultural captivity is transcended, the smothering embrace of the congregation is overcome by the Holy Spirit because this text is more than text; it is Scripture, the possibility of a personal address by Christ.[100]

> Apart from Scripture we have no means of knowing the truth about God. God gives people diverse talents and abilities—the ability to know God isn't one of them. Even when we think we have discovered revelation from elsewhere, we have no way of knowing that our discovery is revelation except through the lens of Scripture.
>
> Scripture is not revelation, but from revelation. Preaching is not revelation or Scripture, but from both. But the Word of God is Scripture no less than it is revelation, and it is preaching no less than it is Scripture. Revelation is from God alone, Scripture is from revelation alone, and preaching is from revelation and Scripture.[101]

Scripture is not revelation, said Barth, though Scripture can be a reliable witness to revelation; it's only human words that witness to the event of revelation. Revelation is always an event instigated by God, even when received through Scripture.

> There is a "beyond" in Scripture. This is the Word of God, namely, revelation. . . . Revelation meets us only indirectly, only in Scripture. . . . The reality of revelation is indirectly identical with the reality

of Scripture. Indirectly, for the Bible is not the same as revelation. The tension remains. The Bible is one thing and revelation another. Nevertheless, we have revelation not in itself but in the Bible. For we have the witnesses of revelation, those upon whom its reflection rests, the prophets and apostles, only . . . in the Bible, in the texts of the Bible.[102]

"The word of our God will stand forever" (Isa 40:8), not as a tombstone but as living address, conversational and relational. *Deus dixit,* Barth notes, is in the Latin perfect tense, an "eternal perfect"—God has spoken and continues to speak.[103]

Scripture is self-presentation by God through human words. "You will be my people and I will be your God" (Jer 30:22) accounts for the ever-present reality of God's speech. To Barth, the "presupposition of the Bible is not that God is but that [God] spoke." And still speaks one Word.[104]

"You will be my people *and* I will be your God" is the twofold character of God's one address. God does not speak into a void; God is engaged in conversation. With human hearing, the circle of God's revelation is complete. Revelation unheard and unheeded is not yet fully revelation.

[What] makes Scripture holy Scripture is . . . the I and Thou encounter, person to person. . . . Only within this I-Thou relation, in which one speaks and another is spoken to, in which there is communication and reception, only in full *action* is revelation.[105]

A Speaking Book

Though Barth didn't, Luther prioritized preaching over Scripture:

The word is the channel through which the Holy Spirit is given. . . . The lips are the public reservoirs of the church. In them alone is the Word of God. . . . Unless the word is preached publicly, it slips away. The more it is preached, the more firmly it is retained. Reading is not as profitable as hearing it, for the live voice teaches, exhorts, defends, and resists the spirit of error. Satan does not care a hoot for the written Word of God, but he flees at the speaking of the Word.[106]

Though preaching and Scripture are two forms of one divine address, human experience is not.

> The Bible is the first mediation and norm, the standard or principle of all communication, the historical basis of all experience, the salutary caveat that must be set over against all experience.[107]

In her sermon on Isaiah 40, Fleming Rutledge says that after listening to "more sermons by more clergy in more churches in more denominations than any other preacher, God plays only a subsidiary or vague role."[108] Our toughest challenge is not that Scripture is written in ancient tongues but rather that we listen within a narcissistic culture that encourages us to listen most intently to ourselves.[109] That's why much contemporary preaching has forsaken theology for anthropology, beginning with the preacher's amateurish assessment of the contemporary human condition—we are depressed, oppressed by unjust social structures, searching for meaning, deeply wounded, or frightened by the future—then the preacher rummages in the Bible, extracts some insight, and applies it to the contemporary human condition, usually something that listeners are to think, do, or feel in order to set themselves right.[110] Preaching in a problem-solution format makes the Bible a helpful, though primitive, often outdated resource among others for solving our problems, as we define our problems.

The problem-solution sermon makes church a place to take our problems.[111] I've heard sermons on "Better Family Life" (based upon the parable of the prodigal son), "Keeping Money in Its Place" (Jesus's call of the rich young man), or "Justice Now!" (Jesus's parable of the laborers in the vineyard). I heard Romans 13 contorted into a defense of Donald Trump, then one week later the same text enlisted by another preacher to attack Trump (joined with Jesus's visit to the house of Zacchaeus). Does Scripture give a rip about either Trump or our obsession with justice, as we define justice?

Little is said in Scripture about human sexuality. Why? The reason I was taught by my church: Scripture was produced by naive, limited, first-century Jews who did not know that sexual self-expression is the most interesting aspect of a human being. At our advanced level—Durham, North Carolina, 2020—we know better.

Anthropological deflection of the theological intent of Scripture takes many forms. As a preacher I was much influenced by George Lindbeck's post-liberal stress upon the formative power of the biblical story. The church is story-formed.[112] Lindbeck helped me critique my sermons that were derived from experiential/expressive interiority, liberalism's "turn to the subject," by pointing me toward a cultural-linguistic understanding of how biblical texts have their way with us.[113] "To become a Christian involves learning the story of Israel and of Jesus well enough to interpret and experience oneself and one's world in its terms, . . . an external word . . . that molds and shapes the self and its world, rather than an expression or thematization of a preexisting self or of a preconceptual experience."[114]

Now I worry that (1) Lindbeck's formative story does little work beyond the church,[115] and more troubling, (2) Lindbeck's narrative-formed church is birthed by a text rather than by Jesus Christ.[116] Preaching is subsumed into the readers' experience of Scripture rather than preaching being driven by the self-revealing Logos. As James Kay asks, if the Gospel narratives are so effective in rendering the identity of Christ, why preach them?[117] Preaching is more than simple repetition of the Gospel narrative or even absorption into the narrative world of Scripture. Reiteration of the text is not enough. At some point preaching "must, in the power of the Holy Spirit risk taking account of the world in which the Christian message is proclaimed, and to which it is addressed. . . . The Word of God attested in Scripture wills to go forth into ever-new situations and therefore the arduous task of interpretation, simply cannot be laid aside."[118]

Though I'm all for the literary interpretation of Scripture, the biblical text is not of interest primarily because of its literary art. A variety of books speak when read well by expectant readers; none speak as Scripture.[119] Though Scripture rarely brags, Scripture has an ontological relationship to Christ (2 Tim 3:16-17); the Bible speaks because of the nature of Christ the Revealer.

The preacher approaches Scripture with the presupposition that a text is not only an address but also a summons, the Word embodied, practiced, God in action, vocation. Preaching is judged by its performance in the lives of the saints.

"Let me clarify for you students who are new at the university," I said one Opening Sunday. "Duke Chapel is not the Department of Religious Studies. They sit back and think religion; here at the Chapel, we enjoy *doing it*. Thank God they aren't the Department of Sex or none of us would be here!"

Another letter of warning from the president.

We impersonate the text in sermons as encouragement for congregational enactment of the text in the world. Preachers worry about performance of the sermon because, as Robert Jenson says, preachers "communicate the gospel by . . . [trying] *to say the same thing* that scriptural . . . texts say. . . . Scripture directly controls our homiletical discourse, it says what God wants it to say," in a similar style to how God says it.[120] Some preachers are unconcerned with style and delivery; God's truth is self-evident, they argue, needing no fancy frills in presentation. This attitude overlooks the breadth of Scripture's literary creativity and diversity, to say nothing of the Lord's ample vocal range.[121] Scripture has a wider array of literary devices than I'll ever utilize. The text disallows me to trim my delivery to my stylistic preferences or vocal limitations.[122] As Rick Lischer says, "The *text* will tell you when to be angry, ironic, funny, or sad."[123]

Gardner Taylor characterized sermon preparation as being taken by the Holy Spirit and a text where the preacher did not intend to go: "A sermon idea has been decided for me . . . rather than I decided it. [It is not] all self-generated. . . . Maybe a great part of it rises out of us, but a part of it comes down upon us. . . . That is the mystery."[124]

Because many of our listeners believe that Christian language no longer describes any objective reality, Scripture is twisted into a means of descending deeper into themselves.[125] Barth counter-asserted the "objectivity of revelation."[126] We think by "thinking of objects," so through Scripture the eternally subjective God graciously becomes objectively present to us. Because God is "pure subject" who always "stands outside at the door" of our human cognitive abilities, we know God only because God graciously makes God's self objectively available to us as God's word.[127]

> We can think about God as an object only in God. This is the miracle of the Holy Spirit—not anything that we can reach . . . or possess or name our own, but the reality of God for us and to us and in us in [God's] revelation. . . .[128]

True proclamation, says Barth, is "human talk about God on the basis of the self-objectification of God which is not just there, which cannot be predicted, . . . does not fit any plan, which is real only in the freedom of [God's] grace, and in virtue of which [God] wills at specific times to be the object of this talk, and is so according to [God's] good pleasure. . . . [Preaching is] human talk about God . . . [which] never passes under our control."[129]

I'm sure that's why I most often experience God's objectivity when I move from text to sermon. There sits the text in all of its obstinate objectivity, unresolvable, impervious to my attempts to adapt it for my own ends, speaking of matters I would rather avoid. I didn't choose the text; it chose me, a wonderful check on my presuppositions and preoccupations.

In the months after 9/11 I collected sermons campus pastors preached the Sunday after that fateful Tuesday.[130] Half of those sermons spoke a reassuring, empathetic pastoral word, many without citation of any biblical text. They portrayed their congregations as anxious, frightened casualties of evil without much awareness of the danger of casting powerful Americans as hapless victims.

A few of the sermons in the collection preached from one or more of the assigned lections for the Sunday, many expressing surprise at the unexpected connections between the biblical text and the national context. Stuck with the independence of Scripture, these sermons put the present moment in a wider, even eternal, context, offering a word that was not being heard elsewhere.

That Sunday after the Tuesday, I preached, not from the assigned lections but from Genesis 1:1-2, stressing that God who created the cosmos continues to create, to bring God's good out of our bad. God will not be defeated by our sin or our foreign policy failures. This ancient text lifts our gaze beyond the confines of the present cataclysm.[131] I was unsure that I had been picked by the right text. Said one worshipper afterward, "I was disappointed that you did not call for national unity." Another, "You implied that we are a bunch of sinners. That's awful. They hate us for our freedom."

Maybe Genesis 1:1-2 was just right.

Originality can't be a chief concern of a preacher. We are servants of and advocates for the text, not its masters. Polls show that contemporary Christians want "authenticity" or "sincerity," as if the value of preaching resides in the disposition of preachers and the judgment of the hearers.[132] The demand that we be authentic or heartfelt in the pulpit is yet another means of listeners trimming divine discourse to suit themselves, as if preaching is self-display by the preacher for self-improvement of self-interested congregations. (How would either listeners or we know when we're inauthentic?[133] Better just to demand that we not screw up the text.)

To be forced by Scripture to be servants of the demanding Word, rather than servile to our congregations, is true pastoral freedom. We are free to speak not out of personal preference, existential concern, or desperation to preserve intramural relationships, but rather to offer what we have received in our encounter with Scripture. The text hoists pastors out of the mire wherein congregations sequester us,[134] demonstrating that "we don't preach about ourselves" (2 Cor 4:5) but rather what we have been told to preach, obedient to the voice on the Mount of Transfiguration, "This is my Son whom I dearly love; I am very pleased with him. Listen to him!" (Matt 17:5).

I'm sure that's the reason many preachers testify that they are less constrained while preaching than in any other act of ministry. Burdened by demands that they have a properly pastoral and emotional disposition, in the pulpit they are free to enjoy the sheer objectivity of Scripture, the way Christ comes to us rather than arises out of us. Carefree, assured that God will say what God wills, to whom God wills, as God wills, regardless of the fragility of preachers or listeners, they are free calmly to say to the congregation, "Having hung the drapes in the parsonage, this is not necessarily what I would have chosen to say to you but I do think it's what the text says. It's my God-given responsibility to say it to you as best I can." That women preachers were recognized and affirmed first in Pentecostal churches shows that "God's Spirit blows wherever it wishes" (John 3:8), descending upon, authorizing, and working through women in the pulpit, listeners ready or not.

"I trembled when I thought, 'I'm twenty-three years old. What am I doing up here talking to people twice my age,'" said a novice preacher. "Then I thought, 'this book has two thousand years more experience with God than any of us.' I'll preach that."

Interpreting Scripture

Historical–critical study of Scripture made much of the historical distance between the ancient text and the church's present performance. Trouble is, Scripture's concerns are not primarily historical; the church listens to Scripture for a contemporary address.[135] As Robert Jenson says, "Between us and Scripture there simply is no historical distance to be kept open."[136] Preachers need not be intimidated by historians. The Holy Spirit loves to take snippets of Scripture that have unknown or limited significance in their original context, whatever that was, in order to speak now.[137] Whenever biblical critics ask us preachers to exaggerate the historical gap, to overlook the theological intent, they are asking the text not to be Scripture.

A popular, generously orthodox preacher began a sermon admitting that lots of people try hard to understand the parable of the dishonest steward (Luke 16:1-13). "But I got to tell you. If you know just a little bit about Palestinian economics of the first century, this parable is absolutely easy to understand and obvious." The preacher explains that "what's happening here" is resistance to Roman economic exploitation. The steward who, to the uninformed reader, appears to be a rascal is "a middle-class guy like most of us," "somebody who saw through the injustice of the economic system and decided to work for the poor." Jesus told this story to urge us to "use our money in the service of relationship."[138] While it's amazing that historians know so much about first-century Judea, the preacher's reconstruction of historical context defuses an otherwise troubling parable, rendering it into amateur economics, moral exhortation, and common sense.

Silly to treat Shakespeare's plays as a valuable source for information about English history, or to think by knowing the historical context of the play, the play speaks more eloquently.[139] As Brevard Childs taught, Isaiah is more than an expression of the faith of ancient Israel; it is a claim about who God is and what God is up to.[140] What is this text about? Rarely will you be far from right if you answer, "God." What is the text's intention? To make God's claim upon God's people here, now.

Scripture spoken expects response. Richard Burnett characterizes this as Barth's "double particularity" of Scripture. Our reading must be dialectical, said Barth, "always a combination of taking and giving, of reading out and reading in, of exegesis and eisegesis."[141] While cautioning against unwarranted eisegesis, Barth says we must be true partners in this dialogue, freely voicing our concerns and questions, even as we submit to the text's speaking to us.[142]

In his Beecher Lectures, Walter Brueggemann said, "The meeting of the community of faith is a speech meeting. We gather for speaking and listening of an odd kind. That meeting has potential of provoking a new humanity. . . . The first partner in the meeting is the text. The congregation gathers with a vague memory of the text . . . mostly reduced, trivialized, and domesticated. . . . All week we have been practicing our nervy autonomy where God is not real . . . trusting excessively and vigorously in our ideological commitments, [more than] . . . the text."[143]

A "speech meeting" of "an odd kind" occurs in Acts 12:20-23. After a nasty rampage of killing and incarcerating, King Herod is petitioned by the starving people of Tyre and Sidon for bread. Herod dons his elegant armor and insists on giving a royal oration. The hungry people exclaim, "This is a god's voice, not the voice of a mere human!" Can we eat now?

"Immediately," Herod was "eaten by worms and died." Tough way to go. God is not nice to politicians who try to sound like God.

Luke, who loves to retell details of long, redundant sermons in Acts, gives not one word of Herod's speech. You've heard one politician, you've heard 'em all.

Luke adds laconically, "But the word of God continued to advance and gain adherents" (Acts 12:24 NRSV).[144]

Who would laugh at this story? Who would be offended by it?

We preach to help our people think like Christians. Few congregations have scriptural imagination greater than their preacher's.[145] Biblical study on the way to a sermon is not monastic, solitary, devotional contemplation of a biblical text. Preachers listen to Scripture from the middle of that busy, dangerous intersection of God and congregation, listening imaginatively, yet submissively, praying that our cultural context and our subjectivity will not overwhelm the text.[146]

Stanley Hauerwas says that we must teach people "to speak Christian."[147] Stephen Fowl agrees: many in the church are no longer skilled listeners to Scripture.[148] A community of informed, well-formed listening must be trained to handle the jolt of God's speaking.[149] True, but I'm grateful that God is no more stumped by poorly formed, uninformed listeners than by my lousy preaching. In even the most adept congregation, the Holy Spirit will still be required for hearing and responding. Among the sorriest, ill-coached, casual, and indifferent listeners, the Holy Spirit may speak, no matter listeners' poor priming for hearing.[150]

For Better, for Worse, God Speaks

"Now Samuel did not yet know the Lord; and the Lord's word hadn't yet been revealed to him" (1 Sam 3:7). In the dead of night, the voice of God awakens the inexperienced kid, "Samuel, Samuel," rather than disturb the sleep of the theologically trained, professional man of God. Both Samuel, the youth, and Eli, the elder, dare to listen, though the content of God's speech to each is quite different. The boy receives God's promise of a bright future; the old priest hears a word of devastating judgment.

As the oldest of the Beecher lecturers, I ask: What is there about the Trinity that speaks so vibrantly and innovatively in young adulthood, summoning many of us to service when we are too young to say no, prodding us to preach some of our most creative sermons before midlife? Is it because as we grow older we are increasingly risk-averse? It's been ages since I've dared charge down the interstate at ninety miles an hour on a Harley. Looking over my earliest sermons, I find God gave me my most brash ideas in my twenties, which I continue to recycle in my last decade.[151]

"Do you ever repreach your sermons?"

"At my age, all my sermons are salvaged," I replied.

Is the Trinity most actively engaged with those who, upon hearing, "Come, throw away your life in an impossible undertaking, prone to failure, and at odds with the world's idea of success," answer like little Samuel, "Tell me more. I'm listening."

But I digress. The story of Samuel and Eli is not about the characteristics of those who hear but rather the peculiar quality of *Deus dixit*.

Eli and his sons, Hophni and Phinehas, priests ordained to speak to the Lord, are evil; their father Eli only old and inept. Eli's sons have turned their priestly vocation into a sinecure to enrich themselves, skimming the offering. Eli rebukes his sons but to no avail. (Clergy are rarely good disciplinarians of our children.) Some unnamed "man of God" gives the word that Eli's house is in trouble. By the word, God "brings death, gives life" (2:6), does a "new thing," displacing the house of Eli with the young prophet Samuel.

The boy Samuel, who is subservient to Eli, is moved center stage for a devastating divine assertion (3:11-14). Eli instructs Samuel on the proper response to God (vv. 9-10), giving Samuel the words with which to answer Yahweh (v. 9). Samuel obediently repeats those very words (v. 10). The roles for speaking and hearing God are being reversed (vv. 15-18). Now Eli is dependent upon Samuel to hear God's direct, living word. Samuel receives God's word but is reluctant to tell Eli the oracle against Eli's house (vv. 15-18). Samuel makes the same response to Eli that he will make to God: "Here am I" (v. 16).

Power has shifted. The once-innocent youth is authorized; the elder, knowledgeable Eli is dependent upon young Samuel. The house of Eli had been promised authority "forever" (2:30), yet the family abused the sacred trust. Now Eli's family receives a promise of punishment (3:13). Samuel hears judgment that he doesn't want to speak, but he dutifully repeats the word anyway. Though the "word is rare" and visions infrequent (v. 1), Samuel receives then speaks the visionary word that nobody wants to hear (v. 11), precursor to a lifetime of delivering unpleasant truth to people you have learned to love.

The word of Yahweh is with Samuel (3:19), the child of miraculous birth, cast into a vulnerable situation by the prenatal prayer of his mother, now bearer of revelation, the one to whom Yahweh's future speaking is entrusted. All is accomplished by "the Lord's word," and yet the outworking of God's will occurs with divinely sought assistance from Samuel's mouth. Yahweh elects to speak to the ecclesiastical establishment with the aid of an untrained, uncredentialled youth.

Not a word from Samuel falls to the ground (3:19). The narrative does not say that Samuel's word is exactly like God's word, and yet they are close, too close for comfort of Eli's house. (We are reminded of Jer 1:1-3, where Yahweh's word is given through young Jeremiah who dares to obey and to speak.)

The vocation of the prophet Samuel, judgment upon Eli's priestly family, occurred in a dry season for spirituality. "The Lord's word was rare at that time; and visions weren't widespread" (1 Sam 3:1). Was the paucity of speech due to a taciturn God or to inept listeners? Finally, God speaks and is heard, not by the aging priest "whose eyes had grown so weak he was unable to see" (v. 2) but by young Samuel who hears his name called. (As a youth I heard a sermon on this passage in which the preacher marveled, "When God calls, God calls you by your very own name, not by somebody else's." I had been warned.)

Though Eli had been living with and working for the Lord for years, young "Samuel didn't yet know the LORD" (v. 7). A second and third time Samuel is called. (In divine vocation, God's call is a hammer, repetitious and persistent: "Moses, Moses." "Samuel, Samuel." "Saul, Saul.")

Typical of Scripture, the story of Eli is reported without moralization, explanation, or exhortation. How much I admire Eli who, upon hearing the verdict from young Samuel, says, "He is the Lord. He will do what he pleases" (1 Sam 3:18). What a well-formed preacher, receiving God's word, even when it causes him and his family such pain. But the most thought-provoking character isn't grieving old Eli or even up-and-coming young Samuel. It's the God who is in conversation with both Eli and Samuel, busy giving and taking, promising, entering into the thick of human life, ending and beginning—with words. As Fleming Rutledge says in one of her sermons on this passage, everything depends upon our understanding "that it is the Lord speaking, not Samuel's religious imagination."[152]

Preachers dare to work with that God, reading a story like that of Samuel and Eli, standing before a congregation and praying, *Go ahead, Lord, pull the trigger, light the fuse.*

Chapter 3

PREACHING: GOD'S SPEAKING

My first attempt at a sermon was in 1968 when I served as a youth pastor in Anderson, South Carolina. Of course, I attacked Lyndon Johnson (maybe Lady Bird too) and denounced the then-current Vietnam War.

After service, an enraged man shouted at the church door, "Punks like you are the shame of America," and "You are a cowardly little pussy who doesn't support our boys fighting in Southeast Asia." After that, he got downright nasty.

I was unsure whether to protect my face, my stomach, or my groin. I staggered back into the church, as far as the vestry. A member of the altar guild, an older woman in a small pink hat, was removing flowers from the brass vases.

"That was awful!" I gasped. "Did you hear what he said to me?"

"Everyone heard," she said, smiling. "I do wish people wouldn't use such language when children are present. Could you hand me that container?"

"He was going to hit me! How could that jerk be that upset by a first-year seminarian trying to preach?"

She looked up from fussing with flowers and said, "Dear, it's not you who upset him. I'm sure you remind him of his son. Both of you have long hair, though you appear to have no tattoos or ear piercing. Tommy is a homosexual, living in California or some such. He's lost the son to whom he gave his life. Tom kept his promise to God to be a good father, but God failed to keep his promise to Tom."

She laughed to herself. "Now, who would be upset with a nice boy like you? No, Tom hates *God*."[1]

Christians are more strange even than the generic "People of the Book." Christians expect God to speak through preachers.

75

> Preaching arises neither out of the mere letter of Scripture nor out of direct spiritual illumination without Scripture, eternal and time-less. . . . Preaching happens when the Holy Spirit works with the words of the preacher, who, after having been tutored by the words of Scripture, speaks.[2]

1. Astonishing to hear Christ reveal, Word of God Incarnate in a Jew.

2. Amazing, in reading Scripture to have God contemporaneously speak through inspired, though thoroughly human, ancient witnesses.

3. Most remarkable is when a preacher like Paul throws caution to the wind and tells the Thessalonians, "when you accepted God's word that you heard from us [Paul, Silvanus, and Timothy], you welcomed it for what it truly is. Instead of accepting it as a human message, you accepted it as God's message, and it continues to work in you who are believers" (1 Thess 2:13). "The message about the Lord rang out from you" contagiously from Paul to the Thessalonians, even them, to the whole world (1 Thess 1:8). High opinion of homiletics, extravagant, threefold theology of revelation.

Preaching is the language act one expects of the Trinity:

> In the past, God spoke through the prophets to our ancestors in many times and many ways. In these final days, though, he spoke to us through a Son. God made his Son the heir of everything and created the world through him. The Son is the light of God's glory and the imprint of God's being. He maintains everything with his powerful message. (Heb 1:1-3)

After this christological opening, the Letter to the Hebrews gives us a sermon that is the most robust, explicit theology of preaching in the New Testament. Divine speech to the Son, then to us, is the theme of Hebrews: "After all, when did God ever say to any of the angels: You are my Son?'" (1:5). How does the Son create and sustain the world? "By his powerful word" (1:3 NRSV). How do believers persevere? "It's necessary for us to pay more attention to what we have heard, or else we may drift away from it" (2:1). Followers of Christ join the ancient Hebrews in a demanding covenantal conversation: "So, as the Holy Spirit says, 'Today, if you hear his voice, don't have stubborn hearts as they did in the rebellion, on the day when they tested me in the desert'" (3:7). "God's word is living, active, and sharper than any two-edged sword, . . . able to judge the heart's thoughts and intentions. . . . Everything is naked and exposed" (4:12-13). In 3:13 believers are urged, "Encourage each other every day"; the whole sermon is a "message of encouragement" (13:22), which is a phrase used in early

Judaism for preaching. When Hebrews quotes Scripture, it is spoken, rather than read, as God's own speech.[3]

Christ of Hebrews is the messenger who is the message. There's no citation of words from the teaching ministry of Jesus; Jesus's death and resurrection render one who teaches now. More than God's spokesperson, Christ is all that God is and does.[4] In saying that God has revealed in "many and various" ways, spokespersons of the past (the Scriptures) are not disparaged but rather Christ is praised as the crescendo of revelation.

The church is born through eyewitness attestation (2:3) and survives only because members exhort one another (10:25).[5] No Christian is self-taught. In some way or another, someone handed over the good news.

Speaking for God is a Christian leader's job (13:7). Exhortation leads to salvation and exposes negligent and unbelieving hearers to judgment (2:3; 12:25). Don't be seduced by strange speaking (13:8). When leaders speak God's true word, they are to be obeyed (13:17). Hebrews has "a clear conscience" (13:18 NRSV) in speaking the word truthfully (13:22).

In summation, the preacher appeals for patience (13:22). Patience awaiting the return of Christ, or in receiving and understanding the word of God? Perhaps both. God is free to speak or not. Listeners must forebear God's veiling and unveiling; God's speech is not at our demand.

Attend to "the one who is speaking" (12:25). Attentive to God or to the writer? Maybe the ambiguity is intentional; attend to a humanly delivered sermon; risk hearing the voice of God.[6]

> Pastors are sinners. . . . Nevertheless, listeners must presume that pastors are servants of the Most High. They speak in God's name, carrying out God's directive, sometimes well, sometimes poorly. That doesn't imply that preachers possess papal infallibility. They know fear and trembling when they enter the pulpit . . . crushed by the knowledge that they are frail humans . . . more unworthy than those who sit before them. Nevertheless, it's still God's Word. The Word of God that they must proclaim judges them. Still, the Word compels them to preach.[7]

The world is affronted that the humanly preached word can nevertheless be God's. Shortly after I entered the ministry, preachers were dropped from the Ten Most Admired Professions.[8] I convened Duke's first Martin Luther King commemoration. Over the years, while listening to the speeches extolling Dr. King, I groused that at the university one is free to praise King for any of his achievements—except for being a Baptist preacher. King is easier to manage as an advocate of social justice or a courageous civic leader than as spokesperson of the Word of God.

Barth admitted to his students that the world often regards preaching as "tactless aggression, presumption, and usurpation." "Who made you guardians and administrators of the sanctuary?" Would it not be better for preachers to "maintain the respectful silence about ultimate things," we "unaccredited blusterers"? Barth says preachers are the first to admit that our sanction is not in "our qualifications and credentials, . . . Christian knowledge, and least of all, . . . experiences and illuminations. . . . [The authority by which we speak] is never our own."[9] We speak only what we have received, and what we receive is not under our control.

As a bishop I've laid hands upon a person's head and said, "Take authority as an elder in the Church to preach the Word of God, and to administer the Holy Sacraments." I then hand them a chalice and paten, symbols of sacramental leadership. But when it comes to preaching, they're empty-handed, totally dependent upon God.[10]

Experienced Preaching

Peter Hawkins opened his Beecher Lectures with a quotation from the end of *King Lear*, "Speak what we feel, not what we ought to say." In his lectures, Peter flipped the reference back on his audience, showing how this Shakespearian sentiment is against everything preaching ought to be. Who cares what preachers feel; we preach what we've been told.

> The promise of the Word of God is the transposing of a [listener] into the wholly new state . . . so that irrespective of [the listener's] attitude to it [the hearer] no longer lives without this promise but with it. The claim of the Word of God is not . . . a wish or command which remains outside the hearer without impinging. . . . It is the claiming and commandeering of the human being. . . . The person who hears the Word [is] now . . . claimed by God.[11]

The crisis that ignited the Barthian theological revolution began when, in his first parish, young Barth's academic theology, "talk about self-consciousness and the 'experience of Jesus' and whatever . . ." went flat.[12] Preaching is in trouble, not because it can't find the proper form or style but because it has tried to preach "whatever," talking about our "experience of Jesus" rather than Jesus.

In the opening volume of *Church Dogmatics* Barth charged that theologians had exchanged the pious experience of moribund "religion" for living revelation and thereby "theology lost its object."[13] "Religion" is God on the cheap, substituting lugubrious spiritual practices for the adventure of God–human conversation. "Religion" is defined by Barth as "a vigorous and extensive attempt to humanize the divine, . . . to make it a practical 'something,' for the benefit of those who cannot live with the Living God, and yet cannot live without God."[14] "Religion," our stand-in for daring encounters with God. Keep Sabbath, plant a garden, work at *lectio divina*, be mindful, find balance, or do whatever keeps you busy now that God has gone silent. Feuerbach set before us our challenge: when we say "God," are we just describing ourselves? Modern theology forsook address from God for examination of human experience of God, justifying Feuerbach's challenge, Barth said. Preachers dare to speak as God has spoken, *Deus dixit*.[15]

Impossible Possibility

Gardner C. Taylor opened his Beecher Lectures admitting that "preaching is a presumptuous business" when a person dares to "stand up before . . . other people and declare that he or she brings from the Eternal God a message."[16]

> Preaching . . . is God's Word in human words, concealed by the total inability of everything human to attain to this object, just as God's Word in Scripture is concealed by the separating distance of everything historical. . . . Preaching has always been sick. It is not self-evident that God's Word should be truly heard and spoken in it.[17]

Preaching is an impossible possibility. Human sinfulness (particularly our propensity toward idolatry) but even more so a crucified, resurrected God, precludes any human faithfully rendering God. So we substitute anthropology for theology, vainly attempting to "speak about God by speaking about man in a loud voice."[18]

> [Remove yourself from] the sphere of the Christian church, do not bother about the church's reference to the Bible or the Bible's reference to the *Deus dixit*, . . . and lo! it is easy to talk about God . . . [safe] from the fatal *Deus dixit*. In the depths of our own soul, or the national soul, or the world soul, you can now find something

that your heart can truly experience, that you can call your God, . . . nonparadoxically . . . fulfilling an inner drive, or proclaiming an ideal truth, or offering kindly service to your neighbors, . . . then happy are those who find it, . . . they can be quiet pastors who never bring disquiet to anyone. . . . They may go their way in peace.[19]

The pacification of listeners by disconnecting preaching from *Deus dixit* had disastrous results in 1930s Germany. Today, anthropocentric talk is the modus operandi of much North American preaching, "fulfilling an inner drive, or proclaiming an ideal truth, or offering kindly service to your neighbors." Ouch. Easier for preachers to prattle about "pious experience or faith," convinced that "certainty about God stands or falls with the certainty about themselves," thinking that "because the idea of God exists in us, therefore God exists."[20]

In making our pious interiority the source of knowledge about God, Barth says we place "a huge demand upon the subject," more weight than human subjectivity can bear. What Christian preachers say presupposes real knowledge of God rather than ourselves.[21]

Anna Carter Florence says, "We will never revive the pulpit with a few fancy pulpit tricks and new preaching styles. We need theological support that goes as deep as the Word itself, because only a theology of the Word that resists idolatry will resist the idolatries of preaching."[22]

Barth repeats the Reformed claim that our chief temptation is Carter's "idolatries of preaching"—using a source for preaching other than that given in revelation.

How lonely are those who dare to speak about God, how far removed from the broad way of the many or even the quiet paths of the finest and noblest among us.[23]

Preachers are lonesome because the world deserts those who dare to preach with the Trinity rather than to serve the world's adorable idols. It's a solitary task to address a need that our people don't know they have.

> To speak about God does not fit in with what [people] are and do even in their best moments. To speak about God is . . . the great divine disruption. . . . Those who speak about God, will have to accept . . . much temptation to confuse human and divine. [Such preachers are produced] neither at university nor at ordination.[24]

Revelation is discontinuous with other events or experiences and does not arise from any human heart.

> God is always the subject, . . . in this concealed and singular address which is not in continuity with other events. . . . Revelation means the knowledge of God through God and from God. It means that the [seemingly mute] object becomes the [speaking] subject . . . if we know God in faith. It is God's work in us. . . . The modern locating of revelation in feeling or experience or . . . inwardness is so terrible just because in relation to God it ascribes to us an organ . . . which is ours apart from God; just because it makes God an object without God, . . . a denial of revelation. Nowhere and never is the Deus dixit a reality except in God's own most proper reality.[25]

In his sermons Barth always dives immediately into the task of explicating the meaning of the word God, using the language of the church. The Christian faith has no need of allegedly neutral apologetic arguments because knowledge of God is a divine gift, not a general human possibility. Instead of engaging in apologetics, building a ramp from something people already worship (reason, sex, prosperity, healing, meaning in life, peace, justice, balance, community) to the God they have yet to worship, Barth says we ought to remember when as infants it was said to us: "I baptize thee in the name of the Father, the Son, and the Holy Ghost," we were addressed without any help from experience and yet, we are, through God's word, baptized.[26] That we do not feel addressed by God does not negate the possibility of being addressed. Before a pastor says, "I pronounce you married," the pastor does not inquire into the couple's prior dating record or the results of their personality inventories. Through promises, words have created something new. God's address is neither a commentary upon nor does it arise out of our experience; God's word creates experience we would not have had without God's word.[27]

> The very reference to the Holy Spirit, that is, to God himself in the present, in the church, and in us, is also a reminder that we have here something neither to be experienced nor to be thought. . . . That [God] does so, not the "heart," is . . . the knowledge, courage, and authority of the Christian preacher. Even for those of us who are not prophets, here is the coal from the altar, which the seraph took with tongs and with which he touched the prophet's lips.[28]

Then there's the problem of self-deception. How does one know that one has had an experience without some means of signification outside experience? Certainly God is able to speak through experience. Yet we are unable to judge the meaning of experience without some means of judgment beyond experience.[29] Trauma and wounds do not speak and therefore can be subjects—but not sources—for preaching.[30] Experiences of oppression and victimization give no advantaged access to the voice even of a crucified God. Rather, the voice of God enables us to name our experience truthfully. How would I know that those whom I treat as outsiders are, in reality, at the center of God's heart, except through Scripture? I would be unable to confess some of the sin of my white privilege apart from knowledge of a gracious God who forgives his crucifers.

The human experience that interests the church is this: God has spoken, humanity has heard. In her classic sermon on Genesis 18:1-16, Fleming Rutledge marvels that the whole story of Israel begins with, "And God spoke to Abraham."

> Abraham has done nothing whatever to deserve this attention. Abraham is nothing in himself. We are given no information about any achievements or qualities that might distinguish him. Abraham comes to the forefront of the world stage for one reason alone; the Lord spoke to him . . . [requiring him to leave] every single thing that gave him his identity . . . ancestors' graves, . . . grandparents, . . . land, . . . friends, . . . life insurance, . . . safe-deposit box, and go to another place far away, unknown.[31]

Abraham's kith and kin are those whom God has addressed and those willing to have their lives transformed in their hearing. Lauren Winner doesn't list preaching as one of the Christian practices that we, in our postlapsarian state, have used, abused, distorted, and "damaged." Still, I expect Winner, fine preacher as she is, would urge us to "depristinate" the practice of preaching, saving it from its anthropological captivity.[32] We can repent, reform, and revamp our distortions of preaching and then happily hope for God's correction and resurrection of this life-giving practice. Considering our degradation of preaching, one must ask, "What sort of God would entrust to us so good a gift as God's word?"

Just the sort of God who would give us Israel or Jesus.

Failure to Communicate

Not all of God's self-unveiling gets through our stiff necks and stopped-up ears. We are, for any of our virtues, self-deceiving sinners, incurable idolaters who have not the truth in us (1 John 1:8).[33] Preachers venture saying to fellow sinners, "Listen up! Here's truth we've been avoiding all week." There will be failures.

> Some congregation might say, how can we . . . hear God's Word in the words of pastors, none of whom we trust? . . . If we expected to hear God's Word more, we would hear it more even in the weak and perverted sermons. The statement that there was nothing in it for me should often read that I was not ready to let anything be said to me. What is needed here is repentance by *both* pastors and congregations.[34]

Some sermon flops are due to God being in Christ rather than in our more comprehensible concocted godlets. As Lischer says, "Preaching bears the impossible weight of its own message, which is God's willingness to be pushed out of the world and onto a cross."[35] Or as Barth put it, "God is so unassuming in the world, but so revolutionary in relation to it."[36] When God embraced a cross as the major means of relating to the world, preaching became a tough way to make a living.

> In no Christian preaching is God's Word so proclaimed that we can exclude . . . the possibility of the minister giving a fine and effective address but nothing else happening. . . . No one has yet found a way . . . [whereby preaching] is always heard and retained by all.[37]

In assessing preaching failure, cross and resurrection ought to be kept together. Some contemporary renditions of the cruciform "suffering God" make empathy the supreme divine attribute, God as the empathetic but inactive fellow sufferer, victim of human rejection. To conceive of the cross as only a sign of human refusal allows human suffering to define God rather than the cross of Christ defining our travail, imprisoning God in the doleful dead end of human history. Fortunately, empathy is not the best God can do. In the cross, our human "No" became God's sovereign "Yes," God refusing to allow our refusal of God's Son to end the conversation.[38]

One Good Friday evening I preached on the parable of the wicked tenants, Mark 12:1-12. I ended my sermon,

Look at us gentiles, we johnny-come-lately guests in God's vineyard, strutting about, acting like we own the place.

Servants were sent to collect the rent, urging us to pay up what we owed. Knowing the magnitude of our debt, we beat them, treating them "disgracefully." In desperation, God sent God's dearly loved Son.

This afternoon between noon and three you know what we did to the Son.

Now what?

Jesus, teller of this violent, true story asks, "So what will the owner of the vineyard do?"

There's a good chance that the owner of the vineyard will "destroy the vineyard and give it to others." That would be justly deserved payback from the master of the vineyard.

We'll have to wait and see if the owner of the vineyard is into justice, won't we? Though we didn't give God what was God's due, maybe God won't give us what we deserve. Who knows? Wait in darkness until Sunday.

Mark says, after Jesus told this story, the religious rulers (people who look and talk like me), "wanted to arrest Jesus because they knew that he had told the parable against them."

The story sure sounds like it is against us. We are justified in taking it personally.

Who would blame God if this is the end of the road, end of God's attempts to be God for us?

You know the sad story: A servant was sent to us (Moses?); we broke the law. Then more servants were sent (the prophets?); we dishonored and ignored them. Then the Son, the only begotten Son. And we responded in unison, "Crucify!" (You heard us say it last Sunday.) End of the story.

The Son, on his way to the cross, tells this parable. Is Jesus's story told "against us" or for us? Is this the last we've heard from the Son?

We must wait and see. In three days we shall know how the story ends. The next move is up to God.[39]

Easter says to preachers that because of God's relentless, cross-resurrection vocalizing we ought not to take our listeners' refusals too seriously. Whether defiant or diffident, their "No" is bracketed by God's dramatic, repeated "Yes." In the light of Christ's determination that "God . . . wants all people to be saved" (1 Tim 2:4), their refusal is only provisional. If even rejection of Christ by Judas is "always relative to the saving action of Jesus,"[40] then the scorn I received from a guy who said last Sunday, "*You* are one of the top twelve preachers in the English-speaking world?" may not be fatal.

Is it wrong for me to want all to respond positively to my sermons? One can understand resisting bad news. But the rejection of *good* news? Refusal to hear God making appeal through us (2 Cor 5:20) is a strange againstness with which Christ contends before his final triumph—baffling, serious but not ultimately so, real but not real, not finally consequential.[41]

In the story of Lazarus and the rich man (Luke 16:19-31), there is a great gap between the rich and the poor, a fissure that also runs through preaching. In misery, the rich man pleads with Father Abraham to warn his rich brothers of the fate awaiting them. Abraham responds that Moses and the prophets preached to them without effect. Even if somebody came back from the dead, they wouldn't listen (16:31).

The irony is that we are listening to the testimony of someone who came back from the dead. While it's hard for the affluent to hear the truth about our ill-gotten gains or our true situation, with crucified and resurrected Christ, even the impossible salvation of the rich may be possible once the camel is shoved through the needle's eye (Matt 19:26). Maybe Abraham was wrong. Maybe our inability to hear has been enabled? Even among those with incomes as high as mine, perhaps there can be hearing, receptivity to the bad news of Christ's good news to the poor, the gap between rich and poor healed by the hearing of news spoken by the resurrected.

"I just can't believe that what you say about God is true," said the young man after one of my most moving sermons. While disappointed—I so yearn to be in control of divine-human communication—I corrected him. "Better for you to say, 'I just can't believe *yet*.' Keep looking over your shoulder. Easter suggests that God's got ways superior to even my best sermons."

Though Paul was mystified that he heard Christ as Lord and most friends and family heard nothing, Paul knew that God is faithful, that the promises of God are irrevocable, and that God will, in God's own good time, have God's way with the world (Rom 11). We preachers may be pessimistic about the effects of last Sunday's sermon, but we are consigned to optimism about preaching's ultimate efficacy. God will have God's say.

It's up to God to produce both truthful preaching and faithful listening. Failure of people to respond positively to our preaching is sometimes a godly reminder that salvation (hearing, receiving, responding to God's address) is God's self-assignment, not ours. Convening this conglomeration of listeners was God's idea of a good time, not mine.

In 1537 Luther began a series of sermons on the Fourth Gospel, not because he wanted to get something off his chest but rather because he had entered a strange land called the Gospel of John. In the sermon, Luther invites his listeners to travel with him:

Therefore we propose to consider his Gospel, . . . discuss it, and preach it as long as we are able, to the glory of our Lord Christ and to our own welfare, comfort, and salvation, without worrying whether the world shows much interest in it. Nonetheless, there will always be a few who will hear God's precious Word with delight; and for their sakes, too, we must preach it. For since God provides people whom He orders to preach, He will surely also supply and send listeners who will take this instruction to heart.[42]

The text and the Lord of the text are more to be loved than our congregational context. Mulish listeners are God's conundrum. In a sermon on Matthew's Gospel, Luther said that the test is "not whether many or few people believe or do not believe, are damned or saved" but rather "fidelity to the Word of God." Nevertheless, the same God who graciously "provides people whom He orders to preach" will "also supply and send listeners who will take this instruction to heart."[43]

The anxiety that ought to keep preachers awake at night is not that people won't listen but rather that God does.

[That which makes preaching tough] is not, of course, the complaining, unfruitful criticism of congregations, not the useless charge that "it has nothing to offer me," not the sorry self-criticism of pastors nor even the useless confession that "I have nothing to say." . . . The true *krisis* . . . is . . . from the words to the Word within the words, and then back again to new and better and more suitable words.[44]

The most intransigent of congregations is no greater judge and jury than our encounters with the Word and the words of Scripture, two forms of revelation judging the third. The scuffle in the pulpit is minor compared with the fearful hand-to-hand combat in the preacher's study. Still, fear of the Lord is the beginning of wisdom (Ps 111:10).

Personable Preachers

In his 1877 Beecher Lectures, Phillips Brooks gave American preaching its most durable definition: "Truth through personality." "Truth through personality is our description of real preaching. The truth must come really through the person, not merely over his lips, . . . through his character, his affections, his whole intellectual and moral being."[45]

"Truth through personality" pandered to the burgeoning science of psychology in late-nineteenth-century America. Today, Brooks's personality preaching has triumphed. When asked, "What do you want in a preacher?" most congregations of my acquaintance will say, "A warm personality" or "Compassion and caring" before "biblical fidelity" or "theological substance."[46]

Still, while personable preaching is popular (anthropology is easier than theology), mining our subjectivity, trusting our experience, or conversing with culture are inadequate sustenance for ministry. Nothing but the truth will do. Karoline Lewis, in her book, *She: Five Keys to Unlocking the Power of Women in Ministry*, shows that to keep at ministry over the long haul, ministry must be tethered to truth.[47] If Brooks were lecturing at Yale today, I hope that he would expend most of his effort on truth—specifically, the One who is "the way, the truth, and the life"—rather than on burdening the preacher's personality.[48]

Christian witness, said Barth, always points away from itself toward that which it sees, like a man standing on a street corner pointing upward into the sky. Of course a crowd gathers, everyone craning the neck, attempting to see whatever he sees. The character or personality of the witness has less value than the witness having seen something. Theology helps us preachers point to something that merits convening a crowd.

> *Deus dixit* . . . is an address. The presupposition of the Bible is not that God is but that [God] spoke. We are directed, not to God . . . but to God communicating. . . . What makes Scripture holy Scripture is not the correctness of the prophetic and apostolic . . . thoughts about God but the I-Thou encounter, person to person. . . . When we do not think of revelation . . . as one person speaking and another spoken to, God revealing . . . to us and we to whom [God] reveals [God's self]; when revelation is seen from the standpoint of the non-involved spectator, then it amounts to nonrevelation. . . . To receive revelation is to be addressed by God.[49]

God's Agency

Yale's Christian Wiman, speaking at Duke, said that people often are drawn closer to God "either by suffering or abundance." In the discussion afterward a participant asked, "What did you do to access God in your own time of suffering?"

Wiman responded, "I didn't. . . . I did nothing."[50]

An audible sigh emerged from the sophisticated audience. Here's a tough lesson for modern, privileged, resourceful people: significant interaction between us and God lies with God, or as Barth said, "All the action that takes place in preaching, . . . between the first advent and the second, is the action of the divine Subject."[51] The Second Helvetic Confession's assertion that "the preached word is God's word" is a remarkable claim.[52] Sinful, limited creatures as we are, we can't speak for God. Only God can speak for God and, in preaching, God does.

The laity think that talk of our sermons as "God's word" flatters us preachers. How little they know! Our homiletical challenge is illustrated by Peter's sermon in Acts 2:32-41. When the smoke settles at Pentecost, with Jews "from every nation under heaven" (2:5) talking funny and hearing funny, the mocking mob in the street sneers that it's as if Jesus is still with them; they're drunk.

Peter faces down the mob: We're not drunk! Yet. It's only nine in the morning.

Peter? Remember where we left Peter? When they were safe at the table, Peter boldly declared, "Lord, I'll speak up for you. Count on me" (Luke 22:33, paraphrased).

A powerless serving maid shut him up: "Weren't you with the Galilean?"

Peter mumbled, "I never really knew him."

Now, in Luke's Acts of the Apostles, *Peter* preaches. You don't believe that the same Spirit who led Jesus to speak in Nazareth has descended on Jesus's betrayers and deniers? Then how do you explain that *Peter* preaches?

> This Jesus God raised up. We are all witnesses to that fact. He was exalted to God's right side and received from the Father the promised Holy Spirit. He poured out this Spirit, and you are hearing and seeing the results. . . . Therefore, let all Israel know beyond question that God has made this Jesus, whom you crucified, both Lord and Christ. (Acts 2:32-33, 36)

This is one of history's worst sermons. Short, ridiculously so. No illustrations, culturally insensitive, accusatory, without intellectual foundation, no connections, no bridge from there to here. And yet:

> When the crowd heard this, they were deeply troubled. They said to Peter and the other apostles, "Brothers, what should we do?"
>
> Peter replied, "Change your hearts and lives. Each of you must be baptized in the name of Jesus Christ for the forgiveness of your sins. Then you will receive the gift of the Holy Spirit. This promise is for you, your children, and for all who are far away—as many as the Lord our God invites."

With many other words he testified to them and encouraged them, saying, "Be saved from this perverse generation." (2:37-40)

A judgmental, accusatory sermon. And yet:

Those who accepted Peter's message were baptized. God brought about three thousand people into the community on that day. (2:41)

Three thousand!

So is my word that comes from my mouth;
> it does not return to me empty.
> Instead, it does what I want,
> and accomplishes what I intend. (Isa 55:11)

Here's my thesis: the best, most frightening thing about being a preacher isn't having to stand and deliver to a conglomeration of ill-formed listeners, half of whom thought it was a good idea to vote for a lying, adulterous, racist casino owner as President. No, the best, most frightening thing is when God takes our words and makes them God's.

We preachers talk a good game: "They don't hear!" Amen. "They don't listen!" How true. I'm up there giving a hundred and fifty percent and the ushers are taking them out on stretchers.

And yet . . . I meant to get around to the sermon before Saturday, but it was one thing and then another. So I jot down some inanities on the back of an envelope. I stand up on Sunday, pull out some sappy illustrations, "tie a yellow ribbon on the old oak tree," "he ain't heavy, he's my brother"—praying it's the first sermon they've heard. Stand for the benediction. I'm done.

He greets me at the door, fighting back tears, and he grips my hand, saying, "Good sermon. God really spoke to me. I'm going to quit my job, sell the pickup, learn Spanish and nursing, and move to Honduras as a missionary."

And what is it a preacher feels when your words become God's?

"Look, uneducated, unsophisticated, poorly defended layperson—*I was just preaching!* You're not supposed to take this literally. We're not fundamentalists! That was a metaphor!"

Here's truth that is both encouragement and warning: Because of the God we've got, we can't trust preaching to be ineffective.

Peter preaches post-Pentecost a poorly prepared, badly delivered sermon, and thousands respond, "What should we do?" God made the worst sermon the most effective ever preached.

It's enough to keep a preacher nervous.

We preachers have adequate defenses for coping with the ineffectiveness of preaching—laity are dolts, biblical illiteracy, half of 'em are card-carrying members of the NRA. They don't hear! What many preachers lack is a sufficiently robust theology to account for why sometimes, despite our worst sermons, God speaks. *They hear.*

A preacher is plagued by questions:

Do I really want that much power over a person's life?

Why should I aid and abet Jesus laying some cross on their overburdened backs?

I lamented to a Duke student the scant attendance at Duke Chapel. He attempted to comfort me, "Go easy on yourself, man. I've heard you preach. It's a miracle you get out as many as you do. Duke is a selective university. Students are smart. They know that if they came to the chapel, and if one of your sermons got to them, their lives would only become more unmanageable."

That's the best reason I've ever heard for not attending church.

Despite the Academy of Homiletics, nobody has ever found a surefire, absolutely effective way to keep the Trinity from insinuating itself into a sermon and having the last word.

After Trump said something stupid about immigration (by reading from a text prepared by Stephen Miller, Duke, 2007), a preacher stood up in the middle of the Sunday service and read Leviticus 19:33 on protecting the resident alien. Without commentary, he just shut the Bible and said, "The Word of the Lord." The congregation responded, "Thanks be to God."

Two well-paying families left his church.

"Perilous times for preachers," I said glumly.

"Still," the preacher quipped, "when I began ministry you had to be something of an artist to preach the gospel, illustrate and embellish, make like an exegetical scholar. These days, all a preacher has to do is stand up, read it straight, and even Floridians get the point. Great time to be a preacher."

Philip is told by an angel to go to the desert at noon (Acts 8:26-40). There, he runs into an Ethiopian eunuch. Somehow the Ethiopian has got his hands on an Isaiah scroll, but he can't understand what he reads. "'Like a lamb he was led to slaughter,' it says. Who's he talking about? Himself or somebody else?"

"We believe he was talking about Jesus," said Philip.

The Ethiopian asks, "What's to prevent me from being baptized in the name of the Lamb?"

Philip said, "Er, uh, nothing would make me happier than to baptize an unclean Ethiopian eunuch, but we need water and we're in the middle of the desert."

"Look! Water!"

And Philip muttered, "The saints were pissed about my baptizing those Samaritans. They'll go through the roof over this!"

God did that, not Philip.

Making our words God's word is God's idea of a good time before it is ours.

Barth said that by God's grace, *aufhebung,* God hefts up our words.

Jonah: "Get up and go to Nineveh, that great city, and declare against it the proclamation that I am commanding you" (Jonah 3:1-4). Go preach to Assad, Kim Il Sung, Putin, . . . Trump! Jonah heads in the other direction. God sends a great fish who swallows Jonah then vomits him on the beach.

"Okay, okay, I'll go preach." Jonah preaches the shortest, worst sermon (until Peter's in Acts 2): "Just forty days more and Nineveh will be overthrown!" There, I've said it. Let's stand for benediction. I got a plane to catch. To hell with all of you.

And in response to Jonah's sulking farewell sermon, the Ninevites repent—people, king, cows.

And the world's most reluctant missionary, Jonah, wishes he were dead. "I knew you were a merciful God who is 'rich toward all' (Rom 10:12), whose salvation does not stop at the US border. I knew!"

If God should take my evasive, cowardly words as an occasion to speak The Word, and if the Holy Spirit should move them to hear the gospel from a reluctant missionary, and in hearing, to turn, return—where then might we be?

Not far from the kingdom.

Chalcedonian Proclamation

In preaching, God solicits our participation in communication, utilizing preachers to draw the world into conversation. No sermon is immaculately conceived; it's words of a thoroughly human preacher delivered in the name of the same relentlessly redemptive God who took interest in Samuel, Eli and sons, Jonah, Peter, and Mary. At the same time, no sermon is merely human public address; God produces more in a sermon than we can tell.

John Calvin marveled at the interaction of the divine and human that is Christian preaching: "When a person goes up into the pulpit, . . . it is in order that God may speak to us through the mouth of a human being, and may be so gracious as to present himself here among us, having willed an ordinary human to be his messenger."[53]

"The preached word is God's word," is best understood by what George Hunsinger calls the "Chalcedonian imagination."[54] From the beginning of *Church Dogmatics*, where Barth tackles "The Word of God, and Experience,"[55] to the end where Barth says that God-human synergy occurs "without any confusion or mixture of the divine and human, or transformation of one into the other,"[56] the Definition of Chalcedon accounts for Barth's view of revelation.

Amid theological dispute among the followers of Apollinarius (overstressing the incommensurability of the two natures of Christ) and Nestorius (accentuating the distinctiveness and differentiation of Christ's two natures), the Definition of Chalcedon delineated the orthodoxy of Nicea. Paradoxical clarification, not simplification, was its aim. Chalcedon celebrates the wonder of the consubstantial God/human Jesus:

> Our Lord Jesus Christ, the same perfect in Godhead and also perfect in manhood; truly God and truly man . . . in all things like unto us, without sin; begotten before all ages of the Father, . . . for us and for our salvation, born of the Virgin Mary, the Mother of God, . . . one and the same Christ, Son, Lord, only begotten, to be acknowledged in two natures, inconfusedly, unchangeably, indivisibly, inseparably; the distinction of natures being by no means taken away by the union, but rather the property of each nature being preserved, and concurring in one Person and one Subsistence, not parted or divided into two persons, but one and the same Son, . . . as the prophets from the beginning declared concerning Him, and the Lord Jesus Christ Himself has taught us, and the Creed of the holy Fathers has handed down to us.[57]

Christ's two natures, unified in one person (hypostasis) yet neither confused, mixed, nor separated and detached. Christ really is entirely, unreservedly divine *and,* in the same person, became fully, completely human.

Barth's reading of Chalcedonian logic enables him to assert a strong claim for divine sovereignty *along with* an affirmation of human freedom without divine determinism. Human agency in preaching is connected to divine agency in a Chalcedonian pattern of *asymmetry, intimacy,* and *integrity.*

> God . . . absolutely precedes and humanity . . . can only follow. Even as sovereign acts and words of God, as [God's] free acts of rule, judgment,

salvation and revelation, these events are also human actions and passions, works and experiences, and *vice versa*.[58]

Asymmetry: God's speaking precedes speech of humanity, which can only follow as response to God's initiative.[59] *Intimacy:* God's words can coincide with human words (and vice versa) in unity rather than separation. *Integrity:* God's words and human words can coexist and inhere in fellowship without merging or mixture of either the divine or the human element.[60]

Patristic formulations like the Definition of Chalcedon keep notions of Christ as complex and dynamic as the Scriptures present Christ to be. Chalcedon rebukes preachers who think our task is to simplify and reduce the gospel, adjusting to the limits of human comprehension unaided by the Holy Spirit. Chalcedon encourages our thought about God to be as imaginative as it must be to talk accurately about its divine/human subject. Furthermore, the Chalcedonian imagination protects our congregations from preacherly attempts to abridge the Trinity to the point where we are not talking about the fully human/fully divine Christ but rather an idol cut down to our size.

Revelation is the action of God in history, that is, the story of the God/human Jesus Christ.[61] We wouldn't need to be so imaginative and dialectical in our talk of God if God had not come to us as the eternal Logos, Son of God *and* human being, in our space and time. The Incarnation tests our claims about God by the person and work of Jesus, the God/human. A sermon's lack of ethical substance is exposed by how often the preacher refers generically to "God" and how seldom the preacher names "Christ." At the same time, a sermon's want of theological substance is unmasked by its depictions of Jesus as human exemplar rather than Christ, Judge of and Atonement for humanity.[62] Rigorous adherence to Christology preserves our preaching from rendering God as a merely spiritual something or as the ideal human somebody—God delivered into our hands to use as we please.

When human speaking in preaching becomes God's speaking, it's the God of Abraham, Isaac, Jacob, and Mary being most godly—that is, God refusing to be God without initiating and sustaining divine/human conversation. God speaks in human speech in order to instigate meeting, to call humanity into fellowship, subsuming us into Christ's history. Christ is not God's Plan B after Plan A fails. Christ is God's eternal self-determination not to be God without us. Humanity's interactions with God are determined by the mystery of the Incarnation, God's binding of God's self to humanity in a way that, though asymmetrical, is thoroughly intimate, without any diminution of God or any merging with humanity.

A nameless serving maid exposes the divinely designated, premier disciple, "The Rock," as a prominent Christ-denier. Peter preaches to the scoffing mob, showing thereby not only human chutzpa but also divine prodding, without ceasing to be the one who had denied his Lord. Chalcedonian dialectic permeates Scripture.

Preaching participates in the Chalcedonian wonder, human speech as God's speech, Bethlehem all over again, miraculous and mysterious, God tangibly enfleshed as a baby born to a thoroughly flawed, utterly human family, infinity dwindled to infancy, without diminution of divinity, God redefining God as God with Us, a Jew.[63] Thus, Barth speaks unashamedly of the divine and human bound, by divine election, as "double agency" in which divine/human words coincide, coexist in undifferentiated, consubstantiated unity because God elects us for fellowship.

Odd that in his early days Barth was known (probably due to our first meeting him in *Romans*) as a theologian of transcendence, of divine and human oppositional distance. The "Chalcedonian pattern," as the recurring center of his theology, leads Barth to say that we "must actually put our hand in the fire"[64] and think the unthinkable—divine/human speaking that, while asymmetrical is also unreservedly intimate, sacrificing neither the integrity of divine sovereignty nor true human freedom.[65]

In *Dogmatics in Outline,* Barth defines faith as the event whereby God makes us "free to hear the word of grace."[66] Faith must be described dialectically as, "Altogether the work of God, and . . . altogether, human work . . . complete enslavement, and . . . complete liberation." From whence does faith come? "[Faith] is raised up, and lives as it is awakened by the word of God."[67] Though divinely initiated, our human faith (our responsive hearing) completes the circle of God's speaking. An unheard address, unreceived, is hardly an address. Our "yes" to revelation is only responsive, reflexive, but it is a significant confirmation of the "Yes" of God's revelation. Even in God's salvific work in Jesus Christ, there is still something for humans to do—listen, hear, respond. Our "yes" may be subsequent to God's world-changing "Yes" to us in Christ (2 Cor 1:20), yet it is a necessary confirmation that God's saving work is not in vain. Chalcedonian faith accounts for preaching being a two-sided exchange. "The one great Yes of God spoken in Jesus Christ includes both the turning of God to [humanity] and that of [humanity] to God."[68] God has spoken; we have heard; and thus we believe.

> [Whenever God's word is received as such] as in creation and the incarnation, so here, too, we have a miracle, an event which has its only ontic and noetic basis in the freedom and majesty of God.[69]

Preachers take especial delight when a parishioner says, "Your sermon really spoke to me today," or "Now I understand in a way I didn't before." Through us, God has succeeded not only in speaking to God's people but also in eliciting their response, the Chalcedonian imagination in motion.[70]

> [Faith] cannot be merely a matter of being justified and believing. With . . . faith there arises the need for repentance, for obedience, for the Christian life. We cannot accept God's answer without placing ourselves under the question that is put to us. We cannot recognize God without accepting [God's] authority. We cannot have knowledge in relation to God without action.[71]

There is no independent, autonomous human believing (Pelagianism), not only because we are sinful, finite, and weak (though we certainly are) but also because we are created for more than belief; we are made for fellowship and conversation with God. We have no innate human capacity for this conversation. "The word of God does not rest at all on a possibility imparted to human existence," is not "integral to it or imminent in it, but in God's word itself, which human existence and its possibilities can in no sense proceed, but only follow."[72] Preaching lives by the Chalcedonian reassurance that God fully human, fully divine is God determined genuinely to be in conversation with us.

Vocation

Still, by God's grace, we hear. Discipleship is confirmation that we have been drawn into the sphere of the divine/human conversation. Human nature, for any of its limits, stands under divine invitation. In Christ, God has inextricably bound God's self to us that we might discover the freedom of being bound to God, the joy of being who we were created to be. We are given our bit parts to play in God's great reclamation of God's world. The church is the visible, bodily form that Christ has elected to be in the world, confirmation that preaching is not in vain (1 Cor 15:14).

Because most of God's speech is in the vocative mood, a sermon must be more than an address; it is a summons. Walter Brueggemann says vocation is definitive for preaching: "The devolution of the task from the divine resolve to human agency is a defining moment for the preacher. The preacher must eventually turn from God-talk to human talk concerning summons, responsibility, vocation, and risk."[73] The word of God seeks to be embodied, performed, enacted by those who have heard a call to mobilization and have said, "Yes."

We preachers are therefore not only heralds, announcers but also recruiters, conveners, a primary means whereby Christ gathers his people in order to send them out as witnesses. "All of these new things are from God, who reconciled us to himself through Christ and who gave us the ministry of reconciliation. In other words, God was reconciling the world to himself through Christ, by not counting people's sins against them. He has trusted us with this message of reconciliation" (2 Cor 5:18-19). The fully human, fully divine Christ has not only brought us near to God but also sends us forth, salvation and vocation inextricably linked in those entrusted to give "the message of reconciliation." Divine "Who will go for us?" followed by human "Here I am Lord," displaying the vocational intent behind the Chalcedonian pattern (Isa 6:8).

In the depths of the recent pandemic, one of my students, pastor of a small African American congregation in Eastern North Carolina, preached (by his phone) to the truck drivers, grocery store workers, health care providers, and sanitation workers in his congregation, taking as his text Genesis 50:20:

> A couple of weeks ago you were just shelving groceries or emptying bedpans. But Jesus has used that evil virus for good by calling you to be a witness that there are people loose in this community who fear disappointing Jesus more than catching COVID-19. Maybe you said, "I got to go to work in order to eat." But Jesus makes you say, "I go to work in order to give a witness." You are now God's secret agents in this town. If they thank you or ask you why you are doing what you do, tell 'em it's because of Jesus! "Want to talk?"

God using a virus, once again to use a preacher, to use a biblical text, to use the baptized to save the world from itself.

The first paper that seminarians are required to write in my Introduction to Ordained Leadership class is "How does God explain your presence here at Duke Divinity?" In ten years of those papers, only a few report some obviously, dramatically divine summoning. The rest tell of a more ambiguous but definite vocational word spoken to them by pastors, random people they met in a bar, grandmothers, or a stranger seated next to them on a bus.

How are most preachers called to preach God's word? Through the words of other people. Chalcedon confirmed.

Human Words as God's Word

Exercise of the Chalcedonian imagination would have saved us from misguided attempts to stabilize (ossify?) and simplify (abridge?) biblical revelation. B. B. Warfield's dictation theory for verbal inspiration defended Scripture against the onslaughts of modernity by arguing that Scripture is pristine, divine speaking, denying Scripture's humanity. Warfield made exaggerated statements that the Scriptures "Affirm, indeed, with the greatest possible emphasis that the divine word delivered through men is the pure word of God, diluted with no human admixture whatever."[74] No. As one of the three forms of revelation, Scripture is theanthropic, without embarrassment human and divine. When Paul speaks in his letters, it's in near hypostatic union, two voices speaking at the same time, Paul's voice and the Spirit.[75]

American evangelicals never accepted Barth due to his dynamic, christological view of Scripture.[76] They attempted to bolster Scripture by arguing that the Bible is the word of God because it contains reliable propositional revelation, deposits of truth, the textual result of God's having once spoken rather than the prior and present actions of a divine agent.[77] Deism.

Historical critics of Scripture thought they had found a historically verifiable nub, extracted from layers of confessional accretion, "what actually happened," rescued from confessional distortion by preachers like Matthew and Mark. Historicism.

Agnostic-atheist Bart Ehrman complains that the biblical text is "corrupted" by inept and inattentive scribal transmissions, gleefully pointing out "thousands" of contradictions and errors in the manuscripts, "scores" of conflicts and inconsistencies in this embarrassingly human Bible that Christians allege to be divine. "Do you really want to trust your faith to such a flawed human product?"[78] asks Ehrman.

Those blessed with a Chalcedonian imagination confront this "nonreligious religious studies professor" with, Why would we seek God Incarnate untainted by the human? Who wants to consort with a god who refuses to embrace flawed humans? If Christians worshipped a text, Ehrman's challenge would be serious. Every week my congregation trusts utterly human me (so full of contradictions and errors) to ponder an utterly human text and then hand over to them the utter truth about God, convinced that

97

this is the way God works, even when they've never heard of the Chalcedonian Definition.

Scripture portrayed as the treasure-trove of stand-alone residue of truth detaches the human words of Scripture from the active self-revelation of a living God. For Barth, revelation is not a lifeless deposit; it is the dynamic, free self-unveiling of a sovereign God whose divine freedom is nowhere more evident than in God's veiled unveiling through Christ, Scripture, and preaching. God's speaking is God present with us, beyond us, God known as the unknown. "God's word is God Himself in His revelation."[79] "God's Word is identical with God himself."[80]

> LORD, . . .
>> You know me.
> You know when I sit down and when I stand up.
>> Even from far away, you comprehend my plans.
> You study my traveling and resting.
>> You are thoroughly familiar with all my ways.
> There isn't a word on my tongue, LORD,
>> that you don't already know completely.
> You surround me—front and back.
>> You put your hand on me.
> Where could I go to get away from your spirit?
>> Where could I go to escape your presence? (Ps 139:1-7)

The Trinity, while not at our command, is so determined to self-reveal, to engage in conversation, that God is unlimited even to Scripture and preaching, God's speech through Balaam's donkey being a beloved instance (Num 22:21-39). First Peter 3:1 urges wives to preach to their husbands "without a word." A burning bush speaks to Moses. Through a meal, bread and cup, "you broadcast the death of the Lord until he comes" (1 Cor 11:26).[81]

> We are not restricting the term "Christian preaching" to sermons from the pulpit, or to the work of pastors, but including in it whatever we all "preach" to ourselves in the quiet of our own rooms. . . . Christian preaching, the Word of God today, . . . not as the mastery of human words over God but as the service rendered to God's own Word, the ministry of the Word of God.[82]

Incarnation

Hans van Balthasar says Scripture and preaching are aspects of the incarnational wonder clarified by Chalcedon, "The Word that is God took a body of flesh, in order to be a [human]. . . . He took on, at the same time, a body consisting of syllables, Scripture, . . . verbal utterance."[83]

Preaching "works" in the miraculous way as the virginal conception of Jesus by the Holy Spirit. The miraculous conception of Jesus in Mary's womb or the Resurrection of crucified Jesus are wonders of similar order, if not the same magnitude, to a sermon. God coming from afar, something born in us that we ourselves did not conceive, a door opened from the outside, life from death, a new world made possible, Easter again. Preaching is God embracing our full, flawed humanity, God taking human form, mortal speaking overshadowed by the Spirit, humanity lifted to God, Bethlehem once more, though still, as Mary was told, a "sign that will be opposed" (Luke 2:34).

> Concerning the miracle of the conception by the Spirit and the virgin birth, we must . . . accept it as a miracle. . . . A miracle is an event that one can only reject, only declare to be impossible and absurd, or only believe. Anything that softens or removes this either/or disrupts the concept of miracle. . . . An explained miracle is obviously a miracle no longer. . . . Those who explain a miracle, even if they do so in a more sophisticated way than we usually find among rationalists, are simply showing thereby that they do not want to have to decide between rejection and belief. . . . On the height of the incarnation . . . miracle cannot be set aside or toned down. If we did not have the "conceived by the Holy Ghost," we would have to have something different but no less pregnant and unheard of.[84]

Rather than treat miracle as an embarrassment, the way of liberal theology, Barth celebrates and relishes the Incarnation as a miraculous act of God, an objective, historical event veiled and concealed precisely because Christ's conception and revelation are miraculous, God-produced.[85]

> [Revelation] may be compressed on the one side into "conceived by the Holy Ghost" as it may be compressed on the other side into "the third day he rose again from the dead." The miraculous conception tells us that the God-man is the objective possibility of revelation, and the resurrection tells us [the same]. The miraculous conception is revelation in concealment, the resurrection [the same]. . . . The miraculous conception discloses, shows itself, and makes itself known by his resurrection . . . the miracle at the beginning and the miracle at the end. . . . Miracle makes miracle known.[86]

Bonhoeffer says, "The proclaimed word is the Christ bearing human nature. This word is . . . the Incarnate One who bears the sins of the world. . . . The word of the sermon intends to accept [humanity], nothing else. It wants to bear the whole human nature."[87] For Almighty God to speak to us in ways that we comprehend is incarnational, God risking enfleshment, bearing "the whole human nature," daring entanglement in our death-dealing evasion of the truth. If Christ had not preached, would we have had reason to crucify him? If he had kept quiet, would he have brought out the worst in us?

> You surround me—front and back.
> You put your hand on me.
> That kind of knowledge is too much for me;
> it's so high above me that I can't fathom it. (Ps 139:5-7)

The sermon is a human activity that can be, by God's grace, God's word. No sermon is immaculately conceived, yet neither is any sermon handed over to our control. Preachers bear a "treasure in clay pots" (2 Cor 4:7). The Word of God is both revealed and arcane, unveiled and veiled. Hearing is hardly ever self-evident, rarely obvious and direct but rather mediated, constrained by the human limits of both the preacher and the congregation yet, at the same time, more than we can say.

We preachers pray for critical self-knowledge, an ability to engage in a lifetime of self-reflection and self-discovery so that we might better know the ways that we adulterate the Word with our words. Sometimes I speak out of my own human striving, self-pity, self-justification, and defensiveness, preaching from a bundle of mixed motives. Speech is not only our way to the truth but also our main means of deceit and misperception. After many of my sermons, surely Jesus has prayed, "Father, forgive him, he doesn't know what he's doing."

Upon exiting the vestry to preach to a highly educated, affluent congregation, the host pastor warned, "Just remember. Half of those to whom you will speak this morning thought universal health care was a government giveaway." I gulped.

"Knowing you," he continued, "I'm hoping you will resist temptation to beat up on the reprobates whom God loves."

When a listener fails to receive the word I have so energetically preached, perhaps the lack of hearing is not due to the listener's limitations but to a gracious God's defense of God's people from falsehood and error. Having preached as well as I know how, I have been amazed (why should I be after Chalcedon?) by the lay listener who comments, post-sermon, "That was fine, far as it went, but why did you ignore the last three verses of the parable? Something there that offends you?"

The fully divine, fully human Christ may account for why if you're not their pastor you shouldn't be their preacher. The one who is daily impressed by the full, flawed humanity of Christ's people—their quiet desperation and inchoate yearnings, their hurt and fear—can best respond to their query, "Is there any word from the Lord?" (Jer 37:17). Paul humanely told First Church Corinth that he fed them baby food because they couldn't take more solid nourishment (1 Cor 3:2). At the same time, being periodically blindsided by the undeniable fidelity of ordinary church people performing miraculous good work enables us to preach without fingers crossed, "You are the body of Christ and parts of each other" (1 Cor 12:27).

The lectionary prods me to preach Jesus on remarriage after divorce (Matt 19:3-12). While I'm listening to Jesus's clear teaching, I see the face of Sarah Jones who has finally summoned the courage to walk out on an abusive marriage.

Paul shoves Romans 1:18-26 at me, inviting me to cuff their godlessness. I can't figure out a way to say what Paul says (and doesn't say) without risking harm to Toby Smith who has finally summoned the courage to be honest about his sexuality. In pastoral counseling sessions, I have promised to stand with him against his parents. Surely Paul understands.

I parachuted into a rural Alabama congregation one Sunday. Jeremiah and I smacked 'em with a stem-winder of a sermon against American adventurism in the Near East. They endured my jeremiad surprisingly well, I thought.

Afterward, making my prophetic, Lexus exit, I passed a bulletin board labeled, "Our Kids in Service." A dozen young adults stared back at me. The host pastor commented, "None of them put on a uniform out of patriotism. Their daddy is so mean, or job prospects in this town are so shitty, the Army is a step up."

Nobody who's not their pastor ought to preach Jeremiah, said I as I scurried back to the safety of my episcopal residence.

God grant me the grace to know the texts that bring out the worst in me and those congregational situations in which *et peccator* gets the best of my *simul justis.* Go ahead and chastise me, Lord, when I refuse to emulate John the Baptist in pointing to you rather than attempting to correct you. Thanks, Lord, for insisting that I lead the congregation in prayers of corporate confession before I preach.

Mea culpa.

Read an interesting lection, say, where Christ urges hatred of mothers (Luke 14:26) and you can hear the sphincters tighten. Then I arise and declaim, "Settle down. He didn't mean 'hate' in our sense of the word. Here's what Jesus would have said if he had the benefit of a seminary education. He meant, er, uh, keep the old lady in her proper place."

Don't be their preacher; be the guy who protects 'em from Jesus.

"He didn't mean 'Go, sell all you have and give it to the poor.' That would be economically irresponsible. Relax; he's not talking about you."

Impugn Jesus's judgment in calling the likes of them to be his disciples.

I read through a folder of my sermons from my first year as a pastor. No matter the assigned biblical text, in the majority I found a way to blast the then-current war in Vietnam, excoriating President Nixon. Tricky Dick heard none of my sermons.

My lingering adolescent authority problems, my need to self-style as a prophet, muscled the gospel out of the pulpit.

When the gospel kicks over the boundaries between Jew and Gentile, and Peter is forced by Christ into the house of the Roman centurion, pagan Cornelius is flabbergasted. In gratitude Cornelius falls prostrate at Peter's feet. (These pagan, military functionaries will worship just about anything if given half a chance.) Peter helps him off the floor: "Get up; Like you, I'm just a human" (Acts 10:26).

Not a bad thing for preachers to admit now and then to our congregations, and to ourselves.

God reveals to the world through the bodily function of human speech. Adequate rest and exercise, in Chalcedonian faith, are theological, moral matters for the preacher. *Soma* and *psyche* together. We must be good stewards of our voice. Teresa Fry Brown's book can show you how.[88] Preachers are not angels or disembodied spirits; we are "human beings like yourselves."[89]

Chalcedonian Preaching

Barth once said that the ideal sermon is like a polished pane of glass that we look through to God.[90] However, Barth's transparency metaphor breaks down in the light of Chalcedonian imagination. In preaching, God does not obliterate our humanity but rather uses, fulfills, commandeers it. Jesus didn't just appear to suffer and die on the cross (the Docetist heresy); he bodily bled and died. The rhetorical husk of the sermon cannot be peeled away any more than one can separate the human from the divine in Christ and still have an incarnate God. We preachers are not obsessing over trifles when we worry about sermon design, form, arrangement, and structure; when we agonize about delivery and presentation; or when we search for illustrations from daily life, no matter Barth's put-down of illustrations in his later homiletics lectures.[91] A sermon is not exalted, disembodied, spiritual ideas, vague, timeless, and abstract, an inspiring public address by anybody to nobody in particular. Sermon structure is no more incidental to the sermon's meaning than Jesus being a Jew from Nazareth.

In tailoring his manner of speech to his demanding subject, Paul says that he chose a foolish style of proclamation congruent with his theological message:

> When I came to you, brothers and sisters, I didn't come preaching God's secrets to you like I was an expert in speech or wisdom. I had made up my mind not to think about anything while I was with you except Jesus Christ, and to preach him as crucified. I stood in front of you with weakness, fear, and a lot of shaking. My message and my preaching weren't presented with convincing wise words but with a demonstration of the Spirit and of power. I did this so that your faith might not depend on the wisdom of people but on the power of God. (1 Cor 2:1-5)

Paul's may be our earliest explicit statement on the peculiarity of Christian preaching and the only place where a New Testament preacher turns aside from proclamation to discuss rhetorical strategies, all the while bragging of not using rhetoric.

If even a cross can speak, it's reasonable to expect an incarnating God to utilize a preacher's humanity to serve divine/human communication. I have seen God use a stammering, unsteady voice to good effect, a sweet man who was admired by his people for his "struggle to speak of the divine."

I know a preacher who was lauded as "the best preacher we ever had" because her sermons "remind me of conversations with grandmother."

"I got a grandson with a smart mouth," said one person in defense of his young preacher's abrasive sermons. "Annoys the hell out of me. Still, church is the only place I get to hear from the young."

As a seminarian, I was self-conscious about my Southern accent; lots of Yalies mocked my Carolina patois. Then Bill Muehl gave me a set of tapes, saying, "These preachers are the century's most acclaimed." Harry Emerson Fosdick's voice was hilariously high-pitched. William Sloane Coffin had a virtual lisp. Halford Luccock spoke with an annoying but riveting speech pattern, raising the pitch at the end of each sentence.

I got Muehl's point. Quirks and flukes of speech can be used by God to grab the notice of listeners.

"You get away with murder in the pulpit due to your down-home, Southern folksiness," said one of my critics. Or was his retort an unintended Chalcedonian compliment?

Women pastors report that they experience a degree of empowerment and freedom when they preach. When women were ordained in Protestant denominations, they immediately rose to prominence, due in part to their authorization being theological rather than the way the world empowers.[92]

The preacher stands up and proclaims in a resonant voice, "Thus saith the Lord!" *and* also confesses with young Isaiah, "Mourn for me! I'm ruined! I am a [person of] unclean lips and dwell among a people of unclean lips" (Isa 6:5). In articulating the truth of Jesus Christ we must boldly believe that we have received the truth of God, *and* humbly admit that truth is given and in no way arises from us. Sad to hear a preacher prematurely relax Chalcedonian tension with, "These are just my ideas, only my suggestions, take or leave them as you will."[93] False humility in preaching sometimes veils arrogance that proudly refuses to bend one's life in obedient service to the Word.

Preachers can't appeal to their finitude as a way to squirm out of our calling to speak the truth. Even when modestly delivered, sermons don't sidestep the Chalcedonian declaration: Jesus may be a crucified Jew, but he is still Lord. Because we preach Jesus, words said in his service are subject to rejection by the world that nailed him to the cross. No one has found a way to talk about Jesus that guarantees that we won't be hurt by those who don't want to hear him. Preachers "take up the cross," if not daily as Jesus warned (Luke 9:23), at least weekly around eleven thirty in the morning.

On the other hand it is also sad to hear the preacher who speaks as if there were no tension, no human limitedness in preaching. There's no surefire, knockdown effective method that frees us preachers from empty-handed dependence upon the Holy Spirit. Only the Spirit can give us the words to cry, "Abba! Father!" (Rom 8:15-16). God's word is never the preacher's unmediated, direct, stabilized possession that compels assent. Ordination does not purge human weaknesses. Words from the pulpit that require no Resurrected Christ, no forgiving Father, no rousing Holy Spirit to make them work are not the Word.

I wish, when I preached, I could break the habit of saying "uh" or "um" at the end of sentences. Still, my unfortunate habit may be testimony that my poor Southern-accented, high-pitched, cracking, aging voice displays the strain of speaking the truth, *Deus dixit*. Preachers speak with un-ease—without polished and perfected oratory free of awkward gaps and pauses, dangling modifiers, ragged conclusions, and lots of hemming and hawing—knowing that God never gives us the last word, that God has not given into our hands direct revelation that belongs only to God. Like John the Baptist, we are witnesses who can only point toward, not encapsulate or control, the terrible, saving wonder of God on a cross.

Still, a Chalcedonian faith reassures that whereas our voices fail, crack under the strain and fade, ricochet off the walls of the church and die, the Word of the Lord endures forever (Isa 4:8; 1 Pet 1:25). Our long, thin, bony fingers of sermons can point to the Messiah, but we can in no way replace Christ as substance and means of preaching.[94] My voice barely reaches the listeners on the second pew; God's voice goes out into the whole world (Rom 10:18). Nail Christ to the cross, seal him in the tomb, he will still have the last word when, "Look! God's dwelling is here with humankind. He will dwell with them, and they will be his peoples. God himself will be with them as their God" (Rev 21:3).

Only the fully human, fully divine God could produce the incident in which I was a participant/observer at Birmingham's Church of the Reconciler—church for, by, and with the homeless. The first time I preached at Church of the Rec, after the call to worship, I gazed at the gathering gleaned off the city streets and realized that my proposed sermon was a stupid mistake. I tossed my sermon, praying, *Come on, Lord, give me something. I'm dying down here. You owe me, Lord. Line?* That frantic prayer, though prayed often, is seldom answered—sometimes the Lord builds character by having a preacher publicly experience being "poor in spirit." But that day, with a congregation of the wretched of the streets before me, the Holy Spirit fed me the words.

"It's always a blessing to be with you," I began. "Here's the question for the morning: What did Jesus do for a living? What line of work was he in?" *No way I could have come up with that on my own.*

Silence. For a moment I wondered if the Lord had overplayed his hand. Finally, someone ventured, "Carpentry?"

"Good guess. No. His daddy Joseph was a carpenter, but no record of Jesus ever helping out in the shop."

"A preacher?" ventured another.

"Right! He was some preacher. But back then, people didn't yet know that you could defang a preacher with a good salary and a fat pension. No, Jesus couldn't have earned a living wage by preaching." *Where did I get that?*

"Did Jesus have an apartment?" somebody called out.

"Great question!" I said. "Nothing about Jesus working, but we do know that 'even foxes have holes to crawl into at night but the Son of Man has nowhere to lay his head.'"

Way to go, Lord.

"Here's the truth: Jesus Christ was an unemployed, homeless beggar. That's why he accepted so many dinner invitations, even to homes where he wasn't liked. He was hungry and had nowhere else to go." *Too direct?*

Somebody down front shouted, "That's all right, Jesus! I ain't got no job neither! That's all right!" Applause in the congregation. "That's all right!"

"No job, no house, no nothin', just like Jesus!" shouted a woman who danced in the aisle as the band struck up. General applause and adoration from the assembly.

I felt nervous and uncomfortable. The Lord is ripping my sermon out of my hands, taking us somewhere I would not have gone with this congregation, left to my own devices.

A few raucous minutes later, I waved the congregation to silence. "You've got my drift. Christians believe that a homeless (drumroll), jobless ('Amen!'), Jew ('Go ahead!') is the whole truth about who God is and what God is up to. If you've never been hungry (crashing cymbal), with nowhere to lay your head ('Godamighty!'), there's a good chance you'll misunderstand Jesus. And I'm not a good enough preacher to explain him to you."

"So," I shouted above the joyful din, "that means that even with degrees from Yale and Emory, even though I can read this stuff in Greek, some of you are closer to Jesus than your bishop!" Dancing and shouting resumed. *I'm not responsible for this.*

After service I walked down the sidewalk and joined a few of the congregants under a nearby highway overpass. They stood warming themselves around a smoky fire in a steel drum. As I approached, a woman shouted, "Some of ya'll ain't right about God. Here comes that preacher who told us the truth!"

I'm unworthy of such sermon response.

Barth taught that revelation is an "event," a miraculous, momentary gift of God that can't be grasped or contained, only received. Barth also called the church an "event," the crater formed by the explosion of the gospel. The church is not an institution, an eternal organization, a continuing community. Church happens whenever the Word makes it so.[95]

The first Sunday of the fall term, ten thirty, I would pace anxiously on the steps of Duke Chapel, wondering whether anybody would show up. Having so many institutional props knocked from under me at a college chapel taught me that God constitutes the church in each generation. Event. Pure grace.

But the eventful nature of the church does not mean that it's fragile. We preachers get a front-row seat to watch the church created afresh in each generation through conversation with the resilient Word:

> As the church that is founded on the apostolic word, the church is never a given factor. It has to become a reality by the calling of God. Ordination is a . . . pointer to God's calling to the extent that in ordination the ordained come to hear the Word of God, which, however, they must constantly hear afresh . . . repeatedly founded anew by an apostolic word. It can exist only in the event of the speaking and hearing of this apostolic word as God's Word. Thus the church is an institution only as an invitation, as a waiting for the church. In the church we are always on the way to the event of the church. Thus the ministry as the stepping forth of individuals is an act which must repeatedly become a reality by the calling of God. Ordination is a . . . pointer to God's calling to the extent that in ordination the ordained come to hear the Word of God, which, however, they must constantly hear afresh.[96]

Maybe you are going through a rough time in your life and your preaching owes more to your reaction to your personal problems than to your exegesis of the Scripture. Perhaps you are preaching for the wrong reasons, improper motivation, the way you were raised as a child, in response to some trauma, or out of your resentment that God has stuck a talented person like you with a congregation of losers like them.

Don't worry. A resourceful, redemptive God who turned a cross into a sign of victory can still figure out how to use you. God's vocation must not be impugned by your reservations. In a Chalcedonian faith, there's no great need agonize over whether what you said in last Sunday's sermon was merely a human rant or a divinely inspired address. You'd be the last to know, wouldn't you? An incarnated God, defined so imaginatively by Chalcedon, sees no reason for rigorous separation of the human from the divine.

In preaching God condescends to use our humanity for all it's worth. I know a distinguished preacher whose shyness has been used by God to deliver the gospel in a way that beguiles and entices her listeners. Then there's the woman who confesses, "I never saw a fight I didn't want to join," whose "in your face" pulpit style has made her a favorite preacher at Christian student conferences. Her sermons intimidate me (she works out at CrossFit), but the kids eat 'em up. I've got a friend with a booming bass voice set in a body that's 240 pounds, six foot three, who reputedly, "Sounds like God if the Lord had played football for Georgia." I can introduce you to a pastor who, when asked about his success in the pulpit, replied, "Once they found out I was a recovering alcoholic in my second marriage, they knew they could trust what I told them about Jesus."

God fully uses our humanity *and* is fully present as the Lord, doing things we could not, speaking a word beyond our words. We must not limit preaching to what the human alone can accomplish. Sometimes I've set up a really good dilemma with my pulpit reflections on a conflicted biblical text but can't figure out how to end the sermon. So I just end. The Lord must do the rest. Mark's abrupt close is a reminder to us preachers that our job is to announce, to proclaim, not to tie it all up with a bow. We speak the gospel on Sunday; it's their baptismally mandated task to perform the gospel the rest of the week.

Preaching, human or divine? The dealings between us and God are so thoroughly incarnational in intent and content, method and means, that preaching can be public demonstration of the Incarnation when the God who was presumed to be distanced and detached is heard in the sound of a human voice.

Because the center is Christ the Lord, preaching may have difficulty finding analogies and allies. Many of the world's ways of making sense are robbed of their usefulness by Christ. Still, because of Christ, human language is under the sphere of divine influence, so we must not ignore insights on human phenomena or dismiss out of hand secular sources of knowledge. Nothing human is beyond the bounds of Christ's redemptive work. God may speak through Cultural Anthropology (I suppose), popular culture, or Economics (maybe), though all must be judged by the three forms of revelation.

There is an inappropriate, non-Chalcedonian spiritualization of preaching in which otherwise good words are filled with helium and floated over the congregation. Words like *liberation, hospitality, community, solidarity,* and *incarnational,* sailing forth from the pulpit, give preachers the illusion that we've actually said something of substance when we've merely mouthed the cliché of the moment. Say "spiritual formation" or "deeper sense of purpose" and watch the congregation's eyes glaze over, the congregation's suspicion that preaching is disincarnate talk about ethereal vagaries reinforced.

Recently I heard a preacher say that "we must continue to show radical hospitality to the poor" as if he were talking about something that's actually occurring in the congregation. His phrase is sentimental bromide to foster the illusion that if we say the words, we've actually done the deed.

A pastor opened a sermon with, "We gather this morning as those who have great anxieties and bear deep, secret wounds." Looking around at the affluent, nearly all-white congregation, they looked in good shape. What is the cost of naming a congregation in this self-aggrandizing, self-pitying way? Even if many are anxious (people with great possessions tend toward anxiety) and wounded (your wounds better be more interesting than mine), they are more than a gathering of the damaged; they are convened as disciples who are expected not only to hear God's word from on high but also to perform it in the world. Jesus doesn't wait for us to be healed, mentally fit, or free of pain and heartache before he calls us to witness. Sometimes, the agony we experience when a sermon goes south relativizes the pain from an aching back.

God grant me freedom from resentment at having to preach the gospel in a neighborhood (relatively affluent, privileged, white, democratic, educated, North American) where there are so many well-wrought, expensive defenses against Jesus Christ. Still, Jesus gives me no role in sorting those whom he will address.

Here's Chalcedonian hope for us deceptive preachers and our prevaricating congregations: the Word has become flesh, our flesh, and tented among us, saying that which we could never say to ourselves.[97]

Temptation to Silence

Because God speaks, for better or worse, sometimes saying things to us we would rather not hear, it's understandable that some extol silence as next to godliness. Preachers are one way that a talkative God ensures that the church doesn't succumb to the lure of the apophatic.

Bartimaeus, a blind man, daringly initiates conversation with Jesus, crying out, "Son of David, have mercy on me" (Mark 10:47). The crowd tries to silence Bartimaeus, to confine him in submissiveness and muteness (v. 48). (Five chapters later a crowd will cry, "Crucify!" to shut up Jesus.) Bartimaeus persists, calling to Jesus, "even more loudly" (v. 48). Jesus hears, heals, and proclaims, "Your faith has made you well" (v. 52). "Immediately, he regained his sight and followed him on the way" (v. 52).

Bartimaeus calls out, defies the crowd's call for silence. Then the crowd says to Bartimaeus, "He is calling you." A now-healed Bartimaeus "followed him on the way."[98] This is the path of the daring sermon: The preacher (in service to the congregation) calls upon God, and congregation and pastor remind one another that Christ "is calling you," resulting in our being called to follow Jesus on the way. Vocational from start to finish.

Meister Eckhart declared, "Nothing creaturely is so like God as silence,"[99] lecturing preachers, "Be silent and do not chatter about God; for when you chatter . . . you are telling lies and sinning."[100] Robert Cardinal Sarah has too much to say about the holiness of saying nothing, calling the modern world an oppressive "dictatorship of noise," "symptom of serious, worrisome illness."[101] "Solitude and silence . . . is where God dwells. [God] drapes himself in silence."[102]

Ironic, don't you think, that the Cardinal could not let silence speak for itself?

"For Zion's sake I will not keep silent" (Isa 62:1), is the preacher's maxim. Even in the face of threats from the crowd made uncomfortable by speech of the marginalized, silence about God is a luxury Zion can ill afford. True, in our wired world, silence can be a gift. Silence gives us room to "hear ourselves think," as we say. But silence is inadequate for thinking about the Trinity.

Amid Revelation's cacophony of speeches, prayers, prophecies, and music, "When the Lamb opened the seventh seal, there was silence in heaven for about half an hour" (Rev 8:1). The silence of awe, fear, or wonder? We don't know, do we? Silence is revealing only with words.

Eberhard Jüngel worries that "God will be talked to death, . . . silenced by the very words that seek to talk about God."[103] Silence is "praised by all religions," claims Dale Allison. "Maybe we have murdered God, . . . finally did away with [God] indirectly, by exterminating silence. Artificial noise has become an unholy liturgy that [draws us away] from nature's God and [God's] self-imposed muteness of love."[104] *Since when is nature silent? Love is mute?*

In her 1997 Beecher Lectures, Barbara Brown Taylor warned preachers that many of our people "have become suspicious if not downright disdainful of the spoken word." She says that our homiletical challenge is "compounded by God's own silence. If God spoke directly to people, preachers could retire. As it is, God's reticence is the problem the clergy think they are hired to address."[105]

Brown Taylor says that the silence of God is the major pastoral challenge. When we cry to God because Scripture tells us that "the faithful receive what they ask for: children, manna, land, health. By implication, those who do not receive are not faithful. . . . If they were, God would speak to them. 'For everyone who asks receives, and everyone who searches finds, and for everyone who knocks, the door will be opened'" (Luke 11:10). "This is the condemnation that hangs over the silence of God."[106]

Ludwig Wittgenstein's dictum "Whereof we cannot speak, that we must pass over in silence" is often used as justification for silencing God. All talk of God is fishy because God is the mystery beyond the limits of verbalization. God, too high to talk down to us or for us to talk up to.

But as Eberhard Jüngel points out, apophatic theologies define God solely on the basis of human limitations, describing God only negatively as inexpressible, unknowable, and therefore unthinkable, the antithesis of Israel's God. To define God's revelation negatively and apophatically, unthinkable and unspeakable, is to negate God—mysticism as prelude to atheism.[107] A Chalcedonian imagination resists negative theology. God has positively self-revealed as a Jew from Nazareth, forever breaking silence between us and God.

In the absence of a Chalcedonian, incarnational theology of God's speaking, metaphysical speculation becomes our only way to talk God.[108] This results, says Jüngel, in the "dumb silencing" of God, exclusion of God from discourse by our "garrulous silencing" of God. Undue humility, sentimentality, and the substitution of other gods permits the word *God* to continue being used, but in a way that excludes God as speaker. God is rendered mute by the philosophical claim that God is unthinkable and therefore unspeakable, depersonalizing God as the unnameable distant one who cannot self-identify through speech.[109]

When he charged that we preachers have "talked God to death," Jüngel was attacking meaningless metaphysical talk about God rather than urging apophatic Deism. God constitutes the world and us by speaking. Theology then "speaks after" God's primary address. So Jüngel brings us back to the Barthian, Chalcedonian theme that God is no more diminished or degraded through human preaching "than is a lover deprived of . . . power through [the lover's] self-communicating love."[110]

As Nicholas Lash says, "The best remedy for our linguistic insufficiency is to confess it" and continue to talk.[111] Preachers know the near-weekly experience of having to say what's hard to say and, after the saying, to admit that we could've said it more clearly, more faithfully. While preaching can be an antagonistic way of life that never quite achieves its aim, daring to express combined with intrepid confession of the limits of our speaking is the way to God provided by God. As Cardinal Newman said, the way to talk about God is by repeatedly "saying and unsaying," though never not saying.[112]

When Paul gets sidetracked by congregational questions about marriage and virgins, he admits that he has no direct word from the Lord (1 Cor 7:12, 25). Candor about the limits of what God gives us to say is admirable. Still, after admitting no revelation, Paul goes right ahead and offers a word on subjects he knows little about. Corinthians, feel free to take it or leave it.

Adrienne Rich says, "Do not confuse silence with absence."[113] And yet, where is "presence" without self-revealing embodiment? Words are not absent even in silence. No place to hide from speech, even when we are not speaking. When asked, "Teach us to pray," Jesus loved his disciples enough to give them words rather than trust the words that might come to them if he abandoned them in silence.

Mystical Evasiveness

Apophatic accounts render God unsociable, God other than the One who called Israel out of Egypt and raised crucified Christ from the dead.[114] "Mysticism" would be Barth's put-down of contemporary spirituality that flirts with apophaticism, the latest attempt to make the church invisible, unrecognizable as Body of Christ. Mysticism is "the way of evasion" that contributes little to preaching.[115]

> Preaching bases itself on the Bible, and the Bible on revelation. Always, then, the knowledge of God . . . [in preaching] is knowledge in the relation of revelation. . . . Hence, despite or because of all its knowledge of God's incomprehensibility (overstressed by mysticism), it cannot avoid saying things about the nature of God.[116]

The notion that God is incomprehensible and therefore inexpressible, dismissed by Barth as "instructed ignorance," stands "very ambivalently between human self-rejection and human self-exaltation."[117]

> God's incomprehensibility stands . . . behind Christian preaching as a decisive factor. As concerns the proclaimed or presupposed nature of God, this preaching must keep silence as well as speak; it must conceal as well as define; it must negate as well as affirm; it must draw back as well as venture forward.[118]

Any apophatic, mystical *Via Negativa* is blocked by the objectivity of a bodily raised, relentlessly revealing Christ. Preachers are theologically cataphatic, suspicious of the apophatic. Just as we can't have relationship without others talking us into ourselves, and others cannot know us unless we speak, a silent God is no God of love.

Oppressive Silence

The silence of those who have nothing to say, the numbed silence of despair post-trauma, the eerie quiet after disaster, the muzzling of those who speak truth to power, rebuke unequivocal praise of silence.[119] The most frequent reason given by members of my congregation for why they did not reach out to someone in pain is, "I didn't know what to say." In encouraging pastors to preach against racism, the predominant excuse for their not speaking out is, "Worried that I might say the wrong thing, I say nothing."[120]

Rachel Muers's theological exploration of silence suggests that my defense of *Deus dixit* could be the expression of male privilege. "The attempt to restore to theology its acknowledgment of God as a speaker sits ill with many aspects . . . of feminist theology. What is the silence of God, after all, it might be claimed, but the long awaited silence of the voice of mystifying male authority, that had itself silenced the voices of women, and of countless others who cannot speak from margins?"[121]

Muers counters that the silencing of God as a defense against "the voice of mystifying male authority" implies (the non-Chalcedonian assertion) that "the speech of God competes with human speech" and fails to see that the "world-constituting character" of God's speech "is the basis of all creaturely freedom—including the freedom to speak a response to God."[122] Speech can be oppressive; so can silence. In preaching, God compliments rather than competes with human speech.

Muers says, "The association of hearing with the non-activity of humanity before God reinforces a pattern of authority [whereby] the power of the appointed speaker [dominates] those who hear," the antithesis of a trinitarian God. Cultural assignation of passive, self-forgetful hearing to women is in no way integral to the Christian view of God.[123] She cites Bonhoeffer who stressed, "Christians have forgotten that the ministry of listening has been entrusted to them by the one who is indeed the great listener and in whose work they are to participate. We should listen to God, so that we can speak the word of God."[124] Listening to God who listens to us, the voiceless discover their voices.

Times of silence in the liturgy ought to foster receptivity to God's speaking. Yet malformed listeners may use liturgical silence as another occasion to fill empty space with individual yearnings. An exception might be times of quiet in the Anglican liturgy where the Book of Common Prayer has so filled us with scriptural thoughts that our moments of silence might be more than a deep dive into our subjectivity.

I admit that my privilege advantages me as the one who does the talking while others with less power listen, making all the more miraculous that God speaks even through privileged people like me to give the good news to the disenfranchised, enabling the silenced to speak.

In a sermon on Psalm 103, speaking of God redeeming us from "the pit" (verse 4), I mentioned, in passing, Virginia Woolf's account of how as a young girl she was sexually assaulted by a relative and, in that moment, looked into a deep, dark, unfathomable "pit."

The next week four women in the congregation made appointments to talk about their experiences with sexual assault.

"I've submitted to years of counseling," said one. "Yet to hear those words spoken by my preacher and then bounce off the rock walls of my church, ricochet back and forth, and sound in my brain, did more good than the therapy."

> In the last days, God says,
> I will pour out my Spirit on all people.
> Your sons and daughters will prophesy.
> Your young will see visions.
> Your elders will dream dreams.
> Even upon my servants, men and women,
> I will pour out my Spirit in those days,
> and they will prophesy. (Acts 2:17-18)

When, from the safety of a protected position, I say, "No comment," or, "Your salvation is not my responsibility," or, "I've been privileged to have pondered the gospel for much of my life, but I'm not going to waste time telling it to you," privilege is at its worst.

I grew up in an unashamedly, legally white-supremacist culture. Each day I boarded a bus that bore the sign: *South Carolina Law: White patrons sit from the front. Colored patrons sit from the rear.* Nobody questioned that sign, especially those who preached to me on Sunday.

In college I attended a student conference on "Christians against War," a protest against the then-raging war in Vietnam. At one of the late-night services, an African American Methodist preacher from rural South Carolina spoke. He didn't have a resonant voice; he made a couple of grammatical errors. A sermon was the last thing we student radicals wanted at this hour on a Saturday.

I remember zingers like, "I'm going to talk to you kids about something I bet you never heard of—*sin.* You think my next line is going to be about sex. Your sexual sin ain't my concern. I'm talking about the sin that you inherited by being born in the South. I'm talking sin worse than this Asian war. I'm talking your sin in black and white, sin that your parents don't want you to hear about. Well, your parents ain't here tonight."

He then pounded us for "giving in to who you were bred to be," for the ways we had benefited from good breaks given to us not because of "how smart you are but only because of the color of your skin." Recounting the Orangeburg Massacre, he mocked the governor of South Carolina and spoke about the defensiveness "of people you love who know better—yes, even grandmamma and granddaddy—but don't know how to get this demon off their backs."

Then he paused for a moment, came out from behind the pine pulpit, pounded his fist on the communion table, and said, "You don't have to keep lyin' and denyin', 'cause here's the good news—*Jesus Christ saves sinners, only sinners.* Some folks sin by tellin' lies about people of other races. Others sin (listen up!) by sayin', 'I'm against this war so my slate is clean, I don't need forgivin'. Well, if you don't need forgivin' then Jesus Christ has got nothin' to give you. *Jesus Christ saves sinners!*"

I left that sermon, better than I was bred to be, weight off my shoulders, a new sense of God commandeering my life. Thank God that preacher took some responsibility for my salvation and refused to bow to tyrannical silence.

I'll admit that despotic silence is not unknown in Scripture: "God isn't a God of disorder but of peace. Like in all the churches of God's people, the women should be quiet during the meeting. They are not allowed to talk. Instead, they need to get under control, just as the Law says. If they want to learn something, they should ask their husbands at home. It is disgraceful for a woman to talk during the meeting" (1 Cor 14:33-35). "I don't allow a wife to teach or to control her husband. Instead, she should be a quiet listener" (1 Tim 2:12). Few verses have been as pernicious.

Hey, Paul, forget about Galatians 3:28? "There is neither Jew nor Greek; there is neither slave nor free; nor is there male and female, for you are all one in Christ Jesus."

Did Paul regret discouraging the testimony of all Christians?[125] I know how my positions, announced with finality from the pulpit, have been destabilized when laity point out my theological inconsistencies and the ways biblical testimony contradicts my preachments. The testimony of fellow Christians has thereby helped me to live into the faith that I have previously only professed. Maybe that eventually happened to Paul.

In 2016 Pope Francis asserted, in the wake of an ecumenical meeting in London, that the subject of the ordination of women is silenced forever.[126] Presumptuous, even for a Pope, to silence God's chosen spokespersons.

When the 2018 UMC General Conference voted to select preachers on the basis of their sexual orientation, I asked, "How will you silence a God who insists on calling LGBTQ persons to preach?"

The psalmist says that "When I kept quiet, my bones wore out. I was groaning all day long. . . . So I admitted my sin to you . . . then you removed the guilt of my sin" (Ps 32:3, 5).

Walter Brueggemann praises preachers when we "interrupt silence," recalling Martin Luther King Jr.'s sermon on April 15, 1967, at Riverside Church in New York, "Beyond Vietnam: A Time to Break Silence." King spoke against US war policy, risking alienation of his followers, even chancing distraction from the perplexing problem of race, and at the same time, noting the connection between government policy and racism. Brueggemann says, "Breaking the silence is always counter discourse that tends to arise from the margins of society, a counter to present power arrangements and to dominant modes of social imagination."[127]

Bruggemann knows that it's preachers who resist the human temptation to leave some things unsaid:

> Alienation and muted rage have a central characteristic in common: an absence of conversation, loss of speech . . . life reduced to silence. Where there is theological silence, human life withers and dies. . . . In the face of that dread silence, the preacher comes to initiate, to reiterate, to read and enact speech that permits communion. . . . It is speech, and only speech that bonds God and human creatures. The preaching task is to guide people out of the alienated silence of exaggerated self, and out of the silence of denial and rage of an exaggerated God, into a serious, dangerous, subversive, covenantal conversation. . . . Communion is not possible where speech is destroyed. . . . In the midst of these reductions, preachers are invited to speak in ways that open a world of conversation, communication, and communion.[128]

"Surely you are a God who hides" (Isa 45:15), which is a proof text for apophatics. Is Isaiah's truth a general principle or a comment on a specific situation in which God was there but not in a way that the prophet knew? Apophatic accounts of God avoid Jesus; there's little of the contemplative or taciturn in that preacher.[129] Though he was "oppressed and tormented, but didn't open his mouth" (Isa 53:7), Jesus would not have been crucified on the basis of his prayers and moments of solitude.[130]

Jesus rarely orders people to be silent and, when he does, the command to silence is ambiguous. Jesus once said to his disciples, "Come by yourselves to a secluded place" of silence (Mark 6:31). But what's the first thing Jesus does after the crowds find him in retreat? He has compassion and begins to teach (6:34). Sometimes Jesus tells those whom he heals to "tell no one" (Matt 8:4), though he doesn't say why. He almost never orders his disciples to be silent, except after Peter's profession of faith (Matt 16:20) and at the Transfiguration (Matt 17:1-13). I suspect Jesus wants more time to preach. Notably, Jesus orders the storms, the winds, and the demons to keep quiet. We may speculate upon the reasons for Jesus's rare counsels to silence, but we do so only through words.

When friend Jason Micheli struggled with cancer and didn't know what to say to God, he says he just prayed the Psalms.[131] God gave words when Jason, the wordsmith, had none, so determined is God to defeat the wound of silence. The great goal of much of pastoral counseling is to bring human anguish to speech, to help pain go public by saying that which we find difficult to say to others. Salvation is rescue from monologue, delivery from the curse of being forced to find words to describe how it stands with you and God.

The Gospel of Mark ends with the women at the tomb commanded by a figure "dressed in a white robe" to "Go, tell." The women are silent "because they were afraid" (Mark 16:8). Eventually the women must have gotten the guts to speak, encouragement for us preachers who, before some unexpected, difficult-to-understand act of God, are fearfully tempted to silence. When Jesus was told by the authorities to keep his disciples quiet, he replied, "If they were silent, the stones would shout" (Luke 19:40). Herein is our hope: God will speak, will resume the conversation, one way or another.

Sentimental Preaching

Gospel preaching in my church family is endangered not by apophaticism, atheism, fundamentalism, or historical criticism; it's sappy sentimentalism. Sentimentality denies human enslavement to evil and sin and reduces the gospel to fantasies of earnest human striving or unjustified positive feelings about human capacity for goodness. Sentimentality is the illusion that once we've said something, sighed deeply, and shed an empathetic tear we've done something.[132] Sentimentality is the pretense of love without justice, forgiveness without reparations, incarnation without atonement, salvation without vocation, the gracious word of the Lord without judgment or reproof from the Lord. We are fine just as we are, without need of divine renovation. Rather than talk about a God who dares to justify the ungodly (Rom 4:5), we, the willfully innocent, boast of our progress toward godliness on our own.[133] In short, sentimentality is all we've got once we've made God mute.

Kierkegaard castigated the Danish church for its sentimental bedding down in "the cordial drivel of family life," as if Jesus's mission is to boost our marriages and families. Sentimental glorification of the family is self-love transposed, "mediocrity"—"nauseating . . . homey, civil togetherness"—substituted for salvation.[134]

The predominately white congregations who inappropriately responded to the killings of George Floyd, Ahmaud Arbery, and Breonna Taylor with "Services of Lamentation," substituted sad feelings in church for angry action in the streets. Better than whining lament psalms they ought to be fearfully chanting those psalms which speak of God punishing the rich and powerful for the violence they work against the powerless. Sentimentality: gospel substitute of the moment. A mass killing? Hand out candles, have a vigil, link arms in the darkness, and declare "this community comes together in times like these."

Racism? "Find somebody of another race and just have a conversation. Discover the richness of this person's experience. See Christ in them. You'll be blessed."

The essence of Christianity? "It all boils down to, 'Love your neighbor as yourself.' Don't worry about believing; Christianity is a practice."

Death? "She will live on in our memories."

A pandemic? "We're going to come out of this as better people."

Mainline church decline? The mission of the UMC is "Making Disciples for the Transformation of the World," with no change in the way that we do church, expend church resources, or train clergy. Failing either to "make disciples" (our membership losses are legendary; we are still white, middle class) or to work world "transformation" (at our last General Conference, in leaning over to speak to the world, we fell in).

I recently heard a bishop say that the question to put to candidates for ordination is, "Do you have a pastor's heart?" I propose, "Have you a theologian's brain and a rabble-rouser's smart mouth?"

When language is used for sentimental effect, and never is heard a discouraging word, particularly in church, the church forfeits its most valuable asset—truthful speech—for a cheap emotional rush. Sentimentality is what Barth had in mind when he charged that some preaching had degenerated into the public display of preachers' "deepest and sincerest inner personal life and experience." Sermons as heartfelt rather than true.[135] Jesus on the cheap.

Though our Lord welcomed children, the moment a child enters a sermon, it goes bad. Tempted toward mawkish, maudlin schmaltz in the pulpit? Listen to a couple of sermons by Lillian Daniel; you may have a headache, but you'll be sober by morning.[136]

Even better than avoidance of cute stories about your children is unsentimental Scripture. Scripture reminds us that our job is not to put emotionally starved, lonely people in touch with their deeper feelings; we confront them with reality: the Trinity. Theology stands, "over against the pious words of Christian preachers . . . [by magnifying] the authority of Word of God as this is spoken in revelation and as witness is borne to it by Scripture."[137]

While rigorous attentiveness to Scripture gives sentimentality the disrespect it deserves, in the hands of a revealing God, even a killer virus can be an occasion for revelation. "In one week, that virus has ruined six months of my preaching," confessed an honest preacher. "Trivial exhortation for the congregation to be good little boys and girls doesn't work in the face of COVID-19."[138]

In the first weeks of the pandemic, many of the virtual sermons I heard served up sentimentality, as if that's the best we had to offer, pleading for kindness, social solidarity (six feet apart), and empathy. Put a stuffed bear in the window. Love your neighbor by keeping distance between you. (Stand-up comics were saying the same.) Then, on Sunday, March 29, Lent 5 in the lectionary, Jesus took a moment from his trek to the cross to prophesy the end of the Temple (Mark 13), the end of religion as we had known it, not due to a virus but to the Lord. Stone not left upon stone. With the Temple knocked out from under us, where will we go for hope and inspiration?

If the CDC can't save us, who can? In such moments, sentimental bromides seem silly. Anxiety overwhelms. Isolated from the crowd, with our securities ripped off, made discontent with our heartwarming maxims, it was as if Mark 13 said: If Jesus Christ is not the full truth about God and what God is up to, we are without hope.

Only Jesus would use a pandemic as an opportunity to wax apocalyptic, preaching an unsentimental sermon that none of us wanted:

In those days, after the suffering of that time, the sun will become dark, and the moon won't give its light. The stars will fall from the sky, and the planets and other heavenly bodies will be shaken. Then they will see the Human One coming in the clouds with great power and splendor. Then he will send the angels and gather together his chosen people. (Mark 13:24-27)

Unsentimental Church

Sentimentality cannot account for the gaggle of ungodly people Jesus gathers to himself. Jesus is why preachers exist in a potentially contentious relationship with their congregations. It's the Body of Christ, convened by God to hear the royal proclamation, but if your evangelism is effective, your church will be full of the same incomprehension, cowardice, disbelief, and rebellion that arise from any human gathering assaulted by the Word. Note: We preachers meet, in our congregations, no resistance to the Word that was not first encountered in our own hearts.

A number of pastoral leadership books say that pastors must win the trust of our congregations before we can truly lead. I worry that most congregations lack the formation to know what they ought to trust their pastor to do. Is their demand for trustworthiness just another congregational attempt to manage and limit what pastors can preach? Paul implies that a congregation ought to trust a preacher for "speaking the truth in love" (Eph 4:15). But is my "love" for the congregation just concealed self-love, my need to be needed, merely an expression of my dependence upon my employer? Sometimes "I love my people" means "I love me and want to use my people as a means of loving me even more." Congregants say, "I don't mind being corrected and criticized by my pastor—as long as it's done in love." How would I, or they, know my real motives for telling the truth?[139]

God forgive me for loving my people in a way that's less painful than how God loves them.

Congregations can love preachers into silence, playing upon innate pastoral empathy that too-easily degenerates into sentimentality. They reward us for compassion and punish us for truth. While it's not wrong to love our people, pastors are called to love them in the name of Christ. In a culture of lies, empathy can be an enemy of the gospel. Because Jesus Christ is not only the way and the life but also the truth, no wonder preachers sometimes get the shakes.

Still, by the grace of God, preachers dare to put in pain people they love and thereby risk being put in pain by their people.

For any of our virtues, never forget that when asked for a verdict on Jesus we unanimously voted, "Crucify!"

Aubrey Spears labels "postmodern homiletics" as preaching that "erases boundaries between Scripture and congregation; [so that] meaning is generated through participatory conversation."[140] When the twofold forms of revelation—Christ and Scripture—are too threatening, "participatory conversation" is all we've got, erasing boundaries between a congregation trying to listen to Scripture and Scripture that often stands in judgment against, and makes a claim upon, the congregation. I began ministry thinking it was my job to narrow the gap between the contemporary congregation and God's word; now I know that my job is to open up the gap. God's ways are not our ways, our thoughts not God's (Isa 55:8).

Preaching is the peculiar speech of the church, though it is neither authorized nor dependent upon the church and therefore may be against the church in order to be for the church. The sermon is not congregationally derived. Preachers risk conflict, resistance, and rejection by the church in order to be faithful to the church's peculiar vocation: joyful subservience to the Word. In a day when pastoral care for the congregation has virtually overwhelmed Christian ministry (visiting old folks, ambulance-chasing, prayer lists, and hand-holding are easier than preaching), Barth reminds us that the most loving service that we clergy render to our people is address by the Word.

So when somebody complains, "I was hurt by what you said in your sermon, and I know you wouldn't want to hurt anyone," you can say, "You seem as weak and deceitful as I am, which makes all the more amazing that Jesus thinks you are his disciple. I didn't call you. If I were assembling a church I would have been more discriminating! *It's about Jesus!* Pain comes with the call."

In our paternalistic/maternalistic attempts to protect Jesus from his crucifiers, we tuck Jesus into people's individual consciences, make Jesus personal, helpful, and empathetic, thereby robbing him of his political intent.[141] Make contact with some inner, spiritual "feeling," pander to their self-pity and preach as if our bottomless need is the equivalent of God.[142]

"Not every [preacher] can [speak the Word of God]. . . . For not every [preacher] has heard it,"[143] says Barth. Many contemporary pastors are only pastors—congregational caregivers, managers, organizational leaders—rather than preachers: those who, having heard, are compelled to preach.

Missionary Preaching

"Christianity in the form we have known it" is ending, wrote Barth as early as 1935.[144] Toward the end of the *Dogmatics,* Barth reiterated, "The Christian West no longer exists."[145]

Obeying Peter's injunction to "Live honorably among the unbelievers" (1 Pet 2:12), I preached twenty years at Duke Chapel. Hired just to be a chaplain, a professor who preached, I got thrust into a continuing argument between God and the university and was made a missionary, witnessing to Christ in a culture that neither knew nor wanted Christ. My preaching was liberated.[146] If preaching no longer bolsters the illusion of a Christian West, aids the improvement of American democracy, or gives the bourgeois a spiritual boost, I'm free to preach what isn't said elsewhere—the gospel.

Disenfranchised and marginalized, North American Christian preaching has been unwillingly thrust back to its missional New Testament roots. What a joy to preach at such a time; more fun than serving as functionaries of the cultural status quo. Without the props we once enjoyed, we are now free to be utterly dependent upon God, testing the veracity of the church's historic claims for God's word in the world, assaying the power of *Deus dixit*, missionaries to the culture we once thought we owned.[147]

In his Beecher Lectures, Fred Craddock repeated Kierkegaard's contention that there is no shortage of information about Christ in Christendom.[148] This is true only if preaching is limited to those who already know. Inductive preaching attempts evocation of the gospel in the cold hearts of those who know the gospel but are no longer moved by it, preserving the Constantinian illusion that "Christian" and "American" are synonymous.[149]

In a post-Constantinian, mission context, preaching accentuates the gap between the gospel and culture, admits the scandal of salvation coming from the Jews going even unto us Gentiles, and knows that our listeners don't know what they mean when they say "God."[150] Missional preaching is more confrontational and formative than evocative, indoctrination of news that is not innate.[151] Rather than make connections with the culture listeners inhabit, missional preaching invites listeners to awake to a new heaven and new earth where Jesus Christ is Lord and Wall Street isn't.

One of my pastors in Alabama served faithfully an impoverished area of Birmingham. His parsonage had been looted numerous times. Neighborhood drug dealers had threatened his family.

"I must get you out of here," said I. "Six years is too long. I'll look for a church in a safer place."

"Bishop," the pastor replied. "Thanks, but I'm not like you. Can't be poetic or come up with those cute illustrations. All I can do is drop a text on 'em and let God do the rest. I can only preach to folks who are going down the third time, people at the end of their rope and without hope. I'm not a good enough preacher to make the gospel relevant to folks who are not desperate."

Do some of my sermons fail because I'm attempting to trim good news meant for the lost and dying to the limitations of the self-satisfied, though mildly discontented upper middle class?

Perhaps there was a time when preaching needed to be beguiling; in a missionary situation, we simply announce, as clearly as we can, the good news that challenges Christendom's comfortable alliances, attempting to get the story of Jesus right for the downcast and dying who are apt to know good news when they hear it. Christ, lover of the lost, will do the rest.

The multicultural, missional context in which we preach to a disestablished, marginalized church, puts preachers in the proper mindset to hear the New Testament again as if for the first time. When the church fought for its life, early Christian preachers like Paul didn't reduce their good news to otherwise widely available common sense. Rather, they carefully articulated the distinctive differences between Christ and Empire. Missiologist David Bosch shows how in a "missionary encounter with the world" the church was "forced to theologize," to make the faith intelligible to others and to Christians themselves while the gospel leapt over every boundary and faced new challenges.[152]

Faithful preaching can never bed down and be merely parochial, in-house speech among Christ's cognoscenti huddled around the Holy Eucharist. In the spring of 1739 George Whitefield wrote John Wesley that the crowds coming to hear him were so great that he needed assistance. His voice could not reach the gathered multitudes. Wesley, the Anglican, Oxford don, was horrified that Whitefield had asked him to engage in unorthodox field preaching. Friends urged him not to go; England was still jittery about Cromwellian rebellion, and speeches at large public gatherings were discouraged.

On Saturday, March 31, Wesley relented and trudged to Bristol where he "submitted to be more vile," descending to open-air preaching. Expositing the Sermon on the Mount the next day, he noted that Jesus preached his greatest sermon in a field, even though many synagogues were available. "I thought saving souls a sin if not in a church," Wesley reflected. *Mission* is when the gospel is taken beyond boundaries, made publicly known, by word and deed, to those who have not yet heard the news that God is taking back what belongs to God. For preachers, sometimes mission begins when the gospel leaps over our own prejudice against making fools of ourselves for Christ (1 Cor 4:10).

My opportunity to become "more vile" came when COVID-19 made me an internet preacher. Though speaking to a computer's camera is not my notion of preaching (anymore than standing in an open field was Wesley's idea of a good time), in a couple of weeks I preached to a larger congregation than in a year's worth of sermons. Much of the response I received came from people who introduced themselves as, "I'm not exactly a Christian, but . . ."

I enjoyed preaching for a year at a declining inner-city congregation, attempting to give some hope and strategies for congregational survival, but my most memorable experience of proclamation occurred when I ventured out on a Saturday night to "Drag Queen Bingo," not two blocks from our church. Attempting to offer the gospel to folk who had been badly wounded by the church reminded me that Jesus is already talking to everybody, whether I'm comfortable talking with them or not.[153]

Barth transformed missiology with his stress upon the *missio dei.* Mission is what God says and does. Even as the Father sends the Son, and the Father and Son send the Holy Spirit, so God sends us. The church doesn't have a mission; the church exists as apostolic (sent) witness to God's mission—God's invasion of God's world with God's news of what God has done and is doing in Christ through the power of the Holy Spirit to restore and recreate God's world.[154]

For preachers who woke up and found ourselves to be missionaries in the culture our churches once thought they owned, the great theologian of mission, Lesslie Newbigin, has been of greatest help. Our challenge is not urbane, critical secularity; it's rampant, governmentally subsidized paganism.[155] George Hunsberger, one of Newbigin's most thoughtful interpreters, says that missionary preaching "invites, welcomes, and enables people to believe things that are at odds with the going versions of reality. It participates in the inner dialogue between the gospel and assumptions of one's own culture and cultivates a community for whom continuing conversion is habitual."[156]

Or as Barth said,

> Jesus is the Conqueror of the powers. If we are His disciples, we are necessarily witnesses of this fact. . . . It must be attested in the world as a declaration of the victory of Jesus. The world which sighs under these powers must hear and receive and rejoice that their lordship is broken. But this declaration cannot be made by the existence of those who are merely free inwardly. If this message is to be given, the world must see and hear at least an indication or sign of what has taken place. The break made by God in Jesus must become history. This is why Jesus calls his disciples.[157]

In a culture that thinks it's already Christian, inanities like "I'd rather see a sermon than hear one" and "Preach the gospel at all times. Use words if necessary" make sense. Who needs preaching for those who are lucky enough to be born in Alabama? For those who've heard, to refuse to tell another who hasn't heard, claiming, "It's imperialistic of me to try to impose my point of view," is Western privilege at its worst. As missiologist Lamin

Sanneh asked, Who told North American Christians that Jesus is our property and that others don't deserve to know the truth of their situation?[158] Not Christ.

Debilitated preaching of North American churches like mine will be renewed by the Spirit-filled, christologically driven homiletics from younger churches in places like Zimbabwe, Honduras, or Korea.[159] Through missionaries unintimidated by our Western arrogance, we—who saw ourselves as givers of the gospel—become receivers.

Christians in Africa, for instance, who received Christianity from Western colonizers, unscrambled the gospel from the perversions of European imperialism, saying, "We'll take what you said about Jesus, but we refuse your colonizing distortions." Now they give the gospel back to the colonizers in deeper, Pentecostal, assertive form, freeing our gospel from its moribund Western, liberal limitations.

Introverts, listen up! Newbigin insists that "There is and can be no substitute for telling the good news. Evangelism, the activity of telling . . . the story of Jesus, is a necessary and indispensable manifestation of the new reality in action."[160] One cannot come to this truth—Jesus Christ is Lord—without mental and moral revolution, *metanoia.* Whenever someone speaks of Christ and another hears, says Kenda Creasy Dean, it's public demonstration of the transformative truth of Christ.[161]

"Just hand people food," chided the manager of the soup kitchen, "You're not here to preach. Just be with people. This is an incarnational ministry." I assured him that neither he nor the homeless had anything to fear—we are mainline Protestants who would rather hand the hungry a plate of tagliatelle than risk telling the truth: we wouldn't be standing with them, in the cold, on the sidewalk if it were not for Jesus putting us here. Somebody ought to tell them that they are not out of work, hungry, and ill-housed because of God. God didn't create Durham; we did.

"Have you got any bread?" may not be the only question of one who is hungry. God may also be prompting the hungry to ask, "Is there a word from the Lord?" (Jer 37:17).

Jesus calls himself the "light of the world," fulfilling the prophet's promise: "I will also appoint you as light to the nations, so that my salvation may reach to the end of the earth" (Isa 49:6b). Elsewhere Jesus turns to his ragtag group of disciples and dares call *them* the light of the world, God's answer to what's wrong. How? "You will be my witnesses in Jerusalem, in all Judea and Samaria, and to the ends of the earth" (Acts 1:8). How? "Whenever you enter a city and its people welcome you, eat what they set before you. Heal the sick who are there, and say to them, 'God's kingdom has come upon you'" (Luke 10:8-9).

Jesus heals a man afflicted by demons, so demented that he has been kicked out of town and is living naked among the tombs (Mark 5:1-20). Jesus casts the tormenting demons into a herd of swine, thus putting the man in his right mind. The grateful man begs to follow Jesus, to become one of his disciples. "But Jesus wouldn't allow it. '[Get some clothes.] Go home to your own people [the ones who threw you out because of your illness],' Jesus said, 'and tell them what the Lord has done for you and how he has shown you mercy.' The man went away and began to proclaim [without any homiletical training] in the Ten Cities all that Jesus had done for him, and everyone was amazed" (Mark 5:19-20). Only Jesus would, the same day, exorcise and then ordain to preach, sending forth a missionary. To those preachers who see themselves as peacemakers, reconcilers, practitioners of civility, healers of wounds, and curers of cognitive dissonance, a missionary context is a threat.[162] Post-Christendom, hearers are summoned to conversion, detoxification, reorientation, and allegiance.[163] Frank Thomas stresses that in dangerous preaching, we're not presenting a personal point of view; we are challenging the gods most adored in a capitalist, heavily militarized economy. Expect trouble.[164] Because no preacher is able to translate the bodily resurrection of Jesus through the limited thought patterns of a scientific rationalist, said Newbigin, North American culture has been the church's toughest nut to crack.[165] If nobody rejects a sermon, missionaries worry that they may have misrepresented God.

"My congregation has never been more divided, blues and reds at war with one another. What can I do to bring people together?" asked the preacher.

"In today's America, if your congregation is not divided, conflicted, and anxious, you may be failing in evangelism," said I. "Church is contentious because Jesus wants 'em all."[166]

The gospel is factual news, an announcement of an historical event that has occurred. Reality. Newbigin criticized some homileticians' characterization of preaching as "dialogue." Inherited from the Greeks, "dialogue" is foreign to world religions, therefore unsuitable for preaching either to those who are not part of the Greek philosophical tradition, or for the announcement of a jarring occurrence like the resurrection.[167] Preaching as congenial, mutual give-and-take rests upon the Constantinian fiction that we've already been evangelized into the faith by virtue of being born bourgeois.[168]

Neither a lecture on religious ideas, advice for better living, nor appeal to our "better angels," preaching "continue[s] that which began to be done when Jesus came into Galilee and preached, announced, proclaimed the Kingdom of God," said Newbigin.[169] "We preach Christ, incarnate, crucified, regnant, as the power of God and the wisdom of God—as in fact, the presence of the reign of God in power and wisdom," provoking an invitation for us to be turned around (repentance) and to join the movement (vocation).[170]

Mission reminds us of what we too easily forget: the gracious, gifted quality of the Christian faith; Christ must be received from the hands of another. The Christian life is training in receptivity and gratitude that "salvation is from the Jews" (John 4:22). No congregation exists without someone, at some time or another, having founded it as a mission. (And no congregation is yet "church" if it's not planting other congregations.) Someone had to love Jesus enough to dare to speak about him. Maybe the evangelical preacher was a sainted grandmother, C. S. Lewis, or an obnoxious fellow student from Campus Crusade; no Christian is self-created. Each believes only on the basis of having received the gospel from some "missionary" sent by God to hand over the truth of Jesus Christ.[171]

I ask seminarians, "Who can remember when you weren't a Christian?" Only a third raise their hands. "If you have no memory of being evangelized, you are disadvantaged in the present moment." Liberated from narcissistic self-concern about our personal salvation, we bear witness to the regime change that God has worked in the world. Christians receive the gospel not for our own sake but for the salvation of the world.[172] Because of the *missio dei*, warm-hearted fellowship rather than daringly trailing Christ across cultural, racial, ideological, and national boundaries (that is, *mission*) is less than church. Therapeutic preaching that accentuates wounds, needs, and anxieties renders the congregation into passive listeners and hapless victims, turning protest into lament rather than equipping them to be confrontive missionaries and evangelists. They need to find their God-given voice, not simply to display their hurt—they already do that without training—but to render witness to the world that Jesus thinks nothing of putting people in pain in service of his word. Paul prayed to be delivered of his "thorn in the flesh" (2 Cor 12:7-9) but also knew that if God continued to refuse his prayer, he was still under orders to preach.

"This is the most loving and caring congregation. When one of us is going through a tough time, we've got one another's back."

Sorry, that's not good enough.

"The pandemic decimated my little church," said the pastor. "We went broke and nobody wanted to stay to pick up the pieces. I assumed I'd be keeping house here for the rest of my ministry. God took advantage of that virus to force me to be an evangelist—damnit. Let's see who in this town is dying to hear a good sermon but doesn't know it."

When Jesus said that whoever listens to us, listens to him (Luke 10:16), he was speaking not to clergy but to all his disciples. The work of the church is "witness," said Barth, "the sum of what the Christian community has to render."[173] The church is defined not by boundaries but by a center: Christ. The limits of the realm of God are unknown to the church. Having witnessed God turning to us, in response we turn toward the world, witnesses to the God who is now known to be *pro nobis*.[174] Says Newbigin, "The great joy of the Christian is that we have gotten the news. The great *responsibility* of the Christian is that we are to bear this news into the world."[175]

"But you are a chosen race, a royal priesthood, . . . *so that you may speak* of the wonderful acts of the one who called you out of darkness into his amazing light" (1 Pet 2:9, italics mine).

Lamin Sanneh notes that Christianity is the only faith that is propagated in languages other than the language of its founder.[176] So determined was the church to get the word out that the church forsook the language of Jesus in order to preach Jesus. One doesn't have to be an extrovert to be a Christian, but it helps. Sorry, if you did poorly in high school French. Missionaries spend their whole ministry acquiring new languages, in the vernacular, no less, so that others may hear.

With Moses, preachers want all God's people to be prophets (Num 11:29). Our task is to teach the saints to preach (Eph 4:12-16). (Priscilla Pope-Levison's *Models of Evangelism* can show you how.[177]) In an Eastertide sermon to my dwindling inner-city church I noted that the New Jerusalem is ridiculously gigantic (Rev 21:16), about the same size as India, and that those white-robed saints raucously processing around the throne were "a great crowd that no one can number . . . from every nation" (Rev 7:9). That's why Jesus is never satisfied with how many are in church, even on Easter. I challenged the congregation to go out and share the gospel with someone who hadn't yet heard, telling them to call me if they needed help with the preaching. I got four phone calls, and the church got one new convert. I told members not to feel bad; my first sermons went flat too. Evangelism has got to start somewhere.

The poor old, compromised, body-full-of-holes church, with all its flaws, is chief witness, showcase for what the risen Christ can do with sinners.[178] We don't need to become more "missional" in our preaching, to work up greater determination to "reach the unreached" or to "win the world to Christ." We aren't awaiting a theology of evangelism and mission that enables us to talk to modern Western pagans in a way that sounds vaguely like what they already believe. What we require is a God who speaks, *Deus dixit*, a Savior who not only makes news but also broadcasts. Just the sort of God we've got or, better, the God who has got us, determined to make us part of God's dare devil mission.[179]

English preacher and Beecher lecturer of a century ago P. T. Forsyth said that

> the one great preacher in history, . . . is the church. And the first business of the individual preacher is to enable the church to preach . . . to preach to the church from the gospel so that with the church may preach the gospel to the world. . . . That is to say, [the preacher] must be a sacrament to the church, that with the church [the preacher] may become a missionary to the world.[180]

"Every Christian is a missionary, a recruiting officer for new witnesses," says Barth. "If our congregations do not recognize this, they cannot be missionary congregations, and therefore they cannot be truly Christian."[181] Preachers proclaim the gospel to the church, "to equip the saints for the work of ministry" (Eph 4:11-12), making missionary preachers of the whole congregation.[182]

The first Bible verse I learned by heart was John 3:16. "For God so loved the church, and people like me in the church, that . . ." No! "For God so loved the world that God gave, . . . that whosoever . . ." That's why preaching must be global rather than parochial, why my church is too small a sphere for divine discourse, and why witnesses must keep talking wherever, however, to whomever.

> The apostle of Jesus Christ not only can but must be a missionary. . . . It is not merely the formal necessity of proclaiming the Word of God, nor the humanitarian love which would rather not withhold this Word from others. . . . The determining factor is the concrete content of the Word itself. The truth . . . about Jesus Christ and human life compels . . . almost as if it were automatically to speak wherever it is not yet known. It is like air rushing into a vacuum, or water downhill, or fire to more fuel. [Human life] stands under the sign of God's judgment. This is not just a religious opinion. It is a universal truth. It applies to all. . . . It leaps all frontiers. It is more urgent and binding than any human insight, . . . enthusiastically embraced. This truth is the driving power behind the Christian mission. . . . It bursts all barriers.[183]

The barriers that we, or the principalities and powers erect against God's speech—indifference, resistance, New Atheism or old-fashioned, blathering sentimentalism, temptations to timid silence and our own hard hearts—are serious. But nothing will defeat a God so determined to have the last word. The conversation isn't over until God says it's over. That's a preacher's best hope, we happy few who next Sunday must arise, mount the steps, clear our throats, shuffle our notes, dare to break the silence, slide out on the high-wire linking text and sermon, and risk giving our congregations news they can't tell themselves: "God has spoken . . ."

Preachers dare.

NOTES

Introduction

1. Karl Barth, *The Göttingen Dogmatics: Instruction in the Christian Religion,* vol. I, ed. Hannelotte Reiffen, trans. Geoffrey W. Bromiley (Grand Rapids: Eerdmans, 1990), 265. Hereafter referred to as *GD.* My translations are of Karl Barth, *Unterricht in der christlichen Religion* 1, 1924, ed. Hannelotte Reiffen (Zürich: Theologischer Verlag Zürich, 1985).

2. "Theology is necessary in order to make preaching as hard for the preacher as it has to be." Gerhard Ebeling, *God and Faith,* trans. James W. Leitch (London: SCM, 1963), 424.

3. The subtitle of Walter Brueggemann's 1989 Beecher Lectures was "Daring Speech for Proclamation." "Preaching as an act of interpretation is in our time demanding, daring, and dangerous." Walter Brueggemann, *Finally Comes the Poet: Daring Speech for Proclamation* (Minneapolis: Fortress, 1989), ix.

4. Barth, *GD,* 31.

5. Did Barth get his "dare" from John Calvin, who said preachers "dare boldly to do all things by God's Word; may compel all worldly power, glory, wisdom, and exaltation to yield to and obey his majesty . . . may command; . . . may build up Christ's household and cast down Satan's; may feed the sheep and drive away the wolves; may instruct and exhort the teachable; may accuse, rebuke, and subdue the rebellious and stubborn; may bind and loose; finally, if need be may launch thunderbolts and lightnings; but do all things in God's Word"? Calvin, *Institutes of the Christian Religion,* 2:1156–57 (4.8.9).

6. Barth, *GD,* 47.

7. "The silence of much contemporary homiletics about the God who speaks through Scriptures, the sermon, and the preacher," begins in the nineteenth century when homiletics forsook theology and focused upon

preaching as a rhetorical act in order to gain academic respectability, thus silencing "discussion about the God who speaks," 14. James F. Kay, "Preacher as Messenger of Hope," in *Slow of Speech and Unclean Lips: Contemporary Images of Preaching Identity,* ed. Robert Stephen Reid (Eugene, OR: Cascade Books, 2010), 13–34.

8. "Women and the Pulpit: An Interview with Leonora Tubbs Tisdale," *Reflection: Yale Divinity School,* Fall (2019): 29.

9. *Voice,* applied to God, appears more than 325 times in the Bible.

10. Barth, *GD,* 201.

1. Christ

1. Nicholas Wolterstorff complains that Barth takes "an idea that plays a minor role in Scripture itself, namely, the idea of God revealing Godself and makes it the major theme of his theology." Nicholas Wolterstorff, *The God We Worship: An Exploration of Liturgical Theology* (Grand Rapids: Eerdmans, 2015).

2. Karl Barth, *Church Dogmatics,* vol. II, part 2, ed. G. W. Bromiley and T. F. Torrance (Edinburgh: T & T Clark, 1975), 121. Hereafter, *Church Dogmatics* referred to as *CD.*

3. Reginald Fuller said that preachers "are concerned with two poles—the text and the contemporary situation. . . . [Preachers] build a bridge between these poles." *The Use of the Bible in Preaching* (Philadelphia: Fortress, 1981), 41. This is the nineteenth-century text-to-sermon bifurcation that Barth deplores.

4. Karl Barth, *Witness to the Word: A Commentary on John I,* ed. Walther Fürst, trans. Geoffrey W. Bromiley (Grand Rapids: Eerdmans, 1986), 66.

5. Nothing can be allowed to supplant the free word of God. *Barmen* is political protest as a declaration of the freedom of preaching. Barth thought that the German Christians were a bigger threat to the gospel than Hitler. See Karl Barth, *Community, State, and the Church,* trans. G. Ronald Howe (Garden City, NY: Anchor, 1960). Also William H. Willimon, *How Odd of God: Chosen for the Curious Vocation of Preaching* (Louisville: Westminster John Knox, 2015), 90–91.

6. Barth, *CD,* II/1, 150.

7. "The paucity of systematic theological attention to divine speaking is surprising in light of its biblical prominence, especially in light of Scriptures' contrast between speaking God of Israel and the dumb pagan idols. . . . False gods tell no tales. But Yahweh talks!" Kevin J. Vanhoozer, "Triune

Discourse," in *Trinitarian Theology for the Church: Scripture, Community, Worship,* ed. Daniel J. Treier and David Lauber (Downers Grove, IL: InterVarsity, 2009), 52.

8. "How can theology make [God's] revelation in Jesus intelligible, and validate its true claim, in an age when all talk about God is reduced to subjectivity?" Wolfhart Pannenberg, *Systematic Theology,* vol. 1, trans. G. W. Bromiley (Edinburgh: T & T Clark, 1991), 128.

9. My theory: Preachers are ridiculed in modern fiction because preachers insist on talking about matters that the modern world wants to keep quiet. See Douglas Alan Walrath, *Displacing the Divine: The Minister in the Mirror of American Fiction* (New York: Columbia University Press, 1993).

10. Immanuel Kant, "What Is Enlightenment?" [1784] in *The Enlightenment: A Comprehensive Anthology,* ed. Peter Gay (New York: Simon and Schuster, 1973), 384–89.

11. William Giraldi, *American Audacity: In Defense of Literary Daring* (New York: Norton, 2018), xix.

12. Stanley Hauerwas, with Robert J. Dean, *Minding the Web: Making Theological Connections* (Eugene, OR: Cascade, 2018), 102.

13. Marilynne Robinson, *Lila* (New York: Picador, 2014), 44.

14. Ludwig Feuerbach, *The Essence of Christianity,* trans. George Eliot (New York: Harper & Row, 1957), 63.

15. Karl Barth, *Barth in Conversation,* vol. 3, 1964–1968, ed. Eberhard Busch (Louisville: Westminster John Knox, 2019), ebook, 95.

16. Barth continually stressed the unresolvable dialectical tension between having to preach and yet being unable. See Barth, "The Word of God and the Task of Ministry," in *The Word of God and the Word of Man* (Boston and Chicago: Hodder & Stoughton, 1928), 183–217.

17. Barth, *CD,* I/1, 116.

18. Cleophus J. LaRue, *I Believe I'll Testify: The Art of African American Preaching* (Louisville: Westminster John Knox, 2011), xiii.

19. Luther admitted that 1 Peter 3:19-22 is an "obscure passage," "so that I do not know for a certainty just what Peter means"; still he saw the text as a kind of parable. Christ is so determined to save that he even preached in hell to those "that lie captive in the prison house of the devil." Luther, *Commentary on the Epistles of Peter and Jude,* ed. Paul W. Bennehoff, trans. John Nichols Lenker (Grand Rapids: Kregel, 1982), 168–69.

20. Barth, *GD,* 14, my translation. Chris Currie says that "the three-fold Word of God is a crucial element in Karl Barth's vision of the church and . . . for the whole of his theological project. Disregarded by the field of Barth studies and rejected by modern ecclesiologists." Currie's work is

the best we've got on preaching as God's word in Barth and is an impetus for *Preachers Dare*. Thomas Christian Currie, *The Only Sacrament Left to Us: The Threefold Word of God in the Theology and Ecclesiology of Karl Barth* (Eugene, OR: Pickwick, 2015), ix.

21. Barth, in *Romans*, following Luther and Calvin, showed that the Bible is first and last, the word, "Jesus Christ." Barth looked upon the Old Testament as "the name Jesus Christ, concealed under the name Israel in the Old Testament, revealed under his own name in the New Testament." *CD*, I/2, 720.

22. John doesn't refer again to Christ as "The Logos." Doesn't have to. The Word is a barrage of words such as the long, rich "Farewell Discourse" in John 14.

23. Later, in *Church Dogmatics*, Barth discusses "The Word of God in its Threefold Form," beginning not with the speaking of the Incarnate Christ but rather with proclamation, "The Word of God Preached" (*CD*, I/1, 88), thus highlighting the Word of God in the present. This move is remarkable, though no ranking or subordination is implied in the way the forms are listed. Barth says, "we can substitute for revelation, Scripture and proclamation the names of the divine persons Father, Son and Holy Spirit and vice versa, that in the one case as in the other we shall encounter the same basic determinations and mutual relationship" (*CD*, I/1, 121).

24. Early in his lectures, Barth unfolds the threefold Word of God through Chalcedonian terminology to describe revelation's unity in differentiation, "neither to be confused or separated," and differentiated while being "trinity in unity, unity in trinity"—one God in three ways. *GD*, 14–15. Helpful on Chalcedon is Christopher A. Beeley, *The Unity of Christ: Continuity and Conflict in Patristic Tradition* (New Haven, CT: Yale University Press, 2013).

25. Barth, *CD*, I/2, part 1. Italics in original.

26. "Revelation is no more and no less than the life of God . . . turned to us. . . ." Barth, *CD*, I/2, 483.

27. The Bible is the word of the living God that says, "Jesus Christ." Even in the Old Testament we have "the name Jesus Christ, concealed under the name Israel in the Old Testament, revealed under his own name in the New Testament." Barth, *CD*, I/2, 720.

28. "The Bible is about Jesus. . . . Jesus was God's plan all along." Sam Wells, *Speaking the Truth: Preaching in a Pluralistic Culture* (Nashville: Abingdon Press, 2008), 40.

29. Will Willimon, "Evangelicals Get Real," April 2020, "Peculiar Prophet," https://willwillimon.com/2020/04/27/evangelicals-get-real/.

30. Except in the sense of Colossians 1:27 and 2:2.

31. Never did anybody suggest *concilium* (church-sanctioned teaching), or *magisterium* (ecclesiastical pronouncements).

32. Barth says, "The word 'announcement' [*Ankündigung*] has the advantage over 'proclamation' [*Verkündigung*]" that in it God is the one "who speaks, and not we, who simply have the role of announcing what God . . . wants to say." Karl Barth, *Homiletics,* trans. Geoffrey W. Bromley and Donald E. Daniels (Louisville: Westminster John Knox, 1991), 46.

33. My teacher Hans Frei said that when Christian interpreters shoehorned the biblical story into the stories dominated by secular philosophy, rather than enfolding the world's account of itself into the biblical story, the battle was lost. Hans W. Frei, *The Eclipse of Biblical Narrative: A Study in 18th and 19th Century Hermeneutics* (New Haven, CT: Yale University Press, 1974), 130.

34. Michael Buckley shows how modern atheism arose out of Christian apologists' depersonalization of God. Michael J. Buckley, *At the Origins of Modern Atheism* (New Haven, CT: Yale University Press, 1987).

35. Barth, *GD*, 368–69, my translation. Schweitzer's famous last paragraph of *The Quest of the Historical Jesus* says: "He comes to us as One unknown, without a name, as of old, by the lakeside, He came to those men who knew Him not. He speaks to us the same words: 'Follow thou me!' . . . And to those who obey Him, whether they be wise or simple, He will reveal himself, . . . as an ineffable mystery, they shall learn in their own experience Who He is." Albert Schweitzer, *The Quest of the Historical Jesu*s, trans. W. Montgomery (London: A & C Black, 1911). Unfortunately, Schweitzer's failed prophet, apocalyptic Jesus, revealed in our "own experience" is a depersonalized "ineffable mystery" who can't offer true "fellowship."

36. Rick Warren, "Learn How to Recognize God's Voice," October 7, 2014, https://www.youtube.com/watch?v=kglsnPp-foU. See also Priscilla Shirer, *Discerning the Voice of God: How to Recognize When God Is Speaking* (Chicago: Moody, 2012).

37. Barth quoted by Gary Dorrien, *The Barthian Revolt in Modern Theology* (Louisville: Westminster John Knox, 2000), 51. Karl Barth, *The Epistle to the Romans,* trans. Edwyn C. Hoskyns, 6th ed. (London: Oxford University Press, 1975 [1933]).

38. Fleming Rutledge, *And God Spoke to Abraham: Preaching from the Old Testament* (Grand Rapids: Eerdmans, 2011), 144.

39. Christ "did not rise to be a disembodied wraith flitting through time; he rose to be a speaking body." Robert W. Jenson, *Visible Words: The Interpretation and Practice of Christian Sacraments* (Philadelphia: Fortress, 1978).

40. In his Beecher Lectures, Brian Blount waxed apocalyptic, celebrating the "reckless implausibility" of the resurrection. Brian K. Blount, *Invasion of the Dead: Preaching Resurrection* (Louisville: Westminster John Knox, 2014), xv.

41. The Roman Empire didn't trouble itself over the Gnostics because the "Gnostic Gospels" aren't good news of an event; they are instructions on how to organize life in accord with a fixed, unredeemed world. No government is made nervous by gnostic spirituality.

42. Richard Lischer, *End of Words: The Language of Reconciliation in a Culture of Violence* (Grand Rapids: Eerdmans, 2008), 66. Christoph Schwöbel says that "the most frequent and most serious" failing of contemporary preaching "occurs where the promise of what God has done for us is turned into a commandment concerning what we should do." Quoted in the introduction to Colin E. Gunton, *Theology through Preaching: Sermons for Brentwood* (Edinburgh: T & T Clark, 2001), 19.

43. "God *has* revealed himself, the Word became flesh. God has assumed human nature. Humanity has become God's in Christ. In Christ God has made fallen humanity his own. Faced with the fall, God did not step angrily aside. Instead [God] has personally united . . . with the race. Lost humanity has been called home" (Barth, *CD,* IV/1, 51).

44. Martin Luther, *A Brief Instruction on What to Look for and Expect in the Gospels*, in *Luther's Works*, vol. 35, Word and Sacrament, ed. and trans. E. T. Bachman (Philadelphia: Muhlenberg, 1960), 120.

45. Luther, *Luther's Works*, vol. 35, 121.

46. Luther said that focusing upon the cross preserves us from thinking we have total knowledge of God. Cited by Lischer, *End of Words,* 102.

47. Mary Magdalene has her homiletical work cut out for her. The response of the male disciples to the death of Jesus? They "go back to their homes." Not the most promising of listeners. Nevertheless, she dares to preach, "I have seen the Lord."

48. William H. Willimon, *Leading with the Sermon: Preaching as Leadership* (Minneapolis: Fortress, 2020), 34–35.

49. "The human nature of Christ (and especially in this connection, his corporality and therefore his spatiality), in his unity with the deity of the Son (unconfused with it, but also undivided from it, in real, indirect identity), is Revelation." Barth, *CD,* II/1, 486.

50. For more on Barth's "eventualism," see George Hunsinger, *How to Read Karl Barth: The Shape of His Theology* (New York: Oxford University Press, 1991), 30.

51. Barth, *GD*, 369–70.

52. "The assertion of God's objectivity is a direct challenge to nearly all theology since the beginning of the nineteenth century." Robert W. Jenson, *God after God: The God of the Past and Future as Seen in the Work of Karl Barth* (Indianapolis: Bobbs-Merrill, 1969), 80.

53. See Barth, *CD*, IV/1, where Barth asserts "the atonement is history."

54. Dietrich Bonhoeffer, *Worldly Preaching,* ed. Clyde E. Fant (Nashville: Thomas Nelson, 1975), 123.

55. Barth, *CD*, I/1, 113.

56. Richard Bauckham, Hayward Lectures, 2018, "Key Moments of Biblical Revelation," https://www.youtube.com/watch?v=t1VkOxsNGSI.

2. Scripture

1. Barth, *GD*, 320–21. I have my work cut out for me. Jörg Lauster charges that Barth's "relentless insistance that God speaks, is an almost violent infantilization of the concept of God," which, for contemporary thinkers, has "a repulsive effect, as it has no connection to modern critical thinking." Jörg Lauster, *Zwischen Entzauberung und Remythisierung. Zum Verhältnis von Bibel und Dogma* (Leipzig: Evangelische Verlagsanstalt, 2008), 22, my translation.

2. Barth declared that, "The New World in the Bible" is "not the right human thoughts about God . . . , but rather the right thoughts of God about humans." The Bible is not about "History! Morality! Religion! Piety!" No. "'God' is the content of the Bible!" See Katherine Sonderegger, "Barth on Holy Scripture," 71, in George Hunsinger and Keith L. Johnson, eds., *The Wiley Blackwell Companion to Karl Barth*, vol. 1 (Hoboken, NJ: John Wiley & Sons, 2020), 70.

3. Barth, *GD*, 58. "The Word of God in all its three forms is God's speech to [humanity], . . . God's act on [humanity]." Karl Barth, "The Need and Promise of Christian Preaching," in Douglas Horton, *The Word of God and the Word of Man* (New York: Harper & Row, 1957), 123 (from a 1922 lecture).

4. Barth, *GD*, 298. Luther said when preachers forsake Scripture and "everyone preaches his own whims and, instead of the gospel and its exposition, we shall again have sermons on blue ducks." Martin Luther, "The

German Mass and Order of Service 1526," trans. A. Steinle in *Works of Martin Luther* (Philadelphia: Muhlenberg, 1932), 6:151–89, 176.

5. Barth, *CD*, I/1, 137–38.

6. Barth, *CD,* I/1, 124.

7. Barth, *CD,* I/1, 137–38.

8. "Revelation is originally and directly what the Bible and the church proclamation are derivatively and indirectly, i.e., God's word. . . . Proclamation . . . must continually become God's word. And we've said the same of the Bible: it must continually become God's word." Barth, *CD,* I/1, 117.

9. Barth, *GD*, 59–60.

10. Barth, *GD,* 59.

11. Barth, *GD,* 37. Barth warns that we must not treat the Scripture as "a ramp" whereby we "climb up from the general history of the spirit and religion to Jesus at the top." Preachers "must smash this ramp." *Deus dixit* is a divinely "qualified history" that is revelation, not a path toward revelation (38).

12. "The God of Israel, willed to be spoken for, but refused to be visually depicted." Robert W. Jenson, *Visible Words: The Interpretation and Practice of Christian Sacraments* (Philadelphia: Fortress, 1978).

13. Luther claimed that within the Trinity is "a pulpit." God's triune being is eternal conversation. By the work of the Holy Spirit, we are taken into intratrinitarian conversation. Christoph Schwöbel, "Introduction," in Colin E. Gunton, *Theology through Preaching* (Edinburgh: T & T Clark, 2001), 2–3. The Bible, said Barth, is the "history of encounter" between God and humanity, most especially between God and Israel (*CD* III/1, 80–81).

14. N. T. Wright says that "biblical authority" makes sense only as shorthand for "the authority of the triune God, exercised somehow *through* Scripture." N. T. Wright, *The Last Word: Beyond the Bible Wars to a New Understanding of the Authority of Scripture* (San Francisco: Harper, 2005), 23.

15. "Word of God" is "the most determinative aspect of the divine-human relationship throughout the Old Testament." Terence Frethcim, "Word of God," in *The Anchor Bible Dictionary* (New York: Doubleday, 1992), 961–68.

16. Aristotle, in *Politics,* wasn't far off the mark in distinguishing human beings as social, political, word-using animals.

17. John Calvin: "The highest proof of Scripture derives in general from the fact that God in person speaks in it." Calvin, *Institutes,* 1.7.4.

18. "Knowledge," Duke University Chapel, October 9, 1998, https://repository.duke.edu/dc/dukechapel/dcrst003287.

19. Rowan Williams introduces his 2013 Gifford Lectures by asking, "Does the way we talk as human beings tell us anything about God?" Rowan Williams, *The Edge of Words: God and the Habits of Language* (London: Bloomsbury, 2014), ix. My question is, "Does the way God talks tell us anything about us as preachers?"

20. I've got my work cut out for me. Elizabeth Achtemeier says that between 1875 and 1933 "the church as a whole lost the Old Testament." Elizabeth Achtemeier, "The Canon as the Voice of the Living God," in *Reclaiming the Bible for the Church*, ed. Carl Braaten and Robert Jenson (Grand Rapids: Eerdmans, 1995), 123. Brent Strawn more recently lamented the silencing of the Old Testament. Brent A. Strawn, *The Old Testament Is Dying: A Diagnosis and Recommendations and Treatment* (Grand Rapids: Baker Academic, 2017).

21. Nicholas Wolterstorff calls our preaching "deputized speech." Nicholas Wolterstorff, *Divine Discourse: Philosophical Reflections on the Claim That God Speaks* (Cambridge: Cambridge University Press, 2000), 38–51.

22. Stanley Hauerwas, "Explaining Why Willimon Never Explains," in *Disrupting Time: Sermons, Prayers, and Sundries* (Eugene, OR: Cascade, 2004), 224–33.

23. Kevin J. Vanhoozer, *The Drama of Doctrine: A Canonical-Linguistic Approach to Christian Theology* (Louisville: Westminster John Knox, 2005), shows that Christian doctrine is meant to be "performed."

24. Walter Brueggemann, quoted in *The Church as Counterculture,* ed. Michael L. Budde and Robert W. Brimlow (Albany: The State University of New York, 2000), 53.

25. See Jon D. Levenson, *Resurrection and the Restoration of Israel: The Ultimate Victory of the God of Life* (New Haven, CT: Yale University Press, 2006).

26. Barth, *GD,* 328.

27. Barth, *GD,* 328.

28. A prophet is unable to be silent, energized by an avalanche of Yahweh's words (Isa 1:1; Ezek 1:1; Obad 1; Mic 1:1; Nah 1:1; Hab 1:1).

29. Calvin, *Institutes,* 4.7.3.

30. Brueggemann speaks of the "untamed witness of the Old Testament." Walter Brueggemann, *Theology of the Old Testament: Testimony, Dispute, Advocacy* (Minneapolis: Fortress, 1997), 107.

31. Brueggemann categorized prophets as daring poets throughout his 1989 Beecher Lectures. Walter Brueggemann, *Finally Comes the Prophet: Daring Speech for Proclamation* (Minneapolis: Fortress, 1989).

32. Will Willimon, *Accidental Preacher: A Memoir.* Afterword by Kate Bowler (Grand Rapids: Eerdmans, 2019), 138.

33. Walter Brueggemann says that "when we face a prophetic text, we face a *text,* not a *role.* Our task is to exposit the text" with all the imagination that we can muster. We are "text interpreters, and not a reiteration of the prophet himself." *Preaching from the Old Testament,* 72.

34. I know the perils of labeling oneself a "prophet." My students labeled my sermons those of a "Peculiar Prophet." It stuck. Michael A. Turner and William F. Malambri, III, eds., *Peculiar Prophet: William H. Willimon and the Craft of Preaching* (Nashville: Abingdon Press, 1984).

35. Michael Pasquarello, III, *We Speak Because We Have Been Spoken: A Grammar of the Preaching Life* (Grand Rapids: Eerdmans, 2009).

36. Nicholas Lash says that God speaks, "But does not shout." Nicholas Lash, *Believing Three Ways in One God* (Chicago: University of Notre Dame Press, 1944), 10–11. I see no scriptural basis for Lash's claim.

37. Rabbi Heschel says that God's anger is "lamentation. All prophecy is one great exclamation: God is not indifferent to evil! He is always concerned, . . . personally affected by what man does to man. He is a God of pathos. This is one of the meanings of the anger of God: the end of indifference!" Abraham J. Heschel, *The Prophets* (New York: Perennial Classics, 2001 [1962]), 121.

38. In *The Intrusive Word* (Grand Rapids: Eerdmans, 1994), I wrote a book out of a Brueggemann quote: "The task of prophetic ministry is to nurture, nourish, and evoke a consciousness and perception alternative to the consciousness and perception of the dominant culture around us," a peculiar way of speaking whose purpose is "to evoke an alternative community." See Brueggemann, *The Prophetic Imagination* (Minneapolis: Fortress, 1978), 13.

39. Barth, *GD,* 56, my translation.

40. Quoted by Richard Schultz, "Hearing the Major Prophets," in *Hearing the Old Testament,* ed. Craig G. Bartholomew and David J. H. Beldman (Grand Rapids: Eerdmans, 2012), 334.

41. I hope never to recover from my first reading of Phyllis Trible, *Texts of Terror: Literary-Feminist Readings of Biblical Narratives* (Philadelphia: Fortress, 1984).

42. See Will Willimon, *Lectionary Sermon Resource: Preaching the Psalms* (Nashville: Abingdon Press, 2019).

43. Dietrich Bonhoeffer, *Psalms: The Prayer Book of the Bible* (Minneapolis: Augsburg, 1970).

44. Bonhoeffer, *Psalms*, 10. Italics in original.

45. Bonhoeffer, *Psalms*, 27.

46. Bonhoeffer, *Psalms,* 15.

47. "Job's great longing is for revelation. . . . He is different from his friends, who . . . need to believe that there are 'explanations' for everything." Fleming Rutledge, *And God Spoke to Abraham: Preaching from the Old Testament* (Grand Rapids: Eerdmans, 2011), 164.

48. Brueggemann says, "The speeches of Yahweh press hard against Job's presumed world and, in the end, destabilize him." Brueggemann, *Finally Comes the Poet: Daring Speech for Proclamation* (Minneapolis: Fortress, 1989), 61.

49. Brueggemann, *Finally Comes the Poet*, 62. Barth reads Job christologically. Job, like Jesus, is the "True Witness," a "free servant of God," who "strides through the hell of affliction to his liberation by and for the free praise of God." Barth, *CD,* IV/3.1, 388.

50. Brent Strawn sermon, Duke Divinity School, Durham, NC, January 21, 2020.

51. Barth, *GD,* 68.

52. Alyce M. McKenzie, *Preaching Proverbs: Wisdom for the Pulpit* (Louisville: Westminster John Knox, 1996), vii.

53. Willimon, *Accidental Preacher,* 142–43.

54. David Schnasa Jacobsen, ed., *Toward a Homiletical Theology of Promise* (Eugene, OR: Wipf & Stock, 2018).

55. L. Susan Bond, "Apocalyptic Vocation and Liberation: The Foolish Church in the World," in *Preaching as a Theological Task: World, Gospel, Scripture: Essays in Honor of David Buttrick*, ed. Thomas G. Long and Edward Farley (Louisville: Westminster John Knox, 1996), 150–64.

56. Richard Dawkins, *The God Delusion* (Boston: Houghton Mifflin, 2006), 51.

57. Literary theorist Terry Eagleton rebuked Dawkins for drawing on the worst examples of God's speech, giving the Old Testament a remarkably wooden, ungenerous reading. Dawkins dismisses God's words as "fiction." Eagleton opines that Dawkins is an inept reader of all literature. Terry Eagleton, *Reason, Faith, and Revolution: Reflections on the God Debate* (New Haven: Yale University Press, 2009).

58. See the thoughtful, almost benevolent critique of Dawkins by Brent Strawn, *The Old Testament Is Dying*, 84–99.

59. Dawkins, *God Delusion*, 287. Dawkins is less dangerous than those who read Scripture a-theistically, though without Dawkins's vitriol, so that it's less obvious that they are dismissing God as a speaking, revealing subject.

60. "What Marcion preferred, linguistically speaking . . . was an *abbreviated language artificially constructed* from the full language of Christian Scripture." Strawn, *The Old Testament Is Dying*, 108, italics in original.

61. Barth, *Homiletics*, 53.

62. Fleming Rutledge, *And God Spoke to Abraham*, xi.

63. Ellen F. Davis, *Wondrous Depth: Preaching the Old Testament* (Louisville: Westminster John Knox, 2005), xiv.

64. Kenneth L. Carder, "Finding Peace in Enemy Territory," Duke Chapel, Durham, NC (October 14, 2001), https://repository.duke.edu/dc/dukechapel.

65. Jerusha Matsen Neal, *The Overshadowed Preacher: Mary, the Spirit, and the Labor of Proclamation* (Grand Rapids: Eerdmans, 2020).

66. Why doesn't God get on with it? When will the promises of Mary's song be fulfilled and Micah's Day of the Lord draw neigh (Luke 21:13)? Jesus says that this time-between-times is time for witness, giving us enough time to preach (Matt 28:18-20).

67. Joel L. Marcus, *John the Baptist in History and Theology* (Columbia: University of South Carolina Press, 2018).

68. "As the church speaks and hears the gospel and as the church responds in prayer and confession, the church's life is . . . none other than our anticipatory participation in the converse of the Father and the Son in the Spirit; as the church is enlivened and empowered by this hearing and answer, the inspiration is none other than the Spirit who is the life between the Father and the Son." Robert W. Jenson, *Systematic Theology: The Triune God*, vol. 1 (Oxford: Oxford University Press, 1997), 228.

69. See Chapter 11, "Delegator," in William H. Willimon, *Why Jesus?* (Nashville: Abingdon Press, 2010).

70. Barth, *GD*, 24.

71. While there are instances of people sharing their own opinions without divine authority, Scripture, Old Testament and New, implies that if all you've got is your personal experience, keep it to yourself. (See 1 Kgs 22:1-40; Mark 13:21-22; Acts 13:4-12; 2 Cor 11:1-15; Rev 2:19-29.)

72. Lischer, *End of Words: The Language of Reconciliation in a Culture of Violence* (Grand Rapids: Eerdmans, 2008), 50.

73. Lischer, *End of Words*, 54

74. "What the preacher comes up with is not so much a new meaning but a new performance of the text, one that will enable its listeners to per-

form it themselves in their daily lives. . . . At the center of our calling lies an imaginative act of reading that culminates in a public performance of what has been read." Lischer, *End of Words,* 92.

75. Much of this material on parables is found in *Stories by Willimon* (Nashville: Abingdon Press, 2020), xi–xvi.

76. See William H. Willimon, *Who Will Be Saved?* (Nashville: Abingdon Press, 2008), 4–6.

77. Barth, *GD,* 93.

78. Barth, *GD,* 33.

79. Barth, *GD,* 337.

80. C. Kavin Rowe, *Christianity's Surprise: A Sure and Certain Hope* (Nashville: Abingdon Press, 2020).

81. Barth, *GD,* 333. As Wittgenstein said, throughout the Gospels there is an imbedded imperative, speaking meant to be obeyed. The Messiah preaches in order to convene a messianic community.

82. Barth, *GD,* 461.

83. Barth, *CD,* IV/2, 21–25.

84. The NRSV renders 1 Corinthians 16:22 as, "Our Lord, come!" but notes that it could also be translated, "Our Lord has come." Jesus has come, is still coming, will come. "Come, Lord" (CEB).

85. Theologian David Ford contends that a main work of the Holy Spirit is to "induce daring." Godpod, June 12, 2019, https://sptc.htb.org /godpod.

86. Barth, *GD,* 342.

87. I'm paraphrasing Robert Jenson's evocative sentence, which Stanley Hauerwas says is the best theological sentence ever written. Robert Jenson, *Systematic Theology Vol 1: The Triune God* (New York: Oxford University Press, 1997), 63. Stanley M. Hauerwas, *The Work of Theology* (Grand Rapids: Eerdmans, 2015), 122–46.

88. Martin Luther, *Commentary on the Epistles of Peter and Jude,* ed. Paul W. Bennehoff, trans. John Nichols Lenker (Grand Rapids: Kregel, 1982), 168–69.

89. Barth, *GD,* 331.

90. Barth, *CD,* I/2, 680–81.

91. Barth, *Homiletics,* 80.

92. Right Rev. Mariann Edgar Budde sermon, the Washington National Cathedral, April 5, 2020, https://cathedral.org/event/holy-eucharist -with-liturgy-of-the-palms/.

93. Barth, *GD,* 15.

94. "Theology is not a private subject for theologians only . . . a private subject for professors. Fortunately, there have always been pastors who understood more about theology than most professors. Nor is theology a private subject of study for pastors. . . . Theology is a matter for the church." Karl Barth, "Theology," in *God in Action* (Edinburgh: T & T Clark, 1936), 56–57.

95. Paul Scott Wilson, *The Practice of Preaching* (Nashville: Abingdon Press, 1995), 92–96, says that sometimes we must make a "theological intervention" in a text "when the text has no apparent theological theme or when there is no explicit focus on either God or Christ." I don't want a text's theological significance to be dependent on our human intervention or upon our judgment of whether or not a text has theological intent.

96. Barth, *Homiletics,* 19.

97. Barth, *GD*, 201.

98. See C. Clifton Black, "Exegesis as Prayer," *Princeton Seminary Bulletin*, July 2008, vol. 29: 131–36.

99. Quoted in Spears, "Preaching the Old Testament," 403.

100. "The gospel is not in our thoughts or heart; it is in Scripture. The dearest habits and best insights I have—I must give them all up before listening. I must not use them to protect myself against the breakthrough of a knowledge that derives from Scripture. Again and again I must let myself be contradicted. I must let myself be loosened up. I must be able to surrender everything." Barth, *Homiletics,* 78.

101. Barth, *GD,* 15. "This is what the Lord says" occurs in more than 420 verses. "The word of the Lord" or "the words of the Lord" occur in over 240 verses. "The word of God" or "the words of God" occur in 40 verses; "the Lord said" in 300.

102. Barth, *GD,* 59.

103. Barth, *GD,* 59.

104. Barth, *GD,* 58.

105. Barth, *GD,* 58.

106. Luther's comments on Malachi 2:7. Rick Lischer was being Lutheran when he said, "The preacher reads the book, then speaks it. The text passes from heart and mind through the lips of the speaker and emerges into an assembly of people." Lischer, *End of Words*, 50.

107. Barth, *GD,* 216.

108. Fleming Rutledge, *And God Spoke to Abraham*, 260.

109. Linguists distinguish between "illocutionary acts" (the word of God, fixed in the past in scriptural texts) and "perlocutionary acts" (Scripture preached, becoming the word of God, received by a contemporary au-

dience). I fail to see the value of such distinctions for the preacher. See Kevin J. Vanhoozer, "Triune Discourse: Theological Reflections on the Claim that God Speaks," in *Trinitarian Theology for the Church: Scripture, Community, Worship,* ed. Daniel J. Treier and David Lauber (Downers Grove, IL: Inter-Varsity, 2009), 25–78.

110. Bonhoeffer read the Bible by asking, "What is God saying to us here? . . . We no longer look for general truths. . . . Any place outside the Bible has become too uncertain for me. I fear that I will only encounter some defined double of myself there." Ralf K. Wüstenberg and Jens Zimmermann, eds., *God Speaks to Us: Dietrich Bonhoeffer's Biblical Hermeneutics* (Frankfurt am Main: Peter Lang, 2013), 30.

111. I have little scriptural evidence that Jesus wants to solve our problems other than occasional healing, exorcism, and raising of the dead. I know, from my own ministry, that Jesus has nothing against stress, pain, and anxiety. Jesus presents us with problems we did not have until Jesus.

112. George A. Lindbeck, *The Nature of Doctrine: Religion and Theology in a Post Liberal Age* (Louisville: Westminster John Knox, 1984).

113. Charles Taylor, *Sources of the Self: The Making of Modern Identity* (Cambridge: Harvard University Press, 1989), 111–210.

114. Lindbeck, *Nature of Doctrine*, 34.

115. See James Kay, *Slow of Speech and Unclean Lips: Contemporary Images of Preaching Identity*, ed. Robert Reid (Eugene, OR: Cascade, 2010), 115–18.

116. David Buttrick in *Homiletic: Moves and Structures* (Philadelphia: Fortress, 1987), claims that if a preacher gets the language right it creates "a faith-world in human consciousness" (20) that "mediates" God (250), thus making exaggerated claims for human speech. Barth quipped that the preacher's job is never "to give birth to God but to give testimony of him." *The Word of God and the Word of Man,* 131.

117. James F. Kay, *Preaching and Theology* (St. Louis: Chalice, 2007), 119.

118. Kay, *Preaching and Theology*, 120.

119. Aubrey Spears gently chides me for speaking of my undergraduate students' reading of Augustine as if their insights are akin to Scripture. Spears, "Preaching the Old Testament," 399, citing William H. Willimon, *Conversations with Barth on Preaching* (Nashville: Abingdon Press, 2006), 33.

120. "The message which Scripture has to give us, even in its apparently most debatable and least assimilatable parts," says Barth, "is in all circumstances truer and more important than the best . . . things that we ourselves have said or can say." *CD*, I/2, 152.

121. Calvin's need for control got the better of him when he expressed enmity to all ostentatious, pompous, contrived speech. See John H. Leith, *Introduction to the Reformed Tradition* (Atlanta: John Knox, 1977), 87.

122. Robert Alter notes how biblical literature "reveals the presence of writers who relished the words and the materials of storytelling with which they worked, who delighted . . . in pleasing cadences and surprising deflections of syntax. . . . The lively inventiveness with which they constantly deploy the resources of their narrative medium repeatedly exceeds the needs of the message, though it often also deepens and complicates the message." Robert Alter, *The World of Biblical Literature* (New York: Basic Books, 1992), 34, 40. Alter speaks of biblical literature as a human phenomenon; I'd like to be more theological. Biblical writers write as they do because the Trinity demands it.

123. Lischer, *End of Words,* 80.

124. Gardner C. Taylor, "A Holy Pursuit," in *Power in the Pulpit: How America's Most Effective Black Preachers Prepare Their Sermons,* ed. Cleophus J. LaRue (Louisville: Westminster John Knox, 2002), 151. Samuel Taylor Coleridge said that his test for the truthfulness of Scripture is "whatever *finds* me, bears witness for itself that it has proceeded from a Holy Spirit." *Confessions of an Enquiring Spirit, 1840* (Philadelphia: Fortress, 1988), 26.

125. Sallie McFague claimed it "idolatrous" to cling to past metaphors for God. Sallie McFague, *Metaphorical Theology, Models of God in Religious Language* (London: SCM, 1983), 8–9. She begins by assuming that theological language is humanly projected (Feuerbach lives!), that language doesn't necessarily refer to a reality beyond language itself. Barth stressed the "objectivity" of our speech about God, as speech from God. Our images of God through Scripture are gifts from God. See the put-down of McFague's position in Colin E. Gunton, *A Brief Theology of Revelation* (Edinburgh: T & T Clark, 1995), 2–7.

126. See Willimon, *Conversations with Barth,* 71ff.

127. Barth, *GD,* 308.

128. Barth, *GD,* 310.

129. Barth, *CD,* I/1, 92–93. "The person who cannot and will not be deprived of the idea that a disposition for God is at his disposal, even without the grace of God, . . . is closed off to the disposition of God" and engaging in sin (which Barth defines as seeking knowledge of God independently of God's grace). *CD,* II/1, 135.

130. William H. Willimon, ed., *The Sunday After Tuesday: Campus Pulpits Respond to 9/11* (Nashville: Abingdon Press, 2002).

131. "The church must not allow itself to become dull, nor its services dark and gloomy. It must be claimed by, and proclaim, the lordship of God in the kingdom of his dear Son rather than the lordship of the devil or capitalism or communism or human folly and wickedness in general." Barth, *CD,* III/4, 69.

132. Brueggemann says that the preacher's attitude is no place to begin a sermon. Begin with "*candor at the throne of God* . . . with what God notices and how God responds." Brueggemann, *Finally Comes the Poet,* 18 (italics in original).

133. Authenticity was forever discredited as a valid criterion for anything by Harry G. Frankfurt, *On Bullshit* (Princeton, NJ: Princeton University Press, 2005), 64–67.

134. Christine Smith believes that problems of patriarchy and hierarchy in preaching are best solved by being in intimate relationship with our congregations, failing to note how preaching is often constrained by a pastor's fear of losing relationships with members of the congregation. Christine M. Smith, *Weaving the Sermon: Preaching in a Feminist Perspective* (Louisville: Westminster John Knox, 1989). As Reinhold Niebuhr reminded us, many sermons are tamed, not from fear, but rather by pastors' love for our congregations. Our maternalistic/paternalistic, overly empathetic pastoral relationship with our congregations stifles truthful discourse. Reinhold Niebuhr, *Leaves from the Notebook of a Tamed Cynic* (New York: Living Age Books, 1957), 128.

135. "Before [the Bible] is read in private, it is heard in public. . . . For most Christians throughout the ages and probably most in the world at present, the norm is listening." Rowan Williams, "The Bible Today: Reading & Hearing," transcript of The Larkin-Stuart Lecture, April 16, 2007, http://aoc2013.brix.fatbeehive.com/articles.php/2112/the-bible-today -reading-hearing-the-larkin-stuart-lecture.

136. Carl Braaten and Robert Jenson, ed., *Reclaiming the Bible for the Church* (Grand Rapids: Eerdmans, 1995), 104. Every interpreter serves some interpretive community. The "Jesus Seminar" showed their irrelevance for preachers when they claimed to represent the consensus "that has come to prevail in all the great universities of the world." Robert W. Funk, Roy W. Hoover, and the Jesus Seminar, *The Five Gospels: The Search for the Authentic Words of Jesus* (New York: Macmillan, 1993), 35.

137. That's why James Forbes said, in his 1986 Beecher Lectures, "The person who preaches the gospel makes a statement about the Holy Spirit just by entering the pulpit." James Forbes, *The Holy Spirit and Preaching* (Nashville: Abingdon Press, 1989), 19.

138. Brian McLaren, A Sermon for Every Sunday, "The Fifteenth Sunday after Pentecost, Year C (2019)," May 14, 2019, https://vimeo .com/336184174.

139. "The contemporary of Jesus is in no better position than we to receive revelation about Jesus." Søren Kierkegaard, *Philosophical Fragments*, trans D. F. Swenson and H. V. Hong (Princeton, NJ: Princeton University Press, 1962), ch. 4.

140. Brevard Childs, *Isaiah* (Louisville: Westminster John Knox, 2001), 307.

141. Richard E. Burnett, *Karl Barth's Theological Exegesis: The Herme- neutical Principles of the Römerbrief* (Grand Rapids: Eerdmans, 2004), 101, 284. See also Barth, *CD,* I/1, 106.

142. Barth, *GD*, 259. "The preacher goes to the biblical text for the congregation . . . with the congregation. . . . Exegesis is a work of the church enacted through the preacher. . . . The move from text to sermon begins, not with a decision about how to inform the congregation about the results of the preacher's personal exegesis of the text but, rather, a decision about what aspect of the congregation-text encounter will be carried over into the sermon itself. The bridge the preacher must now crawl is one between the text-congregational-context and the sermon-congregational-context." Thomas G. Long, *The Witness of Preaching* (Louisville: Westminster John Knox, 1989), 79.

143. Brueggemann, *Finally Comes the Poet*, 7.

144. See William H. Willimon, *Acts: Interpretation* (Louisville: West- minster John Knox, 1988), 113.

145. "The sermon is not normally the place for concrete moral admo- nition, because such admonition will only enhance the partisan distortion, either an agreement or disagreement, rather than feed the imagination. Nor is a sermon the place for concrete instruction about public policy. Con- creteness about policy questions . . . takes place more effectively in other contexts. The sermon is a place where the church is free to imagine what it would be like to be intentional about mission." Brueggemann, *Finally Comes the Poet*, 88–89.

146. Richard Hays and Ellen Davis urge creative attentiveness to the text without mechanistic moves from text to sermon. Ellen Davis and Rich- ard Hays, *The Art of Reading Scripture* (Grand Rapids: Eerdmans, 2003).

Barth advises preachers to forswear speculation about what might lie behind the texts and "turn with all the more attentiveness, accuracy and love to the texts as such." Barth, *CD*, I/2, 494.

147. Stanley Hauerwas, *Working with Words: On Learning to Speak Christian* (Eugene, OR: Cascade, Wipf and Stock, 2011).

148. E. Stephen Fowl, *Engaging Scripture: A Model for Theological Interpretation* (Oxford: Blackwell, 1998), 211.

149. "Hearing the voice of God . . . requires a body of believers manifesting a particular type of common life in the Spirit. . . . One may discern the quality . . . of one's hearing of the voice of God by whether or not it draws one into closer communion with those who have already faithfully heard. . . . Our brothers and sisters in Christ, both past and present, who are also engaged in that same journey." Stephen Fowl, "In Many and Various Ways," in *The Voice of God in the Text of Scripture,* ed. Oliver D. Crisp and Fred Sanders (Grand Rapids: Zondervan, 2016), 55. Chuck Campbell says that we "require a disciplined community of hearers grounded in the practice of Scripture, sacrament, and discipline." Charles L. Campbell, *Preaching Jesus: New Directions for Homiletics in Hans Frei's Postliberal Theology* (Grand Rapids: Eerdmans, 1997), 247.

150. To self-identify as a "public theologian" leads to speech trimmed to the limitations of the group that presumes itself to be "public." Miroslav Volf says that "a vision of human flourishing and the common good is the main thing the Christian faith brings into the public debate." I believe the best thing we bring is Jesus. Miroslav Volf, *A Public Faith: How Followers of Christ Should Serve the Common Good* (Grand Rapids: Brazos, 2011), xvi.

151. See *The Collected Sermons of William H. Willimon* (Louisville: Westminster John Knox, 2010).

152. Fleming Rutledge, *And God Spoke to Abraham*, 127.

3. Preaching

1. From Will Willimon, *Accidental Preacher: A Memoir* (Grand Rapids: Eerdmans, 2019), 143–44.

2. Barth, *GD*, 37–38.

3. "The writer of Hebrews is concerned that his addressees are in danger of losing confidence in the message they received, and his strategy for buttressing their faith is to effect a renewed encounter with God's word." Jonathan I. Griffiths, *Hebrews and Divine Speech* (London: Bloomsbury, 2014).

4. Noting that Hebrews speaks of faith as "the conviction of things not seen" (Heb 11:1), Barth interprets "things" to be "things whose truth lies in God alone. Hence the believer . . . has God alone and nothing else as . . . support and basis." *CD*, III/2, 156.

5. "For since the church owes its birth to the word, is nourished, aided and strengthened by it, it is obvious that it cannot be without the word. If it is without the word, it ceases to be a church." Martin Luther, *A Brief Instruction on What to Look for and Expect in the Gospels*, in *Luther's Works*, vol. 40, Word and Sacrament, ed. and trans. Conrad Bergendoff (Philadelphia: Muhlenberg, 1958), 37.

6. Griffiths, *Hebrews and Divine Speech*, 165.

7. Barth, *GD,* 36, my translation.

8. Vikas Shukla, "Top 10 Most Respected Professions in the World," ValueWalk, March 25, 2019, https://www.valuewalk.com/2019/03/top-10-most-respected-professions.

9. Barth, *GD*, 52.

10. "In the shadows of a dying Christendom the challenge is how to recover a strong theological voice without that voice betraying the appropriate fragility of all speech—but particularly speech about God." Stanley Hauerwas, *The Work of Theology* (Grand Rapids: Eerdmans, 2015), 113.

11. Barth, *CD,* I/2, 152.

12. Karl Barth, *Barth in Conversation,* vol. 3, 1964–1968, ed. Eberhard Busch (Louisville: Westminster John Knox, 2019), ebook, 95. Theology gets dangerous when we're faced with preaching it.

> If we reduce theology to a matter of generic "religion" or even Christianity in particular, there's nothing dangerous or suspect about it, assuming we know how to walk warily around the burning bush. We have made theology into another field of scholarship like any other. On these academic pastures, and in good company, one can honorably spend one's life. Or we can study theology as practice, aligning theology with our assessment of human need or drinking from the fount of our own experience, focusing on the practically helpful aspects of faith. No danger in that either. But there comes a point—no theologian can evade it—when the question is forced upon us: *what will you say*? (Barth, *GD,* 6, my translation)

Marilynne Robinson says that some of the students who go to seminary from the Iowa Writers Workshop find that the domesticated theology they receive "doesn't speak to them or enable them to speak to other people." It doesn't preach. (Marilynne Robinson, interviewed by Jane Williams at https://sptc.htb.org/godpod/godpod-112.)

13. Barth, *CD*, I/2, 294.

14. Karl Barth, *The Epistle to the Romans,* trans. Edwyn C. Hoskyns, 6th ed. (London: Oxford University Press, 1975 [1933]), II, 332.

15. "Experience is indeed a teacher, but only as a member of a larger faculty." Fred B. Craddock, *Preaching,* 25th Anniversary Edition (Nashville: Abingdon Press, 2010), 75. For Luther, as for Barth, the Word of God requires neither "experience" nor "reason" to make its way to the congregation. "Christ cannot be set forth," said Luther, "any other way than through the Word, and cannot be grasped any other way than through faith." George Hunsinger, "Barth and Luther," George Hunsinger and Keith L. Johnson, eds., *The Wiley Blackwell Companion to Karl Barth,* vol. 1 (Hoboken, NJ: John Wiley & Sons, 2020), 460–71.

16. Gardner C. Taylor, *How Shall They Preach?* (Elgin, IL: Progressive Baptist Publishing, 1977), 24. James Kay quotes Bultmann: "Christ is correctly preached not where something is said *about* him, but only where he himself becomes the proclaimer." James F. Kay, "Promissory Kerygmatics," in David Schnasa Jacobsen, ed., *Toward a Homiletical Theology of Promise* (Eugene, OR: Wipf & Stock, 2018), 90.

17. Barth, *GD,* 39.

18. Karl Barth, *Word of God and Theology,* trans. Amy Marga (London: T & T Clark, 2000), 196.

19. Barth, *GD,* 64–65.

20. Barth, *GD,* 38–48. Chuck Campbell charges that advocates for preaching from and to personal experience show a "naive confidence in individual experience and choice, just at a time when the very notion of the free, autonomous 'self' is being questioned." Charles L. Campbell, *Preaching Jesus: New Directions for Homiletics in Hans Frei's Postliberal Theology* (Grand Rapids: Eerdmans, 1997), 144.

21. Barth, *GD,* 49–50.

22. Anna Carter Florence, *Preaching as Testimony* (Louisville: Westminster John Knox, 2007), 103.

23. Barth, *GD,* 50.

24. Barth, *GD,* 51.

25. Barth, *GD,* 62–63.

26. Barth, *GD,* 68–69. Eventually, Barth had reservations about infant baptism. Here he extols the practice as counter to Pelagian assumptions. Madeleine L'Engle chastises preachers for attempting, without aid of the Holy Spirit, to make God comprehensible to the "naked intellect," "domesticating" God in an effort to make God "easy to believe in." *The Irrational Season* (New York: HarperSanFrancisco, 1977), 49.

27. Lisa Thompson extols personal experience as source for our sermons, provided our experience is that of the "outsider." Thompson seldom refers to Scripture; her claim to be an "outsider" gives her unmediated access to the truth of her experience. But we haven't had an experience just because something happened to us; interpretation is needed, particularly if one privileges one's experience to be that of "outsider." Lisa L Thompson, *Ingenuity: Preaching as an Outsider* (Nashville: Abingdon Press, 2018).

28. Barth, *GD,* 68.

29. Mary McClintock Fulkerson shows how appeals to "women's experience" can ignore the particularity and limits of "experience," and lead to a hegemony of experience. Mary McClintock Fulkerson, *Changing the Subject: Women's Discourses and Feminist Theology* (Minneapolis: Fortress, 1994), 384.

30. Shelly Rambo shows the fruitfulness of looking at Christian theology through the lens of trauma studies. *Resurrecting Wounds: Living in the Afterlife of Trauma* (Waco: Baylor University Press, 2017). Unfortunately, Rambo leaves victims of trauma at Good Friday and Holy Saturday rather than moving to Easter. For a more theologically disciplined approach to trauma, see Deborah Hunsinger, *Bearing the Unbearable: Trauma, Gospel, and Pastoral Care* (Grand Rapids: Eerdmans), 2015.

The Academy of Homiletics made "Preaching and Trauma" the theme of its 2020 meeting. Preachers must take care not to give human trauma undeserved revelatory significance.

31. Fleming Rutledge, *And God Spoke to Abraham: Preaching from the Old Testament* (Grand Rapids: Eerdmans, 2011), 55.

32. Lauren Winner, *The Dangers of Christian Practice: On Wayward Gifts, Characteristic Damage and Sin* (New Haven, CT: Yale University Press, 2018).

33. Not thoughtful atheism but unconscious idolatry is the preacher's bane. Barth considers the fools of Psalm 14:1, who say, "there is no God" to be those who feel "no need of enlightenment by the revelation and Word of God," irrationally assuming that life can be lived "on the basis of the resultant vacuum, and therefore by the norm of maxims and motives." Their disbelief is (quoting Anselm on Psalm 14:1) "insipid." Barth, *CD*, IV/2, 411.

34. Barth, *GD,* 33–35.

35. Richard Lischer, *End of Words: The Language of Reconciliation in a Culture of Violence* (Grand Rapids: Eerdmans, 2008), 8.

36. Barth, *CD*, IV/2, 291.

37. Barth, *GD,* 444.

38. Whereas Paul said that among the Corinthians he knew nothing

but Christ crucified (1 Cor 2:2), in many of the depressed and depressing congregations where I preach, I wonder if I ought to say, "You were so disheartened that I preached nothing but Christ resurrected."

39. William H. Willimon, "End of a Violent Week," Good Friday evening service, Northside United Methodist Church, Greenville, SC, March 1981.

40. Barth, *CD*, II/2, 504.

41. Barth, *CD*, II/2, 140–42.

42. Quoted in Hughes Oliphant Old, *The Reading and Preaching of the Scriptures*, vol. IV, 20 (Grand Rapids: Eerdmans, 2007), 98.

43. Cited by Ewald M. Plass, *What Luther Says* (St. Louis: Concordia, 1959), 208.

44. Barth, *GD*, 37.

45. Eberhard Busch, *Karl Barths Lebenslauf: nach seinen Briefen und autobiographishcen Texten* (München: Kaiser, 1976), 89–90.

46. Charles Fuller, *The Trouble with "Truth through Personality"* (Eugene, OR: Wipf & Stock, 2010), counters Brooks with a questionable defense of Scripture as a repository of propositional truth.

47. Karoline Lewis, *She: Five Keys to Unlocking the Power of Women in Ministry* (Nashville: Abingdon Press, 2016).

48. "Not every [one] can do this [speak the Word of God]. Not every [one] can speak God's Word. For not every [one] has heard it." Barth, *CD*, I/2, 490–91.

49. Barth, *GD*, 58.

50. Christian Wiman, Duke Divinity School, Durham, NC, September 6, 2019. Of the birth of the Reformation, Luther said: "I simply taught, preached, wrote God's word. . . . Otherwise I did nothing. And then, while I slept, or drank Wittenberg beer with my Philip and with Amsdorf, the Word so greatly weakened the papacy . . . I did nothing; the word did it all." Martin Luther, "The Eight Wittenberg Sermons 1522," trans. A. Steimle, in *Works of Martin Luther* (Philadelphia: Muhlenberg, 1943), 2:387–425.

51. Barth, *Homiletics*, 47.

52. James Kay says that the Second Helvetic Confession's "The Preaching of the Word of God Is the World of God" may well be "the most influential theological sentence ever written about preaching." James F. Kay, *Preaching and Theology* (St. Louis: Chalice, 2007), 8. *Praedicatio verbi Dei est Verbum Dei* ["The Second Helvetic Confession"], in *The Constitution of the Presbyterian Church (U.S.A.)*, pt. 1, Book of Confessions (Louisville: Office of the General Assembly, 1994).

53. Quoted by Philip W. Butin, "Preaching as a Trinitarian Event,"

in *Trinitarian Theology for the Church: Scripture, Community, Worship,* ed. Daniel J. Treier and David Lauber (Downers Grove, IL: InterVarsity, 2009), 205.

54. George Hunsinger, *How to Read Karl Barth: The Shape of His Theology* (New York: Oxford University Press, 1991), 234–80.

55. Barth, *CD,* I/1, 198–227.

56. Barth, *CD,* IV/1/3, 63. Barth makes no explicit references to Chalcedon in *GD,* but the "Chalcedonian Pattern" permeates the Barthian corpus, including *GD,* coming to its explicit fruition in *CD,* IV/3.

57. https://simple.wikipedia.org/wiki/Chalcedonian_Creed.

58. Barth, *CD,* IV/3, 63.

59. As the eternal, divine Son of God who became human, Augustine and Cyril (I think) would say that Christ's divinity is his truest identity; his humanity is the instrument of his revelation and connection to us. In other words, Christ's two natures are not symmetrical.

60. Hunsinger, *How to Read Karl Barth,* 86–87.

61. Nicholas Wolterstorff complains that Barth is too Christocentric, restricting divine revelation to Jesus Christ, citing, "God's Revelation is Jesus Christ, the son of God." *CD,* I/1, 137. Wolterstorff fails to appreciate the danger of disconnecting "revelation" from this Jew from Nazareth. Nicholas Wolterstorff, *Divine Discourse: Philosophical Reflections on the Claim That God Speaks* (Cambridge: Cambridge University Press, 2000), 68.

62. Barth, *CD,* IV/3, 520.

63. Edward T. Oakes, S. J., *Infinity Dwindled to Infancy: A Catholic and Evangelical Christology* (Grand Rapids: Eerdmans, 1999); the title is taken from Gerhard Manley Hopkins's, "The Blessed Virgin Compared to the Air We Breathe," which speaks of "infinity dwindled to infancy . . . grace that does now reach our race."

64. Barth, *CD,* IV/3, 160.

65. Nicholas Lash notes that during the seventeenth and eighteenth centuries, in English and German culture, the word "God" came to name the ultimate explanatory principle. God as master lawyer, a mechanic, or technician rather than the One with whom we are in a speaking/hearing relationship. This "god" is the antithesis of the God/human, Jesus, and a "god" more easily defeated by modern philosophy. Nicholas Lash, *Holiness, Speech and Silence: Reflections on the Question of God* (Aldershot, UK: Ashgate, 2004), 13.

66. Karl Barth, *Dogmatics in Outline,* trans. G. T. Thomson (New York: Harper & Row, 1959), 15.

67. Barth, *CD,* III/3, 247.

68. Barth, *CD*, IV/3, 1, 5.

69. Barth, *GD,* 176.

70. Evans Crawford praises the "hum" of the African American church's call-and-response tradition as a "responsive chord" when pastor and congregation "affirm and celebrate the gospel together," reminding preachers "that they are not gods, but persons who themselves need to be spoken to as hearers." Evans Crawford, *The Hum: Call and Response in African American Preaching* (Nashville: Abingdon Press, 1995), 60.

71. Barth, *GD,* 87.

72. Barth, *CD*, I/1, 223.

73. Brueggemann, *Preaching from the Old Testament,* 50.

74. Benjamin Warfield, *Inspiration, and Authority of the Bible,* 2nd ed. (Phillipsburg, NJ: P&R Publishing, 1980), 86. See Kevin J. Vanhoozer, "Triune Discourse: Theological Reflections on the Claim That God Speaks," in *Trinitarian Theology for the Church: Scripture, Community, Worship,* ed. Daniel J. Treier and David Lauber (Downers Grove, IL: InterVarsity, 2009), 31–33. Barth accused literalists and verbal inspirationists of making the Bible a "paper Pope" that brought the Bible "under human control." Barth, *CD*, I/2, 522.

75. While Chalcedon clarified the being of Jesus Christ, not Scripture, especially not preaching, I think a Chalcedonian imagination illuminates preaching. Kevin Vanhoozer thinks otherwise ("Triune Discourse," 41).

76. See Mark Galli, *Karl Barth: An Introductory Biography for Evangelicals* (Grand Rapids: Eerdmans, 2017).

77. Gerhard Forde said that conceiving of the biblical text as self-sufficiently revelatory, preachers are tempted, "instead of *doing* the text with the hearers [to] *explain* it . . . with as many clever and appealing illustrations as one can muster. . . . The text does not do anything . . . to change us or incorporate us into its story; rather the text is changed to fit our story. The Word becomes mere information or description or instruction . . . an occasion for us to exercise our powers; it becomes a law, perhaps inevitably a club with which to beat people." Gerhard O. Forde, "Preaching the Sacraments," in *The Preached God*, ed. Mark C. Mattes and Steven D. Paulson, 89–115 (Grand Rapids: Eerdmans, 2007), 93.

78. Bart D. Ehrman, *God's Problem: How the Bible Fails to Answer Our Most Important Question—Why We Suffer* (San Francisco: HarperCollins, 2008) and *Misquoting Jesus: The Story Behind Who Changed the Bible and Why* (San Francisco: HarperCollins, 2005).

79. Barth, *CD*, I/1, 295.

80. Barth, *CD*, I/1, 304.

81. Barth said that the way the Roman Catholic Church of his day viewed the real presence of Christ in the Eucharist was how we ought to see preaching. See Amy Marga, "Barth and Roman Catholicism," in George Hunsinger and Keith L. Johnson, eds., *The Wiley Blackwell Companion to Karl Barth,* vol. 2 (Hoboken, NJ: John Wiley & Sons, 2020), 845.

82. Barth, *GD,* 161.

83. Hans Urs van Balthasar as quoted by Vanhoozer, "Triune Discourse," 53.

84. Barth, *GD,* 162.

85. Asked if we should demythologize miracles, Barth responded, "Demythologize? No, the miracles shall be regarded as comforting protest against *our* myths!" *Barth in Conversation,* vol. 3, 18.

86. Barth, *GD,* 162.

87. Dietrich Bonhoeffer, *Worldly Preaching,* ed. Clyde E. Fant (Nashville: Thomas Nelson, 1975), 126.

88. For preaching as a bodily activity, see Teresa Fry Brown, *Delivering the Sermon: Voice, Body, and Animation in Proclamation* (Minneapolis: Fortress, 2008).

89. See Jerusha Neal's critique of theologically inadequate "embodiment" language applied to preaching. Jerusha Matsen Neal, *The Overshadowed Preacher,* 100–101. Deborah Hunsinger uses Chalcedon as a sound theological basis for pastoral care. Deborah van Deusen Hunsinger, *Theology and Pastoral Counseling: A New Interdisciplinary Approach* (Grand Rapids: Eerdmans, 1995).

90. Barth, *Homiletics,* 121. The best way to understand Barth's tour de force *Homiletics* is through Angela Dienhart Hancock, *Karl Barth's Emergency Homiletic, 1932–1933: A Summons to Prophetic Witness at the Dawn of the Third Reich* (Grand Rapids: Eerdmans, 2013).

91. Barth, *Homiletics,* 130.

92. See the difference that the preaching role makes for the authority of women in Kate Bowler, *The Preacher's Wife: The Precarious Power of Evangelical Women Celebrities* (Princeton, NJ: Princeton University Press, 2019).

93. Lucy Atkinson Rose says traditional preaching is "potentially dangerous" (133) but then exchanges dominance from the pulpit for that of the authoritarian, sharing, "roundtable" congregation. *Sharing the Word: Preaching in the Roundtable Church* (Louisville: Westminster John Knox, 1997).

94. See Willimon, *Conversations with Barth,* 6.

95. North American Christians have reason to believe that the church as we have known it is passing away. I once thought that Barth, unlike us, simply assumes that the church as he knew it will continue into the future.

I now believe that Barth's lack of anxiety about the future of the church is based on his great faith in the triumph of the Word.

96. Barth, *CD,* IV/3, 76.

97. Matthew Kim thinks preachers must analyze the listeners' culture and the way they process information. Matthew D. Kim, *Preaching with Cultural Intelligence: Understanding the People Who Hear Our Sermons* (Grand Rapids: Baker Academic, 2017), 10. Kim has great faith in our skills of listener context and analysis. Barth contended that, because we have a revealing God, preachers always know more about God than our arcane, secretive listeners.

98. Walter Brueggemann, *Interrupting Silence: God's Command to Speak Out* (Louisville: Westminster John Knox, 2018), 77. See also Stephen H. Webb, *The Divine Voice: Christian Proclamation and the Theology of Sound* (Eugene, OR: Wipf & Stock), 2004.

99. Quoted by Rachel Muers, *Keeping God's Silence: Towards a Theological Ethics of Communication* (Oxford: Blackwell, 2004), 6.

100. See "Introduction," in *Apophatic Bodies: Negative Theology, Incarnation, and Relationality,* ed. Chris Boesel and Catherine Keller (New York: Fordham University Press, 2010), 1.

101. Robert Cardinal Sarah, with Nicolas Diat, *The Power of Silence: Against the Dictatorship of Noise* (San Francisco: Ignatius Press, 2016), 27.

102. Robert Cardinal Sarah, *Power of Silence,* 30.

103. Eberhard Jüngel, *God as the Mystery of the World: On the Foundation of the Theology of the Crucified One in the Dispute between Theism and Atheism,* trans. Darrell L. Guder (Grand Rapids: Eerdmans, 1983), vii.

104. Dale C. Allison, Jr., *The Silence of Angels* (Valley Forge, PA: Trinity Press, 1995), 36, 37, 40.

105. Barbara Brown Taylor, *When God Is Silent* (Cambridge, MA: Cowley, 1998), xi.

106. Brown Taylor, *When God Is Silent,* 52.

107. "God is the one thing Christians cannot cease to communicate." Robert W. Jenson, *Visible Words: The Interpretation and Practice of Christian Sacraments* (Philadelphia: Fortress, 1978), 32.

108. Barth dismissed metaphysical attempts to talk about God as "*Gnosticism* . . . where the gospel is understood and explained with the help of certain metaphysical, ontological, and anthropological presuppositions—instead of listening to its good *news,* to which . . . such principles have to be *subordained.*" *Barth in Conversation,* 2.

109. Jüngel, *God as the Mystery of the World,* 251.

110. Jüngel, *God as the Mystery of the World,* 298.

111. Lash, *Holiness, Speech and Silence,* 13.

112. Quoted in Lash, *Holiness, Speech and Silence,* 17.

113. Muers, *Keeping God's Silence,* 41.

114. "God's otherness is one of communion." Christopher Morse, *Not Every Spirit: A Dogmatics of Christian Disbelief,* 2nd ed. (New York: Continuum, 2009), 86.

115. Charles Taylor says modern, secular folk hunger for the mystical: "People sense a terrible flatness in the everyday . . . identified, particularly with the commercial, industrial, or consumer society. They feel emptiness of the repeated, accelerating cycle of desire . . . ; the cardboard quality of bright supermarkets, or neat row housing in a clean suburb." Preachers ought to be suspicious of speaking of the gospel as cure for our mystical hankering. Charles Taylor, *A Secular Age* (Cambridge, MA: The Belknap Press of Harvard University Press, 2007), 309.

116. Barth, *GD,* 355.

117. Barth, *GD,* 359–60.

118. Barth, *GD,* 359–60.

119. Rachel Muers gives thoughtful, qualified praise for silence but warns that silence, "affirmed as a phenomenon with positive significance, would be politically and ethically irresponsible . . . particularly . . . in the light of twentieth century critiques of acts of violent silencing, historical and contemporary." Muers, *Keeping God's Silence,* 10.

120. Those who work for racial justice say, "If you see something, say something." William H. Willimon, *Who Lynched Willie Earle? Preaching to Confront Racism* (Nashville: Abingdon Press, 2018).

121. Muers, *Keeping God's Silence,* 46.

122. Muers, *Keeping God's Silence,* 47. Muers asks, "Is it possible to understand and speak of God's communicative action in a way that does not perform some further act of silencing?" (72). It's my belief that God's communication incites human speaking, otherwise known as preaching.

123. Muers, *Keeping God's Silence,* 112.

124. Bonhoeffer, *Life Together,* 83–84.

125. Brueggemann says that such a move is "inchoately present from the outset in the baptismal community, so that relationships in the new regime of Christ are radically changed from conventional practice." Brueggemann, *Interrupting Silence,* 99.

126. Laurie Goodstein, "Pope Says Ban on Female Priests Is Likely to Endure," *The New York Times,* November 2, 2016, https://www.nytimes.com/2016/11/02/world/europe/pope-francis-women-priests.html.

127. Brueggemann, *Interrupting Silence.*

128. Brueggemann, *Finally Comes the Poet,* 49.

129. Bonhoeffer urged us to forsake abstract assertions about God and to risk an "encounter with Jesus Christ," incarnate, "God in human form." Dietrich Bonhoeffer, *Letters and Papers from Prison,* ed. Eberhard Bethge, trans. Reginald Fuller et al. (London: SCM, 1971), 558. The incarnation poses a challenge for any who would extoll silence as theologically virtuous. See Chris Boesel and Catherine Keller, eds., *Apophatic Bodies: Negative Theology, Incarnation, and Relationality* (New York: Fordham University Press, 2010).

130. Lamin Sanneh pointed out to me that God (Gen 1:1) is talkative Creator rather than silent contemplator, distinguishing Jews and Christians from other religions of Asia.

131. See Jason Micheli, *Cancer Is Funny: Keeping in Stage-Serious* (Minneapolis: Fortress, 2016).

132. On the perniciousness of sentimentality, see Jeremy S. Begbie, *A Peculiar Orthodoxy: Reflections on Theology and the Arts* (Grand Rapids: Baker Academic, 2018), ch. 2. "The sentimentalist . . . (1) misrepresents reality by evading or trivializing evil, (2) is emotionally self-indulgent, and (3) avoids appropriate costly action" (27).

133. Barth perceived the arrogance hidden within our sentimental faith in human ability to speak "God" on our own: "What are you doing . . . with the word of *God* upon *your* lips? Upon what grounds do you assume the role of mediator between heaven and earth? Who has authorized you to take your place there and to generate religious feeling? And, to crown all, to do so with results, with success? Did one ever hear of such overweening presumption, such Titanism, . . . such brazenness! One does not with impunity cross the boundaries of mortality! One does not with impunity usurp the prerogative of God!" (31). Barth, *The Word of God and the Word of Man,* 125–26 (emphasis in original).

134. Cited in William H. Willimon, *How Odd of God: Chosen for the Curious Vocation of Preaching* (Louisville: Westminster John Knox, 2015), 94.

135. Observing the unctuous piety of some clergy, Barth smirks, "The prophets and apostles . . . do not seem to have been recruited as a whole from among the most pious circles." *GD*, 282. Richard Ward says the chief question for new preachers is, "Can I be myself as a preacher and proclaimer of the Word?" Richard Ward, "Finding Your Voice in Theological School," in *Preaching and Performance*, ed. Clayton Schmit and Jana Childers (Grand Rapid: Baker Academic, 2008), 140. Ward erroneously implies that there's some "self" that is in danger of being violated by the act of preaching, a "self" untouched by having hands laid on the head. Rowan Williams knows

that "myself" is invariably an imagined ideal of myself, "So that my self-perception remains firmly under my own control." Rowan Williams, *On Christian Theology* (Oxford: Blackwell, 2000), 241.

136. See Lillian Daniel, *Tell It Like It Is: Reclaiming the Practice of Testimony* (Herndon, VA: The Alban Institute, 2006).

137. Barth, *GD*, 280.

138. Trump tried to rush an end to national quarantine by Easter, predicting "churches will be packed," illustrating Begbie's insight that "Christian sentimentalism arises from a premature grasp for Easter morning, a refusal to follow the three days of Easter . . . in an irreversible sequence of victory over evil," Easter without Good Friday and Holy Saturday. Begbie, *A Peculiar Orthodoxy*, 41.

139. We must have "courage (*Mut*) before both the text and the people, and also the right kind of humility (*Demut*) before the text." Barth, *Homiletics,* 116.

140. Aubrey Spears, "Preaching the Old Testament," in *Hearing the Old Testament*, ed. Craig G. Bartholomew and David J. H. Beldman (Grand Rapids: Eerdmans, 2012), 391. Others who portray preaching as dialogue between preacher and congregation: John McClure, *Other-Wise Preaching: A Postmodern Ethic for Homiletics* (St. Louis: Chalice, 2001), 13–26; Lucy Rose, *Sharing the Word: Preaching in the Roundtable Church* (Louisville: Westminster John Knox, 1997), 98–113, 130–31; Joseph Webb, *Preaching and the Challenge of Pluralism* (St. Louis: Chalice, 1998); and Christine Smith, *Preaching as Weeping, Confession, and Resistance: Radical Responses to Radical Evil* (Louisville: Westminster John Knox, 1992). These calls for preaching as dialogue are race and class connected and typical of a privileged church that thinks it's already Christian and a suitable partner for dialogue with God without need of the church's continuing conversion.

141. The progenitor is Schliermacher. See Daniel J. Price, *Karl Barth's Anthropology in Light of Modern Thought* (Grand Rapids: Eerdmans, 2002), 61–84.

142. Daniel Price describes the Barth/Schliermacher divide: "Either we can explain religious beliefs as a projection of human needs for love, or we can explain human love as a reflection of divine love. In Schleiermacher's theology we arrive at God by analyzing religious consciousness. Barth had decided that . . . predications about God based on religious consciousness could only lead theology into a cul-de-sac of subjectivism." *Karl Barth's Anthropology,* 291.

143. Barth, *CD,* I/2, 490–91.

144. Quoted by Eberhard Busch, *The Great Passion: An Introduction to Karl Barth's Theology,* ed. Darrell L. Guder and Judith J. Guder, trans. W. H. Rader (Grand Rapids: Eerdmans, 2004), 242.

145. Barth, *CD,* IV/3, 525.

146. This is the move that Hauerwas and I named in *Resident Aliens.* Stanley M. Hauerwas and William H. Willimon, *Resident Aliens: Life in the Christian Colony* (Nashville: Abingdon Press, 1989).

147. "The Christian West, *i.e.,* the society in which Christian and non-Christian existence came together, . . . no longer exists. . . . There can be no escaping the startling recognition that a [person's] being as a Christian is either grounded in . . . vocation or it is simply an illusion which seems beautiful perhaps in the after-glow of a time vanished beyond recall." *CD,* IV/3.2, 524–25.

148. Fred B. Craddock, *Overhearing the Gospel: Preaching and Teaching the Faith for Persons Who Have Already Heard* (Nashville: Abingdon Press, 1978). Craddock's usage of Kierkegaard was unfair to the thought of the one who saw himself as a missionary to Danes who, having been inoculated with a mild form of Christianity were immune to the real thing.

149. Charles Campbell says Craddock confuses the Word of God with "the presuppositions of modern, liberal American culture." Campbell, *Preaching Jesus,* 130.

150. Philip Jenkins, *The Next Christendom: The Coming of Global Christianity* (New York: Oxford, 2002).

151. Evangelizing is a continuing project. "Christians find that they themselves are nominal Christians and urgently need to receive the gospel afresh." Barth, *CD,* IV/3.2, 873. See Darrell L. Guder, *The Continuing Conversion of the Church* (Grand Rapids: Eerdmans, 2000).

152. David J. Bosch, *Transforming Mission: Paradigm Shifts in Theology of Mission* (Maryknoll, NY: Orbis, 1991), 16.

153. Emily M. D. Scott, in *For All Who Hunger,* shows the adventure of going out into the world to see what God is up to, then inviting those who didn't know they are God's people to God's table at St. Lydia's. Scott shows how evangelism (though she would be loath to use the word) compels us to talk about Christ to those to whom Christ is already speaking, even when they don't know it. Emily M. D. Scott, *For All Who Hunger: Searching for Communion in a Shattered World* (New York: Random House, 2020).

154. See Hanna Reichel, "Barth on the Church in Mission," in George Hunsinger and Keith L. Johnson, eds., *The Wiley Blackwell Companion to Karl Barth,* vol. 1 (Hoboken, NJ: John Wiley & Sons, 2020), 327.

155. Patrick W. T. Johnson in his article, "Call to Conversion: Lesslie

Newbigin on Preaching," *Currents in Theology and Mission,* 37.1 (Feb 2010): http://www.lstc.edu/resources/publications/currents/, helped me organize my thoughts on Newbigin. See also William H. Willimon, "Preaching as Missionary Encounter with North American Paganism (in homage to Lesslie Newbigin, 1909–1998)," *Journal for Preachers,* 22, no. 3 (1999): 7.

156. George Hunsberger, "Renewing Faith during the Postmodern Transition," *Transmission Special Edition* (1998): 10–11.

157. Barth, *CD,* IV/2, 544.

158. Lamin Sanneh, *Whose Religion Is Christianity?: The Gospel beyond the West* (Grand Rapids: Eerdmans, 2003).

159. Jung Young Lee, *Korean Preaching: An Interpretation* (Nashville: Abingdon Press, 1997).

160. Lesslie Newbigin, *A Faith for This One World?* (London: SCM, 1961), 90.

161. Kenda Creasy Dean, *Almost Christian: What the Faith of Our Teenagers Is Telling the American Church* (Oxford: Oxford University Press, 2010), 12, says American teenagers are blasé toward the church because we communicate "a watered-down gospel so devoid of God's self-giving love in Jesus Christ, so immune to the sending love of the Holy Spirit that it might not be Christianity at all."

162. In leading conversations on racism in white congregations I have noted that the white demand for "civility" is a major impediment to honest conversation, an aspect of white fragility. Duke historian, William Chafe shows that civility is "the cornerstone of white progressive mystique . . . encompassing abhorrence of personal conflict, courtesy toward new ideas, and a generosity toward those less fortunate than oneself," all of which can be used by white Christians to muffle the anger and protest of black Christians. William H. Chafe, *Civilities and Civil Rights: Greensboro, North Carolina, and the Black Struggle* (New York: Oxford University Press, 1980), 8. Chapter 4 of Elaine Heath's *The Healing Practice of Celebration* (Nashville: Abingdon Press, 2020) evinces the dangers of advocacy of "civility" in speech when applied by Christians to important arguments.

163. Newbigin describes conversion as "a personal commitment to Jesus Christ as Savior and Lord, which means, 'a final surrendering of the self to the person of Jesus Christ.' Second, . . . turning toward a pattern of conduct that is consistent with a life wholly committed to Christ, and turned toward the neighbor in love. Third . . . participation in a visible fellowship that is centered in Jesus Christ. . . . [Yet] conversion is never only for the sake of those who are converted, but for the sake of all . . . the converted are sent to testify—in word and deed—that the reign of God has come in Jesus

Christ. . . . The continual conversion of the church is to the world and for the world." Johnson, "Call to Conversion," 14.

164. Frank A. Thomas, *How to Preach a Dangerous Sermon* (Nashville: Abingdon Press, 2018).

165. Lesslie Newbigin, *Foolishness to the Greeks: The Gospel and Western Culture* (Grand Rapids: Eerdmans, 1986), 1.

166. Leah D. Schade, *Preaching in the Purple Zone: Ministry in the Red-Blue Divide* (London: Rowman & Littlefield, 2019), thinks that, in lieu of preaching, we ought to give Sunday to dialogues with our congregations and thereby come to common ground, making the achievement of common ground more important than telling and hearing the truth.

167. Dialogue is the guiding metaphor for John S. McClure, *The Roundtable Pulpit: Where Leadership and Preaching Meet* (Nashville: Abingdon Press, 1995).

168. James Davison Hunter advocates "faithful presence" as the uniquely Christian way to change the world. James Davison Hunter, *To Change the World: The Irony, Tragedy, and Possibility of Christianity in the Late Modern World* (Oxford: Oxford University Press, 2010). The church is called for more than Hunter's presumed humble presence; we are called to *witness*.

169. Lesslie Newbigin, "Preaching Christ Today" (The Eighteenth Joseph Smith Memorial Lecture, Overdale College, Birmingham, UK, 1979), Newbigin.net Online Bibliography.

170. Newbigin, "Preaching Christ Today."

171. Robert Wilken says, "The Word of God makes its way not by argument but as men and women bear witness to what has happened." Robert Wilken, *The Spirit of Early Christian Thought: Seeking the Face of God* (New Haven, CT: Yale University Press, 2003), 6. Preaching "is not a matter of apologetics, but rather of evangelization . . . part of the whole church's ministry to convert our lives by having them constituted by a narrative that we have not chosen, but which has chosen us." William H. Willimon and Stanley Hauerwas, *Preaching to Strangers: Evangelism and Today's World* (Louisville: Westminster John Knox, 1992), 10.

172. "The Church is the bearer of the work of Christ through history, but not the exclusive beneficiary. God purposes the salvation of all. For this purpose [God] has chosen a people. Because that people have over and over again fallen into the sin of supposing that they have a claim upon God which others do not have, they have over and over again been punished and humiliated and have had to hear the word of God spoken to them from others. . . . Whenever the Church has imagined that it had a claim upon

God which others did not have, it is already fallen away from grace. The church is servant and not master. It is appointed to a stewardship on behalf of all, not to a privilege from which others are excluded." Lesslie Newbigin, *Christian Witness in a Plural Society* (London: British Council of Churches, 1977), 14.

173. Barth, *CD*, IV/2, 843.

174. Barth, *CD*, IV/3.2, 865ff.

175. Lesslie Newbigin, *The Open Secret: Sketches for a Missionary Theology* (Grand Rapids: Eerdmans, 1995), 4, italics in original.

176. Lamin Sanneh, *Translating the Message: The Missionary Impact on Culture*, rev. exp. 2nd ed. (Maryknoll, NY: Orbis, 2009).

177. Priscilla Pope-Levison, *Models of Evangelism* (Grand Rapids: Baker Academic, 2020).

178. Barth, *CD*, IV/3.2, 844.

179. "The task of the *church* is to *witness* and to *announce* his deed and work—inside of its own boundaries (regular worship + evangelization) and to the whole world (mission)." *Barth in Conversation*, 1.

180. P. T. Forsyth, *Positive Preaching and the Modern Mind* (New York: A. C. Armstrong, 1907), 71.

181. Barth, *CD*, III/4, 515.

182. Barth, *CD*, IV/3.2, 845. There's no such thing as "apostolic succession," says Barth except as applied to missionary proclamation by all the baptized. *CD*, I/1, 106.

183. Barth, *CD*, III/2, 607.

INDEX OF NAMES

SCRIPTURE INDEX

New Testament